Islamic and Je

'*Islamic and Jewish Legal Reasoning* is a series of thoughtful scholarly essays in which recognition of differences becomes the starting point for mutual understanding. The essays introduce the reader to pairs of outstanding scholars who reflect together on legal questions regarding animals, sovereignty, the status of women, and other issues. Their conversations provide a wealth of detail on these two important traditions, and they remind us again that to know our own law and culture, we must first understand the questions others raise about them.'

ROBIN W. LOVIN,
William H. Scheide Senior Fellow in Theology,
Center of Theological Inquiry, Princeton

'*Islamic and Jewish Legal Reasoning* is daring and innovative. The book is a conversation among scholars of law and religion in these two great traditions, based on intensive collective readings of and reflections on each other's key texts, specifically concerning the role of reason and authority in determining law. The result is a fascinating and highly readable account of this dialogue.'

ZIBA MIR-HOSSEINI,
SOAS, University of London

'Designed for the non-specialist, this fascinating book invites the reader to listen in on a conversation about law, Jewish law and Islamic law, among distinguished scholars thinking about modern questions—the nature of law and judicial authority, the status of women, animal rights, and sovereignty—with ancient and medieval texts. It is a deeply serious book which models an informed and open dialogue about consequential matters rather than providing packaged pieties.'

WINNIFRED FALLERS SULLIVAN,
Chair, Department of Religious Studies, Indiana University Bloomington

Islamic and Jewish Legal Reasoning

—Encountering Our Legal Other—

Edited by
ANVER M. EMON

ONEWORLD

A Oneworld Book

First published by Oneworld Publications 2016

Copyright © Anver Emon 2016

All rights reserved
Copyright under Berne Convention
A CIP record for this title is available from the British Library

ISBN 978-1-78074-880-1
eISBN 978-1-78074-881-8

Printed and Bound by Clays Ltd, St Ives plc
Typeset by Tetragon, London

Oneworld Publications
10 Bloomsbury Street
London WC1B 3SR
England

Stay up to date with the latest books,
special offers, and exclusive content from
Oneworld with our monthly newsletter

Sign up on our website
www.oneworld-publications.com

Contents

PART II

Acknowledgments

P reparing a volume like this requires a coordinated and collective effort from those willing to engage and otherwise support such an innovative approach to both research and pedagogy. At a time in higher education when institutions look for distinct impact and research outputs by which to assess the value of scholarship, a project like this promises something that is not susceptible to quantification or easy prediction. Those who participated in this project—from the workshops over a period of years to the production of this book—evince a hope in the possibilities attendant to reflective reading practices that we imagine will occur in universities, seminaries, reading groups, and private homes. That hope—which of course includes the possibility of failure—is often bemoaned as lacking in today's seemingly risk-averse institutions of higher education. This is not the place to recount whether such risk aversion is as prevalent as critics suggest or, if it is prevalent, to inquire into the whys and hows. Rather, prefacing this acknowledgment with this broader concern about higher education is intended to deepen my expression of gratitude to those who helped make this book possible.

Throughout the process, Robert Gibbs has been a confidant, collaborator, and trusted friend who brought his energy and vision to the project. Moreover, all the authors in this volume have worked diligently to create something new; that took courage as well as considerable energy, since we were all forced to engage with a research and writing process that departed from what is most comfortable and familiar to us in the academy. Canada's Social Science and Humanities Research Council supported this book with a grant to bring all the authors together to discuss earlier drafts of their chapter; having that authors' workshop allowed us to collectively imagine the final vision of the book and helped give cohesion to the volume. Various units at the University of Toronto also provided support for this project. They are, in no particular order: the Jackman Humanities Institute, the Faculty of Law, the Department of Philosophy, the Faculty of Arts and Sciences, and the Center for Jewish Studies, in particular the Roz and Ralph Halbert Endowment in Jewish Studies. I also want to thank the Dean of the Faculty of Law, Edward Iacobucci, for his commitment to this project.

Lastly, I want to thank Oneworld Publications, in particular Novin Doostdar and Jonathan Bentley-Smith, for their exemplary and expert attention to every detail of book production and distribution. It is a real pleasure and honor to have this book featured in their innovative and path-breaking publication list.

INTRODUCTION

Islamic and Jewish
Legal Reasoning—Beginnings

ANVER M. EMON AND ROBERT GIBBS

ON READING TOGETHER

The story of this book reveals the sometimes circuitous path that research can take, especially if the research does not adhere to certain orthodoxies on research, or if it is designed to do something whose ultimate end product is unpredictable. It began in the offices and homes of Anver M. Emon and Robert Gibbs in 2006 in and around the University of Toronto. Robert Gibbs had already written extensively on topics in Jewish philosophy and ethics. Anver M. Emon was writing about various approaches to legal reasoning in Islamic law. They met in the Law Library and began conversations in the Philosophy of Law discussion group at the Faculty of Law, in which members from across the university would reflect on law, philosophy, and competing disciplinary approaches to the topic. The conversation developed further when Emon went to Cambridge University to join Gibbs and others in the Scriptural Reasoning project, where scholars read the scriptural texts of multiple traditions with scholars from those different traditions.

These three moments remain central to the book before you. The most basic is the library. The contributors to this volume are academic scholars—people who read in the library, write books and articles for the library, and hold within themselves their own *internal* libraries that situate them as readers of other texts that they subsequently make their own. This project draws upon each contributor's internal library, where each has a home. The library as metaphor situates each of us in a tradition of law and scholarship that both informs our study but also limits what questions we ask and how we may go about answering them. As we inhabit our own internal libraries but also bring them into conversation with each other, we are confronted by their inherent limits—limits that become apparent only through this conversation. Those internal libraries, which each of us have, not only privilege certain questions about what we read when we read together, but also alert us to the questions we do not ask when we are confronted with the internal libraries of our colleagues. Indeed, to read together as we did for five years, and even to write together, requires a new context where our libraries can intersect and reveal to us new insights not only about other traditions, but also (and most interestingly) about our own.

The second moment, the Philosophy of Law discussion group, provides a metaphor that frames the conversation between the internal libraries of the commentators in this volume and all those who joined us over the years in our workshop. Philosophy of law is not so much a common ground as a common site for discussion and for a truly wide range of approaches to questions about law. In the specific Philosophy of Law group in Toronto, there were often participants who knew diverse legal traditions (e.g., common law, Jewish law, Islamic law, civil law, Roman law) and who had different philosophical heroes (e.g., Kant, Hegel, Levinas, Maimonides, Ibn Rushd). The practice was to read philosophical texts—sometimes current, sometimes historical— and to attend to the diverse perspectives brought to the group. The social interaction was governed by conceptual interaction, based on reading philosophical texts. The contributors in this book were not participants in that weekly Philosophy of Law reading group, in large measure because they were not resident in Toronto, and both Gibbs and Emon over time withdrew from this specific law reading group, even though the task of this sort of interdisciplinary and philosophical engagement remained desirable. But that moment provided a third tradition of law that was implicitly in the room when Jewish and Islamic legal scholars convened together in discussion workshops. As much as the discussion among the scholars in this volume focused on Islamic and Jewish legal reasoning in the early texts of each tradition—we often joked that anything after 1500 C.E. was too young—scholars of both traditions could not escape the ever-presence of a legal order shaped by the modern state and characterized by secular models of law and governance. Whether working from the Jewish legal tradition or the Islamic one, scholars of both traditions were keenly aware of the way both of these legal traditions were implicated in the ongoing development of statist regimes, whether as part of formal law or as a feature of public debate about the scope of accommodation of religious minorities such as Muslims, Jews and Christians.

The third moment, Scriptural Reasoning, served as a short-term catalyst for pursuing a different line of research and inquiry. Scriptural Reasoning began as a collaboration between Jewish, Christian, and Muslim scholars who convened (and many still do) semi-annually to read from each other's holy scriptures together in small groups. The practice of reading in small groups with short texts allowed the texts to mediate differences that could remain unresolved. Textual exploration allowed each community of readers to offer its own texts, to learn from the others how they read their texts, and to learn from others how they read their own "other's" texts.

The virtue of Scriptural Reasoning—the focus on a narrow set of scriptural texts (Hebrew Bible, New Testament, Qur'an)—was also its vice for some scholars of Islam and Judaism who considered the *sola scriptura* model of Scriptural Reasoning as too indebted to a Protestant tradition to embrace the salient role of the interpretive tradition in Judaism and Islam. Each tradition has a signal place for these scriptural texts, which it holds to be revealed. But for both Jews and Muslims access to these texts is always through traditions of interpretation. What would happen if the texts we read together stretched forward in interpretative history? Relatedly, Scriptural Reasoning often prioritized theology over and against other fields of inquiry, specifically the legal field that features so prominently in both Judaism and Islam.

Taking the three moments together, a new project came into focus. Because law is central in many historical and ongoing concerns about both Judaism and Islam, and given the richness of both centuries-long legal traditions, we hoped to frame a new practice of reading. Could the two traditions be read together without driving the interest in the discussions to reducing the two traditions to a common ground? At this point, the new project seemed to be best construed as a dialogue and not a three-part conversation, and Christianity was omitted.

Of course, there is a long tradition of canon law, but the centrality of law has been suspect within Christianity since its founding. Moreover, Christian theologians have tended to be interested in other worthy matters much more than law; and the political philosophers in the modern world, who descended from the Protestant Reformation, were largely unsympathetic to religion. Indeed, this new project grew out of an interest to problematize both the post-Westphalian presumptions that inform debates in philosophy of law, and the category "religion" which is profoundly informed by Protestant traditions. Together these concepts of law and religion serve as assumptions that shape how the relationship between law, religion, governance, and religious pedagogy is construed for the deeply historical and yet also very contemporary religious traditions of Islam and Judaism. Thus, when scholars of the two traditions convened, a third legal tradition—the secular liberal state and its philosophical tradition—was a tacit point of reference to the work to be undertaken.

The working title that emerged was "Reason and Authority." The questions we addressed revolved around the general concern of the roles of reason and authority in interpreting and determining law in religious traditions. While the question of authority and reason arises in every legal culture, the Islamic and Jewish legal traditions offer explicit and extensive reflection on what reason is and how it can interpret sources in juxtaposition with both political and religious authority. By looking at juristic and judicial practices, by following lines of interpretation that originate in revealed texts and flow through chains of multiple and evolving interpretations, the scholars discerned important relations between the authority of the revealed text and the reasoning of the community of scholars. In interpreting legal matters, human reason is not only required, but also plays a contributing role in rationalizing, even in developing, the authoritative tradition. Indeed, the ideal is to discern the precise role of reason internal to the legal religious traditions. Thus each term of the title must undergo exploration.

Authority is not simply an end to debate and legal process, but is put to work in different ways and is discerned through different modes of inquiry. While both Islamic and Jewish law claim some form of divine authority for their tradition, each engages in complex negotiations with political and institutional authority. More to the point, however, each tradition articulates and contests claims of authority and so makes explicit for itself these questions about authority. Juxtaposing these accounts illuminates a more complex map of what authority is and how it is felt in the law.

Reason is far from being a simple or stable term. The reason of legal reasoning is not identical to what a philosopher would define as reason. Instead, juridical reasoning draws on specific texts, cases, precedents, principles, and pragmatic concerns associated with resolving very particular, narratively rich disputes between parties. What counts as reason changes through a tradition and is not uniform across traditions. But in so far as it is accessible to a human as human, without private or superhuman aid, it stands in legal systems as a pivot point for the collective work of thinking in law.

Of course, the third term, *and*, is the most important. For the other two terms are not simply separate and independent from each other, nor do they simply coincide or even derive one from the other. It may be that for governing societies, whether as states or as communities within states, some form of authority is essential. Certainly, for both of these religious legal traditions, there is a claim of divine origin; but the claim of divine origin is not the same as the claim of authority. Because law involves social processes, it also involves some sort of reasoning by human beings and thereby raises fundamental questions of the conditions under which certain forms of reasoning (or reasoners) are able to exercise the authority of judgment, decision, and guidance. How do we make sense of these two terms? One popular view is that religious law depends only on authority. On this view of authority, reason itself may not have much to do with positive law, because if it did the result would be purely secular law. Thus the choice of *and* directly challenges the presumption that any assertion of authority in these traditions must be irrational, thus demanding that we choose between *either* reason *or* authority.

Another way of thinking about the salience of juxtaposing reason and authority is to consider the implications of thinking law as both pedagogic and coercive. These legal traditions require both the possibility of education and the possibility of force. Pedagogically, the two legal traditions of Islam and Judaism generate and inform how members of these two traditions see themselves in their world. Religious legal traditions such as Islam and Judaism today often play a pedagogic role in inculcating in members of each tradition specific content about what it means to be Muslim or Jewish in contemporary, often secular, worlds, such as in North America and Europe. In the interstitial details of ritual requirements, legal rulings on complex and fact-specific mundane affairs, these legal traditions today often express and inform religious identity claims in a world in which the Westphalian state claims a monopoly on the legitimate coercive force of the law.

On the other hand, for the members of our workshop and the authors of this book, there was a ready awareness that what may be pedagogic in one instance can also become coercive in another. The possibility of these traditions being more than pedagogic and obliging others to obedience (with formal or informal modes of coercion or sanction) offered a site for examining different features of authority and the way in which they are rationalized, justified, and legitimated, especially in relation to differences between groups of people (men and women, believers and non-believers, etc.). Although *reason* may represent a more educational attitude, it also crosses over into compulsion or "the force of the better argument;" relatedly, *authority* often represents sanctioned coercion, but it may also incorporate the formative and educational practice that legitimates legal rulings.

These questions on reason and authority could have been undertaken by any single one of us in our group, alone in the library. (And indeed, unavoidably for purposes of research, each of the participants had to do just that, more or less.) But by attending to the textual particularities of Islamic and Jewish law it became possible to frame a discussion about reason and authority across the differences between Islamic and Jewish law. The possibility became a reality through the exploration of a key hypothesis: how might we better appreciate the traditions that we study if we also study the tradition of our "other"? In other words, how could a scholar of Islamic law better appreciate the Islamic legal tradition when studying the texts and traditions of another? Likewise, how could a scholar of Jewish law better appreciate the Jewish legal tradition when studying the texts and traditions of another? This practice was not designed to be an exercise in comparative law. Nor was it meant to be an attempt to find that ever-elusive "common ground." Rather it was a defamiliarizing effort to think about our individual scholarly enterprise in a group using the lens of difference, both in terms of the two traditions and of the members within the group.

FORMATION OF A READING PRACTICE

In order to explore and test this hypothesis, various units at the University of Toronto offered aid in hosting our first workshop. The Centre for Ethics, the Faculty of Law, and the Faculty of Arts and Sciences contributed funding that enabled us to convene our first working group of Jewish and Islamic law scholars in 2007. Then a generous grant from Canada's Social Sciences and Humanities Research Council supported annual meetings of this working group from 2008 to 2011. There were many who joined us for these workshops; some of them joined us once or twice, whereas others were core members who returned year after year. We were privileged to have the chance to work with so many impressive scholars, and want to take this time to acknowledge them all and extend our deepest thanks: Rahel Adler, Rumee Ahmed, Kecia Ali, Beth Berkowitz, Jonathan A. C. Brown, Ayesha Chaudhry, Aryeh Cohen, Arye Edrei, Yaacov Elman, Mohammad Fadel, Shari Golberg, Marion Holmes Katz, Joseph Lowry, David Novak, David S. Powers, Abdulaziz Sachedina, Adam Seligman, Amira Sonbol, Suzanne Last Stone, and Ernest Weinrib.

These scholars are some of the recognized leaders in the fields of Jewish and Islamic law. Some are in the ranks of emerging scholars. Several graduate students also participated in these workshops: Jonathan Crane, Shari Golberg, Syed Adnan Hussain, Ari

Mermelstein, Paul Nahme, and Ahmed Saleh not only helped with the logistics, but also sat in and watched the scholars try something new and challenging. Many of those graduate students have now graduated, are pursuing their own research agendas, and in one case (Golberg) continued to work on this project and has a co-authored a chapter in this volume. Although this specific form of workshop may not be repeated frequently, the intergenerational work links up with a specific aspect of this endeavor—namely a desire to generate something from the workshop that could aid classroom courses on law in either or both religious traditions. There are larger and more challenging topics about the role of these practices in academic fields, but the first steps were to convene the workshops and then to produce this volume.

At each workshop, Rabbinic and Islamic law scholars convened at the University of Toronto for two or three days to read texts from the two legal traditions. The goal in selecting the texts was to set up two roughly parallel lines: one in each tradition. Each line followed ongoing debates and concerns across different strata of textual genre, commentary, and analysis.

Each workshop had a theme. For each theme a set of texts reflecting different strata of legal authority and analysis would be read. The themes of the workshops were: adjudication (2007); law and the other (2008); history and law (2009); boundaries of the law (2010); and neighbors and neighborhood (2011).

Adjudication explored lines of interpretation that addressed the need for judges and their authority, looking also at who is qualified to judge as well as differences in authority between different generations and different levels of appellate jurisdiction.

Law and the other examined questions of multiple legal systems in places where one community has political rule over another. To what extent are Jewish or Islamic laws binding on others living among them? May one seek relief from another's courts?

History and the law posed fundamental questions about the relationship between history and law, looking directly at the reflections about history within legal texts. Although there is a distinct emphasis on evaluating and weighing the authenticity of different texts and their lines of transmission in the Islamic tradition, there is a surprising silence and a willingness to view historical change as bound to the original revelation in Rabbinic law.

Boundaries of the law explored strings of texts that asked whether and to what extent these religious legal traditions imagined limits to the reach of the law. In both traditions, legal reasoning extends to permissible and recommended actions, but they also examine the possibility of gaps in the legal systems that require judicial intervention.

Finally, *neighbors and neighborhood* addressed basic questions on how we construct neighborhoods and how we interpret the levels of responsibility for different neighbors. A series of texts on pre-emption in selling adjacent land in each tradition revealed the legal construction of neighbors and further explored the question of the status of those who do not belong to the religious community.

The most innovative contribution to the practice of this studying together was how discussion was bound to the texts. It is not that the text became or ought to become hegemonic over the flow and dynamic of conversation. But, as a site (or is it "cite"?) of authority, it also allowed us to hold ourselves and each other accountable for our readings and representations of the text and what it may or may not imply. To ensure that function of the text, we quickly adopted a protocol for introducing the text for purposes of discussion. At the outset of each plenary discussion of a text, the text was introduced by a scholar for whom the text was "other." In other words, a Jewish law scholar would introduce an Islamic legal text, and an Islamic law scholar would introduce a Jewish legal text. By adopting this protocol, scholars of one tradition could not help but encounter their other amid the internal library of their own tradition, which remained ever present and effective for them. To introduce a textual other was not to abandon or forgo one's expertise, but to allow all of us to reflect on how such an encounter with difference had the potential to raise new questions about things that we assumed we knew or believed about what we considered both as familiar and as foreign. Expertise was invoked not for the expert to tell everyone what the expert knew, but rather to respond to a sympathetic but inexpert question. Hence this work together was less the familiar seminar where each gets a chance to speak about what she or he knows, and more like a masterclass where each helps the others to sort out questions, sometimes basic and sometimes surprisingly rich. It was a real privilege to be able to explore with each other texts that were largely unknown by half of the room. But this activity also elicited a specific kind of play, since one was free to admit ignorance in a university context, and in that ignorance improvise and take risks in interpretation.

At the end of each workshop meeting, we would reflect on the entire set of texts and discussions in light of a discussion memorandum that would outline key issues at the intersection of philosophy of law, law and religion, and the often taken-for-granted assumptions about law in an international state system. In these reflective moments, engagement in the play of textual interpretation was then bound to other planes of conceptual reflection.

FROM READING TOGETHER TO WRITING TOGETHER

At our final workshop in 2011, it became clear that, for many group members, there was something unique that happened in these workshops which needed to be expressed and shared. The result of our discussions is the present book. To capture the spirit of the workshops, we have organized the book as follows. The first part consists of five chapters. Each chapter is co-authored by a dyad of scholars, one of whom is a scholar of Islamic law whereas the other is a scholar of Jewish law. Moreover, the first part is subdivided into two sections. The first section consists of three articles written in the style of a dialogue between the two authors (Ahmed/Cohen; Adler/Chaudhry; Berkowitz/Katz). These three essays reflect the reading practices of our group and the ethics of exchange that came with reading traditions both familiar and unfamiliar. The second section consists of two articles that reveal the implication of juxtaposing our internal libraries (Chaudhry/Golberg; Edrei/Emon). The second section is less dialogic but it showcases the kind of scholarship that can arise when we encounter the limits of our own tradition as it frames for us the questions we ask and research. Importantly, the book does not offer novel scholarly research, but rather aims to reveal the kinds of scholarly insights that can be gleaned by our pedagogy of research through difference.

The second part of the book consists of two essays reflecting on the five co-authored chapters, from the perspective of philosophy of law (Gibbs) and the sociology of religion (Seligman), two disciplines that were certainly in the room at each workshop and whose insights lurked in the backdrop to our discussions about the texts that were foregrounded.

The essays themselves reflect each contributor's internal library and its intersection with the themes of the workshop. The first essay, by Rumee Ahmed and Aryeh Cohen, focuses on the issue of authority, in particular on judicial authority. Examining texts that we read together as a group on adjudication, they reveal through their dialogue and exchange how reading one's tradition in light of another offers new opportunities to rethink received truths that may presume too much. The issue for them centers on whether and to what extent the judge holds authority against the laity, and what that implies about the judge as link between the lay believer and his or her attempt to abide by the demands and will of God. Through a discussion of the judge and the law as metaphor, both authors speak about the way in which the law is implicitly made to stand for more than may be explicitly stated.

In their dyadic contribution, Rachel Adler and Ayesha S. Chaudhry ruminate on the marital contract, and in particular the role of guardian-ship of brides, in both Islamic and Jewish law. Of particular importance to them is recognizing their own otherness to their own respective traditions. They emphasize the fact that, as women and as feminist readers, they would not have been part of the intended audiences of the texts they read together. Nor would their questions have been the ones that animated the texts they read. As new readers in a textual conversation that has historically excluded them, they do more than query the texts; they model an ethics of reading (and reading together). Everyone has the option to disregard a text or a tradition or a con-versation. Indeed, there are many who might suggest that feminists ought to give up on religious traditions in which patriarchy has been the rule. But, as both Adler and Chaudhry suggest, to do so imposes an artificial choice that some may not wish to make. Their important essay, therefore, not only reveals the boundaries and exclusionary capacity of texts and traditions, but also the limits of readers who must expand their own boundaries and capacities if they are to enter into a conversation from which they have been precluded. This is not to say that critique must be dulled or numbed. As they say, there is more for feminist readers of these traditions to do than merely *understand* historic traditions. They can, with their new readings of marriage, raise important questions that shift the center of conversation by no longer presuming patriarchy is normal in these traditions, and instead make it explicit it and lay it bare.

In their article on animals, Beth Berkowitz and Marion Katz present two pairs of texts dealing with non-human animals and their treatment by human beings. The first pairing juxtaposes texts (one from the Mishnah/Talmud, the other from a pre-modern Muslim legal manual) dealing with legal obligations to assist animals in need; the second (one from the Talmud, another from a pre-modern Muslim hadith commentary) brings together narratives revolving around the merit that accrues from attending to animal suffering. Each selection is followed by a short explanation provided by the scholar who studies the relevant tradition, followed by a dialogue between the two of them that brings out the themes and shared resonances of the texts. Although the specific texts (and their topic) are not from the Jewish and Islamic law workshop, the form of their contribution (as in the case of Chaudhry and Adler) is inspired by the dialogic experience in the workshop.

Taken together, the articles by Ahmed/Cohen, Adler/Chaudhry, and Berkowitz/Katz are inspired by the conversational, dialogic protocol of the workshop. All three essays speak to specific texts, which they outline, present, or reproduce for the reader. The texts helped generate the conversation, but it was the back-and-forth of a dialogue between scholars (and their internal libraries) that informed the flow and ultimate insights of the conversation. As a group, these three essays characterize the real-time experience of the working group as scholars sat around a table, working through discrete texts together.

The second set of dyadic articles reflect the ever-present significance of the internal libraries that each scholar unavoidably brought to bear in all of our discussions. We all have these internal libraries, which inform the questions asked and answers given. Putting these internal libraries in conversation with each other, though, illuminated the limits and parochialisms of each tradition, which became more obvious and challenging through the pairing with the other tradition. So, for instance, Ayesha S. Chaudhry and Shari Golberg explore how each tradition employs women as informal (and even formal) policing agents of women's sexuality. Juxtaposing the role of virginity checkers in Islamic law with the Rabbinic tradition on the *sotah*, or accused adulteress,

Chaudhry and Golberg explore how religious texts in both traditions transform women into agents of patriarchy. Their essay draws upon a selection of texts that they address through close reading together. In that sense, their essay reflects the dialogic spirit of the working group's protocol and shares certain affinities with the articles in the previous section. However, the style of their engagement and the materials they bring to bear on their analysis reveal the role in which internal libraries speak to the construction of a legal idea and its application.

This dynamic is especially evident in the essay by Arye Edrei and Anver M. Emon, who address a wide range of texts on the Religious Zionist literature on the halakha on the law of war, and the early Islamic legal treatment of the non-Muslim permanent resident, or "dhimmi." The two sets of texts, on first glance, do not seem connected. But what links them are the presumptions both sets make about the sovereignty of the underlying governing enterprise. Together Edrei and Emon reveal an inversion in the political imaginaries underlying the Halakha of Judaism and the *fiqh* of Islam. The Halakha was developed in a context of diaspora whereas the *fiqh* was developed in light of the ideal of an expansive empire, whether real or imagined. In the twentieth century, however, these assumptions were confronted by certain new realities. The creation of the State of Israel cut against the presumed state of diaspora for the Jewish people, whereas the creation of multiple sovereign states in the Muslim-majority world created a plurality of sovereigns in contrast to the pre-modern ideal of the unified, monist caliphate. What do these changes in political reality imply about the intelligibility of a halakha developed in diaspora or a *fiqh* tradition developed with an empire in mind? In other words, what is the implication of historical change for the intelligibility of a legal tradition that presumed very different historical realities?

With these two essays Part I of the book comes to an end. Part II offers two reflective essays on the implications for scholarship which this sort of research project poses. Robert Gibbs offers his reflection from the vantage point of philosophy of law and Adam Seligman does so from the perspective of the sociology of religion.

In Gibbs' essay a philosophical perspective draws new insights from the dialogic work of this group. The dialogic nature of the work allows Gibbs to emphasize how study itself represents a specific non-coercive space, particularly valuable for philosophy. Throughout his essay, Gibbs sets up a philosophical framework that uncovers the salience of the workshops and the writings for philosophy of law and ethics. He argues for an extensive engagement with contrasting jurisprudence as a method for thinking philosophically. The interplay of scholars expert in the different traditions allows contrasts between the traditions to expose key concepts against the background of well-developed academic expertise. The engagement of our authors, in the room and then on the page, as individual readers and experts contributes directly to his claim about what philosophy should be. His essay then tracks along the five essays and describes the philosophical questions that comes into focus through the dyadic interplay on the page.

Seligman's piece steps back and looks at the collected essays in this volume from the perspective of tradition, specifically the role of tradition in paving the paths of reason and reasoning through which legal, social, and even personal decisions are made and relationships negotiated. He furthermore looks at past dialogues across traditions and thereby embeds the enterprise of this book in a history of such pedagogic dialogues. Critically, he focuses on the role of modesty, not least epistemological modesty, as a necessary perquisite for such dialogue and as a focus of much traditional wisdom within the three monotheistic religions. Finally, he makes explicit the connection between tradition and authority as these inform any ethical stance that we adopt in our worldly actions. He ends with a meditation on how traditions and traditional authorities negotiate (or fail to negotiate) the existence of those others who stand outside of their tradition but nevertheless exist as "strangers in our midst."

PART I

1

Assuming Power

Judges, Imagined Authority, and the Quotidian

RUMEE AHMED AND ARYEH COHEN

INTRODUCTION

As part of the fascinating and edifying project of "Jewish–Islamic Legal Reasoning," several scholars of Jewish and Islamic law met over several years to discuss pre-modern legal texts on varying subjects. Each year brought new texts and new subjects, which resulted in innumerable points of view, conclusions, and disagreements. At the end of the project, we formed groups of two—each composed of one scholar of Jewish law and one of Islamic—and reflected further on a single topic with a single set of texts.

The authors of this article were drawn to the texts on "Reason and Authority" with a focus on adjudication of disputes.[1] These texts

---

[1] The Islamic legal texts were provided in Arabic and English translation. Most translations were done by the workshop organizers. Listed here, with one exception, are the Arabic citations for the text passages reviewed: Qur'an 4:59; Ibn Kathir, *Mukhtasar Tafsir Ibn Kathir* (Beirut: Dar al-Qur'an al-Karim, n.d.), 1:406–408; Fakhr al-Din al-Razi, *al-Tafsir al-Kabir* (Beirut: Dar Ihya' al-Turath al-'Arabi, n.d.), 4:112–119; Ibn Abi al-Damm, *Kitab Adab al-Qada'*, ed. Muhammad al-Qadir 'Ata (Beirut: Dar al-Kutub al-'Ilmiyya, 1987), 19–43, 53–55; Abu al-Hasan al-Mawardi,

represented Jewish and Muslim legal reflections on the topic from different contexts across many centuries. The authors engaged in long debates on the meaning of these texts—both what they mean on their own and what they mean for each other.

Through the course of our discussion we uncovered many layers of meaning in the texts and, more importantly, uncovered many of the biases that we brought with us to the texts. We found that these biases sometimes overdetermined our reading of the texts, leading us to assumptions about the texts that may not have been warranted. That is not surprising—such biases likely overdetermine the way that most people read pre-modern legal texts. It is almost impossible to recognize those biases when reading solely within one's own tradition. We found that reading Jewish and Islamic texts side by side opened up new possibilities for thinking about religious law that would have been otherwise inconceivable.

It is difficult to describe the process of Jewish–Islamic legal reasoning and to explain why it is so important for our study of pre-modern religious legal texts. So, rather than recount our conclusions, we decided to try to capture a key conversation that we had about the texts. As you will see, reading one's own texts *through* another's leads to new insights and possibilities about one's own tradition. However, reading

---

al-Ahkam al-Sultaniyya wa al-Wilaya al-Diniyya (Beirut: Dar al-Kutub al-'Ilmiyya, 1985), 83–96; Abu al-Hasan al-Mawardi, *al-Ahkam al-Sultaniyya*, trans. Asadullah Yate (London: Ta-Ha, 1996), 98–114.

The Jewish legal texts were provided in both Hebrew and English translation. Given the availability of published English translations of Hebrew texts, the list of text selections is followed by the translations used. The Jewish law texts reviewed were: Deuteronomy 1:16–18 and 17:8–13; Sifre Devarim, Piska 17 and 152; Mishna, Sanhedrin 86b; Babylonian Talmud, Sanhedrin 88a–88b, Baba Kamma 84a–84b; Maimonides, *Mishneh Torah* (Chapter 1, "Law of Rebels"). For the relevant sources for translation, see: Reuven Hammer, *Sifre: A Tannaitic Commentary on the Book of Deuteronomy* (New Haven: Yale University Press, 1987); I. Epstein, ed., *The Babylonian Talmud* (London: Soncino Press, 1935–59); Maimonides, *The Code of Maimonides* (*Mishneh Torah*), trans. Abraham M. Hershman (New Haven: Yale University Press, 1949).

one's own texts *with* another leads to a rethinking about tradition as a whole and invites us to reimagine both how pre-modern legal texts should be read and what legal traditions mean in the modern day.

RUMEE AHMED

The texts on "Reason and Authority" from the Islamic legal tradition included selections from pre-modern Muslim luminaries including al-Mawardi (d. 1058), Fakhr al-Din al-Razi (d. 1209), Ibn Abi al-Damm (d. 1244), and Ibn Kathir (d. 1373). These scholars worked in different times and different places, with varying relationships to power: some were employed by the state; others were critical of it. It is therefore striking that all of the Islamic texts under study mention—explicitly or implicitly—the Qur'anic verse 4:59:

> O you who believe! Obey Allah, and obey the messenger, and those in authority amongst you.

This verse might have been unambiguous in Muhammad's time; one must obey God, Muhammad, and anyone whom Muhammad appointed. However, once Muhammad died, identifying "those in authority amongst you" became much more important, and much more ambiguous. The verse seems to suggest that Muslims are bound to obey "those in authority" just as much as they must obey God and his prophet. Once the prophet is gone, the obvious question that the jurists were preoccupied with is, "Who has authority in the absence of the Prophet?" The answer to that question hinged on the identity of "those in authority amongst you."

In our selection of readings, we had two types of Sunni texts, each attempting to tell us exactly who "those in authority" might be. The first type of text is exegetical (*tafsir*) and the other type legal (*fiqh*).

The exegetical texts define "authority" in clearly political terms. Ibn Kathir, for example, defined "those in authority" as "rulers," despite also mentioning that the towering historical figure Ibn 'Abbas believed that "those in authority" were religious scholars.[2] The exegete al-Razi took a similar tack, regularly conflating the terms "authorities" (umara') with "political rulers" (salatin).[3] This would suggest that, for Ibn Kathir and al-Razi, Muslims must obey their political rulers just as they would obey God and his messenger, and that these rulers are authorities in the absence of the Prophet.

The Sunni legal texts confirm the authority that exegetes conferred onto political rulers, but they add an important intermediary in the chain of authority. This intermediary is the judge, whom the political authorities appoint to adjudicate legal issues in Muslim communities. The sultan, after all, cannot solve all the problems of the community himself and cannot be expected to both define and apply the law. Thus, much like God appoints messengers from among humans, so the sultan appoints judges from among the scholars. The judge then articulates the law, and the laity is beholden to their rulings. If the laity were to revolt against the judge, it would be akin to revolting against the sultan, which would be tantamount to revolting against God and his messenger.

There is, therefore, a distinct chain of authority that links obedience to the judge, obedience to the sultan, obedience to Muhammad, and obedience to God. Certainly, the judge is a representative of the sultan, but, more importantly, he represents God and God's messenger on earth. Thus, the sultan–judge–laity relationship is a symbol of the God–prophet–human relationship. Once a person has reached the position of "judge," he cannot be questioned or subverted, just as one cannot question or subvert God or God's prophet. The populace is

---

[2] Ibn Kathir, Mukhtasar, 1:406–408.
[3] Al-Razi, Tafsir al-Kabir, 4:113.

theologically helpless in the face of his decrees, and, though they can try to ensure that judges are righteous before they are appointed, they can only obey once that title has been conferred. One hopes that the judge is merciful just as one hopes that God is merciful, but if the judge/God decides to be vengeful, then humans have nothing to do but to acquiesce.

Of course, this is not actually how pre-modern Muslim societies functioned; there are many documented instances of the populace rejecting the ruling of a judge, and the judiciary clearly had limited power to enforce judicial decrees. Normative texts—like the ones under study here—described the world as it ought to be, rather than the way that it actually was. In that sense, the texts describe the ideal power relationship between political authorities and the laity as top-down. That is, God *gives* authority to the ruling elite, who in turn *take* authority from the people through their appointed judges, such that the people are compelled to hand over whatever power and authority they may have to the judges' decisions in order to live in fidelity with the ruling and cosmic order. Though the sultan is encouraged to appoint upright judges—and despite the prophetic commandments to obey only in matters that are acceptable (*ma'ruf*)—the Islamic legal scholars effectively gave judges the power of demigods, the judges' will being almost as inscrutable as God's own.

Whatever one thinks of the merits and demerits of such an order, it makes it very simple for common folk to live in fidelity with God's will. All they need to do is obey the judge and the sultan and they will be guaranteed God's favor, just as they would by obeying Muhammad. This same simplicity makes things very complicated for modern Muslims, for whom there is no sultan and no appointed judges. In modern times, the absence of the sultan begs certain questions. What if there were no ruling elite to appoint judges and thereby take power from the people? Would that result in an irreparable disconnect between God and the laity? How does Islamic law get adjudicated, and—more importantly—how do Muslims "obey those in authority" when the authorities themselves are gone? To whom does God give his authority if there are no representatives to act on his behalf?

None of the Islamic readings under study helps us to answer those questions. We could suppose that, in the absence of the sultan, people might *give* their power up to God. In other words, they could appoint a judge for themselves and agree to abide by his or her rulings. But such democratization of authority goes unconsidered in these texts and in fact goes against the spirit of obedience presented therein. People cannot simply choose a judge and decide to follow that judge's rulings; obedience is found in obeying the commands of an externally appointed judge regardless of personal preference. Even as meticulous a thinker as al-Mawardi could only imagine a world in which a judgeship goes vacant, thus devising rules for filling that office. He could not imagine a scenario, or at least an intelligible scenario, in which judges could never be appointed. Would the pre-modern scholars have seen the present situation as one in which Islamic law ceased to function, authority was in the hands of no one, and obedience to authority an impossibility? How, in such a situation, could Muslims demonstrate their obedience to God?

We can only guess what the pre-modern Muslim scholars might have to say about the modern Muslim legal context, but in the Rabbinic texts under study we have something of a parallel to the situation in which modern Muslims find themselves. Engaging in counterfactuals is always a risky game, but it is hard to miss that the rabbis seem to have been asking the same questions that Muslims are asking today about obedience and authority. The fundamental question in the Rabbinic texts appears to be: in the absence of the Courts of Israel, can any judicial body adjudicate law? When read in light of the Islamic texts, the question becomes a bit more dire: in the absence of the Courts of Israel, can any judicial body serve as a symbol for the entire God–Israel relationship? This may not have been the overriding

Rabbinic concern, but approaching the Rabbinic texts in this way helps us understand the stakes involved in modern Muslim discourse.

The Babylonian Talmud seems to express grave reservations about adjudicating any criminal or civil case in diaspora except in the cases of property damage and debt-servicing. Rabbi Menachem Hameiri (d. *ca.* 1316), reflecting on the limited mandate of courts-in-exile, suggested in his *Beit HaBechirah*, a commentary on the Talmud, that the courts only assumed these roles when absolutely necessary.[4] Certainly, the tone of the Babylonian Talmud and the Tosafists' reflections on it suggest as much. The rabbis seem careful to restrict their exilic jurisdiction to minute subfields so as not to overstep their bounds and to ensure that they do not unintentionally stand in for the Courts of Israel. The rabbis-in-exile appear to go to great lengths to clarify that they do not endorse the idea in the Muslim texts that the sultan–judge–laity relationship is a symbol of the God–prophet–human relationship and that no court can serve as such a symbol outside of the Land of Israel.

This judicial neutering of courts-in-exile is underscored by the limited punitive power that these courts assumed. Rabbi Yitzhaq alFasi (d. 1103) seems to have suggested that courts-in-exile have the right to set the amount that, in the case of injury, should be deemed sufficient recompense to the injured party:

> It is the custom of the two Academies that even though we do not collect fines in Babylonia, [the court] bans [the guilty party] until he appeases the injured party. When he gives [the injured party] the amount that is appropriate [for the damages], [the court] immediately releases the ban whether he is actually appeased or not.[5]

---

4 Menachem Hameiri, *Beit HaBechirah*, Baba Kamma 84b.
5 *Halakhot: Baba Kama*, 30b (Vilna edn.).

Note that if the guilty party fails to remit an appropriate amount to the injured party, then the punishment is merely that the guilty party be banned until the amount is remitted. But "banned" from what, exactly? It would appear that, since the courts have no state power, the guilty party could only be banned from the Rabbinic court. Thus, if the banned party had need to go to court for some other matter, she or he could theoretically have recourse to a state court. And so, apart from the social or religious stigma that might be attached to not paying a fine, the guilty party had little incentive to remit payment.

Surely, this was not lost on the Babylonian sages and the Tosafists. There is evidence in the Rabbinic texts under study that the rabbis knew that they had insufficient power to enforce the law. They gave themselves a very limited jurisdiction to begin with, and they gave themselves little power to punish delinquency. The obvious question is "Why?" Part of the answer is surely pragmatism; in diaspora the Jews were subject to non-Jewish law and had, by definition, limited jurisdiction. Further, Jews would have recourse to non-Jewish courts if they felt that the Rabbinic courts were unfavorable to their position. So, the courts-in-exile needed to restrict their jurisdiction to that in which they had the power to adjudicate without appearing ineffective owing to their inability to exact punishment.

This raises the question, "If courts-in-exile have the power to adjudicate and punish, should they?" Would they, in effect, be standing in for the Courts of Israel, potentially serving as a symbol of the God–prophet–human relationship? Rabbi Hameiri, surely reflecting on the Geonim in the Abbasid Empire, suggested that the courts-in-exile could adjudicate and punish if and when Jewish law happened to coincide with the non-Jewish law of the land. He described the situation where the will of the non-Jewish people nicely aligns with Jewish law. In that case, he wrote:

it is as if the litigants had accepted to adjudicate upon themselves according to Jewish law. Even capital crimes are judged by the power of their agreement.[6]

According to Hameiri, the will of the people gives the Jewish courts-in-exile legal authority. In this scenario, the courts are *given* authority by the people, since they cannot *take* authority from them.

This makes perfect sense in terms of governance: the judiciary is merely a branch of government, and the government is only legitimate if the people give it some measure of authority. However, as a symbol of the God–prophet–human relationship, it is a disaster, at least from the perspective of a commanding deity. If the courts are such a symbol in the Hameiri model, then God only has as much authority as the people are willing to give. Such a perception of the commanding deity is anathema to Muslim conceptions of God and law, and I would hazard it be anathema to Jewish conceptions as well. It would seem that courts cannot serve as a symbol of the God–prophet–human relationship in the absence of an overarching government within which the courts *take* authority from the citizenry.

However, the fact that the courts do not serve as a symbol does not restrict all applications of the law; modern Muslim and Rabbinic Jewish attempts to apply whatever law they can in the absence of state power are a testament to this. It does, nevertheless, require reconceiving law so that it is not *supposed* to symbolize the God–prophet–human relationship. Rabbi Hameiri gives us a clue as to how this reconceiving might be achieved. He wrote that, in the absence of ordained judges, lay judges must "adjudicate as if they were fulfilling the commission of the ordained judges, for if not all law would be nullified and the world destroyed."[7] In this conception the judges are not the link

---

[6] Menachem Hameiri, *Beit HaBechirah*, Baba Kamma 84b (emphasis added).
[7] Ibid.

between God and humans; rather, the link is the application of law, however limited its jurisdiction. The application of the law serves as a justification for God's continued relationship with the world. If the law were not applied, the world would be destroyed. Conversely, so long as the law is applied, in some form or another, the world will not necessarily be destroyed.

Judges are thereby removed from the immediate equation of giving and taking authority, having been replaced by the world. God takes authority from humans by threatening to destroy the world if the law is not applied in some measure. Humans give authority to God by applying the law in the world and creating a just society. In this new conception, one no longer obeys judges to please God; rather, humans must apply law to validate the world. Obedience, it would seem, is less about listening to one person, and more about saving the world.

If we step out of the text a bit, we find a parallel to Rabbi Hameiri's reconception of law as previously mentioned in modern Muslim appeals to apply sharia. Many of these appeals discuss the importance of applying law, but not because God commanded it; in fact, God is often an afterthought. Instead, the focus of these appeals is how beneficial sharia would be for individuals and society, how beneficial these laws are for human coexistence, and how deleterious the social and physical ramifications of ignoring divine law. Modern Muslim discourse on religious law seems to mirror the Rabbinical move away from courts symbolizing the God–prophet–human relationship, and toward basic human survival and flourishing.

To return to our earlier questions—namely, "Whom do Muslims obey when the authorities are absent?" and "How does God take authority when there is no one to represent him"—we see that, for the rabbis and many Muslims in the modern period, authority is not given by God to judges and then taken from the laity, but rather given to God for the sake of the world. God gives the world no legitimacy if the law is not applied, and sharia-minded Muslims see a world without sharia law as illegitimate. Put another way, God takes authority from humans by demanding the application of law for the world's continuation, and humans give authority to God by applying the law in the world. The relationship in this new model is bi-directional; whereas in the pre-modern model God gives authority to judges and judges take authority from the laity, now humans give authority to God and, in return, God gives authority to the world. Because of this new model, the courts cannot serve as a symbol of the God–human relationship because it turns God into a deity that receives authority; or perhaps that simply points to a need for a new theology that can handle this new model.

All of this requires us to answer, in this new model, who are "those in authority amongst you" who must be obeyed? It cannot be the laity, who are giving their authority to God and to the world. It certainly cannot be the world; whereas judges could certainly stand in for God and command obedience, the world cannot command at all, let alone command obedience. Who, then, are "those in authority" who must be obeyed? It would seem that the honest answer in the new, diasporic conception of law is: no one. If obedience to the arbiters of the law is no longer seen as a symbol of the God–human relationship, then no one has the authority to command obedience unless the populace chooses that authority for themselves. Even then, disobedience to that authority is not tantamount to disobedience to God. Humans, in this new conception, have full authority to choose whom they will and will not obey without immediate theological ramifications. Whether or not modern Jews and Muslims acknowledge this conclusion, it is manifest in the modern communities that they create in which law as applied in the world is of deep importance, but in which obedience to those articulating the law is not.

ARYEH COHEN

A number of distinct though overlapping issues are touched upon in these texts. On the one hand is the question of authority. What is its source? Is the source of authority God? Is the source of authority a certain body of knowledge and the ability to apply that knowledge to cases at hand? Is the source of authority purely political (i.e., appointment by a caliph)? Is this latter a stand-in for a connection to God (i.e., the caliph is to the jurist as God was to the Prophet)? Is the source of authority the community's acceptance (*ijma'*)?

A second question is the theological question, which is, perhaps, an ontological question. Is the judgment that the judge renders the word of God? Is it actually the word of God? That is, is the judge in some way channeling the actual revealed word of God in the same way as verses of the Qur'an were revealed to Muhammad in various times and places as necessary? Or is the judgment the word of God only by analogy? In perhaps the same way as the Supreme Court is, as Justice Robert Jackson said, not final because it is infallible but, rather, is infallible because it is final?[8]

Finally, the epistemological question. Is the purpose of the judge to find truth? Can the judge find Truth, capital T?

At times it seems that the judge is the arbiter of truth by means of his superior knowledge and intellect, his grasp of the Qur'an, and the Sunna, and the early interpretations, and also the ways of analogy. It is only by these means that a judge may be appointed, and if he does not live up to these expectations he may not be appointed and his judgments will be rejected. However, here things become fuzzy, since the judgments of the judge who does not meet the requirements, if he was appointed anyway, are rejected *even if they corresponded to the truth and were correct.*[9] On the other hand, al-Mawardi, the author

---

[8] *Brown v. Allen*, 344 U.S. 443 (1953).
[9] Al-Mawardi, *al-Ahkam al-Sultaniyya*, trans. Yate, 100.

of *al-Ahkam al-Sultaniyya*, also states firmly that "If a judge comes to a judgment and the same case comes up later, he should again make *ijtihad* and pronounce a judgment in accordance with what his *ijtihad* leads him to, *even if it conflicts with the judgment he made before.*"[10] Truth, then, is the function of the judgment and not something that the judge must excavate to find. One's appropriateness to be a judge is thus very important, since it is that aura (of appropriateness) that guarantees, or constructs, the integrity of the system.

At the same time it may be noted that the qualifications for being a judge are such that it may only be Muhammad himself who could be a judge. According to al-Mawardi, the judge "must be of just character." This is defined as:

> being true in speech, manifest in his fulfillment of a trust, free of all forbidden acts, careful to guard himself against wrong actions, free of all doubt, equitable both when content and when angry, chivalrous and vigorous both in his *deen* and his worldly affairs. When such qualities are perfected in him, this quality of justice—by which his testimony is permitted and his judicial authority is acceptable—may be said to be present. If, however, he is lacking in any of these qualities, his testimony is not accepted, his words are not accepted and his decisions are not executed.[11]

It is this last statement that moves this description to the realm of the mythical. Is it possible that there is one who is not lacking "in any of these qualities?" Perhaps this is the aim of this passage, to mythologize the judge.

This same paradox is available in the Talmudic statement (Shabbat 10a), "Any judge who renders a completely truthful judgment, Scripture

---

[10] Ibid.
[11] Ibid., 99.

ascribes to him as if he was made a partner with the Holy One of Blessing in the act of creation." Is this because the judge has discerned the Truth and then revealed it to the world, in the same way as God revealed the world itself at Creation? Or is it rather that the judge who judges truthfully, using the tools of his intellect and his understanding of the principles and substance of the oral and written law, is, in his creation of this truth in this case, likened to God who created the world?

The answer to this dilemma is not obvious and both traditions have discussions about mistakes. According to Ibn Abi al-Damm, the adjudicator gets a reward for judging using *ijtihad* even if he has made an error, although if he had judged correctly he would have gotten two rewards.[12]

The very practice of adjudication renders the answer to the question of the meaning of authority all the more fraught. Once it is acknowledged that the job of the judge, when there is no clear source in the Qur'an or the Sunna, is to use his rational capacities to analogize existing law to a case not covered, then the parallel to Muhammad's relation to God breaks down or at least becomes ambiguous.

However, at least in this set of texts it is that very anxiety—that the judges in every generation operate under the paradigm of prophetic justice or at least by claiming an authoritative relationship to the originary scene of judgment—which haunts these texts. The relative freedom of adjudication by analogy is itself inscribed upon that originary scene in which Muhammad praises Mu'adh when he sends him to Yemen for saying that when he (Mu'adh) finds no source in the Qur'an or the Sunna he will "exert [his] analysis."[13]

The set of Jewish texts is haunted by the anxiety of exile. It is the geographical brokenness of the chain of authority that bedevils their

---

[12] Ibn Abi al-Damm, *Adab al-Qadi*, 20.
[13] Ibid., 21–22.

ability to adjudicate. The solution that they come up with renames their lack of authority as something else. It is seemingly a technical fix that evades the fundamental problem. Hameiri's robust statement of the solution creates a new ground for adjudication, the prior agreement of the people (a version, perhaps, of the idea of *ijma'*).

There are those who answer regarding all those instances that are recorded in the Talmud that were judged in Babylonia, that the reason was because they came before us to be judged and since they accept upon themselves the judgement, we judge any type of case with which they come. However, as long as both parties do not come before us we do not judge the one, even if his complaint against his fellow is based in law. However they come to this from a new ordinance which is that in any event the Gaonim agreed to judge now [in the diaspora] all matters of theft and larceny because of the good order of the world. Alfasi wrote that this is so even in regards to fines, that even though they are not judged in Babylonia we ban him until he appeases his fellow. The greatest of the Geonim write that [it is permitted to the courts in the diaspora] even to levy monetary fines and mete out lashes as is required by the situation. We say that in those places where their governments permitted the use of Jewish law, and there was a general consensus to act in such a manner, behold, it is, apparently, as if the litigants had accepted upon themselves to adjudicate according to Jewish law. Even capital crimes are judged by the power of their agreement according as it is necessary...Some have written that this is the law since ordained judges were necessary for theft and larceny cases as long as only while there were ordained judges somewhere. However, when there are no ordained judges [lay judges] adjudicate as if they were fulfilling the commission of the ordained judges, for if not all law would be nullified and the world destroyed.[14]

The Tosafists' solution is more quotidian. We judge these cases on a regular basis because we cannot abandon the project of justice.

A question: There are several places [in the Talmud] where they would adjudicate cases of theft. (*citing Baba Kamma 96b and 115a*)...One can dismiss this challenge by saying that all the cases refer to situations in which the injured party seized [property of the injurer for payment of damages] or in which the plaintiff said let us move the judgment to the Land of Israel as in the first chapter (Baba Kamma 15b). There are those who explain [these "anomalous" cases] that they are specifically cases of theft tangential to physical injury, such as two people who were fighting until one attacked his fellow and stole from him. Theft in this manner is highly unusual and we are not fulfilling the commission of the courts in the Land of Israel [in those cases]. *It is a matter of daily occurrence that we [i.e., the Tosafists themselves] adjudicate cases of theft.*[15]

Hameiri's solution turns the line of authority on its head. The authority to judge does not descend down the chain from Moses through the sages to the judge in any generation. Rather, it flows upward from the (Jewish) people to the judges. (This despite the fact that the people were never actually consulted and therefore their acquiescence is itself an artifact of the judicial system.) The Tosafist solution merely bypasses the problem with a hermeneutic of the quotidian. They raise as a principle of authority the claim that "it cannot be

---

[14] Menachem Hameiri, *Beit HaBechirah*, Baba Kamma 84b (emphasis added).
[15] *Tosafot*, Baba Kamma 84b (emphasis added).

that we would not judge the daily occurrences of theft and so forth that come before us."

The theological issues are almost irrelevant. This is fascinating, since for many places the whole discussion was theoretical. Although we know that the Tosafists did adjudicate, the Jewish community in Provence, where Hameiri lived, did not have judicial autonomy. However, neither authority raises any theological question. The adjudication is assigned to the realm of the human intellectual interaction with the tradition, within the constraints of exile, without any attempt to reconcile the solutions with any claim of revealing the divine will in judgment.

RUMEE AHMED

There is an interesting irony in the two pieces that we have written; namely, a preoccupation with the ontological and epistemological connection of jurists and law with God, whereas the texts that we studied hardly mentioned God at all. As Cohen points out, in the texts that we read, "the theological issues are almost irrelevant." If a jurist's conclusions can be dismissed "even if they corresponded with the truth and were correct," one has to wonder why we were concerned about whether the texts analogized jurists with God. We considered whether the jurist stands in for God, or the jurist uncovers the Truth through a godly method, but Cohen is right to conclude that the jurists under study seem unconcerned with either of these questions.

Why, then, are we so intent on answering these questions whenever we approach legal texts when the jurists don't seem to care? No doubt the impetus behind our reflections comes from modern preconceptions and anxieties around the derivation and application of law to which we assign the appellative "religious." Religious law is supposed to be about God, it is supposed to represent God, and following it is supposed to make us godly. When we read pre-modern juridical texts, we tend to assume that they share those presuppositions across time and space. Moreover, we assume that a Muslim writing in the Abbasid Caliphal court in Baghdad shares many of these presuppositions with a Talmudist writing in Provence. We assume that, since they are both deriving a "religious" law, they can be seamlessly placed in a shared conversation with one another. That is a rather large—not to mention bold—assumption to make. One would not, for instance, assume that a scholar of religious music at Yale University and a scholar of religious music in Carolingian France would share the same presuppositions. Why, then, do we assume that Jewish and Islamic law may be animated by a shared latent concern for theology?

There are at least three assumptions at play about the role and definition of God, law, and religion in our reflections above. The first assumption—about God—seems informed by a particularly Christian view of theology as central to the religious enterprise. When one looks at pre-modern Jewish and Muslim religious treatises, there is a clear emphasis on law over and above theology. In the Islamic tradition, dialectical theology (*kalam*) is usually bypassed in favor of creed (*'aqida*), wherein simple formulations trump complex discourses on the Godhead. Yet, when one reflects on pre-modern Jewish and Muslim works, there is often an enduring belief that it is all, really, about and in service to theology. In that conception, all of religious writing is basically about how to get to God—or Truth. But what if that was not actually the case? What if pre-modern religious writings were primarily about right living, or right thinking, or right governing, with God as an accepted reality, albeit a peripheral one?

This leads into the second assumption, which concerns religious law. The dominant assumption is that religious law must be enacted correctly so that believers may be godly, or at least be in God's good graces. However, the texts themselves do not demonstrate such a concern with God or with the Truth. In fact, they are strikingly mundane and somewhat cynical in their approach to adjudication. The cynicism might be missed, though, in light of the mythic status that our jurists seem to accord judges and the law. Both reflections above noted that the law could not have practically worked in the way the jurists suggested, and that judges could not have lived up to the impossible standards imposed on them by the jurists. It is easy to conclude that the mythos of law is linked to the transcendence of God and "the religious mindset." What if, however, the mythos was a function of explicating law for its own sake; that is, describing an ideal law that would ensure that a society achieved, if not justice and the Truth, at least good governance? What if the primary function of law was not so much to place one in fidelity with God as it was a pragmatic and/ or philosophic argument for a soundly functioning society?

This leads us to our final assumption, which concerns religion. When "law" is fronted with "religious," we tend to think of a different kind of law than the secular, governance-oriented law to which we are used. This presumption is, of course, well warranted; secularism is a modern dogma and was not the primary concern of pre-modern religious jurists. What comes to light is that we are viewing pre-modern religion—and by extension religious law—in response to secularism. That is, we assume that pre-modern religious law must not have been secular at all, and so impose modern ideas of religiosity onto the law to make it "religious." The pre-modern jurists, however, were not thinking in this way, which does not mean that they were not religious. If their law was formulated in a way that we do not recognize as religious, that does not mean that they were secular. It more likely means that they understood religion and religious law very differently than we do. Their religion may have been much more pragmatic; concerned with the workings of the community and society before it was concerned with metaphysical realities. This is a religion in which the community does not have to prove its religiosity or godliness by applying the law; religiosity appears already assured by the presence of the community

ISLAMIC AND JEWISH LEGAL REASONING

and its interest in religious law. The work of this religion, then, is not so much about creating a theological link between God and human, but about using the link that God sent to humans—religious law—to adjudicate in a way that balances coherence, practicality, and ideals.

ARYEH COHEN: CODA

Religion then, in this *practice* of it, is not something that is added onto the law. This may very well be its defining attribute *as* religious law: the law is the tool by which people in and with their considered judgments keep the world going. And thus, and for no other reason, it is the judge who judges truthfully who is a partner in creation. This aspect, however, and importantly, is neither apparent in the practice nor present in the discussion of the jurisprudence. Even the discussions of ritual law, which is—standing on this side of the construction of secularism—the most religious of laws, is not religious in essence. The "religious" aspect of religious laws and especially ritual law is expounded in the mystical and philosophical literature, not in the legal writings.

This suggests, perhaps, a reconfiguring of the field, discipline, or perhaps just the topography of pre-modern Jewish (and maybe also Islamic) studies. The field has always given privilege of place to the philosophers, and then, for the last fifty years or so, mysticism has gained centrality. However, the Talmudists, the jurists who explicated and commented upon practice, who created the intellectual vocabulary and also the guidelines to it, have never been seen as central to the Middle Ages by the majority of scholars and students of Jewish studies—save for a small band of diligent scholars of enormous intellect (Urbach, Twersky, Soloveichik, Ta Shma, Kanerfogel, Libson, Brody, Fishman, and some others) who have struggled mightily to rectify that situation. Aside from pride of place, however, the sidelining of this eminently Rabbinic enterprise of commentary and code from the discussion of pre-modern philosophy and mysticism supports a very modern idea of religion. Religion after secularism is that which is left over when the affairs of the world are taken care of. Religion before secularism, however, is just that—the everyday affairs of the world. It is, then, the province of the philosophers or the mystics to lay another layer of metaphysics over this quotidian practice. It is the quotidian practice, though, which is at the heart of the "religious" texts and commentaries.

CONCLUSION

Finally, it is important to remember the intellectual/religious situation of this pre-modern discourse. In an important discussion of what he calls ancient ritual theory, commenting on the discussion of the Temple service in both legal writings (Mishnah Yoma) and liturgical poetry (the so-called *avodah*), Michael Swartz writes, "Ancient ritual discourse has also been known to constitute a form of ritual itself. That is, the act of speaking about ritual, in the form of philosophical or legal study, recitation of ritual prescriptions, or the creation of artistic works portraying existing rituals, can itself become a ritualized activity and thus enter a liturgical system."[16] This understanding can, *mutatis mutandis*, be transferred to the pre-modern writers that we have been reading.

The basic site of the commentary discussion on the Talmud, a discussion that is overwhelmingly legal in context and form, is not the courtroom but the study hall. This does not mean that no actual

---

[16] Michael Swartz, "Judaism and the Idea of Ancient Ritual Theory," in *Jewish Studies at the Crossroads of Anthropology and History: Authority, Diaspora, Tradition*, ed. Ra'anan S. Boustan, Oren Kosansky, and Marina Rustow (Philadelphia: University of Pennsylvania Press, 2011), 297.

adjudication was based on these texts. However, the commentary tradition is a tradition of Torah study. The study itself is seen as a religious practice, a form of worship. For this reason the practical end of the study (an innovative understanding of a legal situation, for example) is important *tout court*, not because of the litigation it may or may not resolve. In the years and centuries following the inscribing of these discussions, some of the resolutions and interpretations had actual impact on litigation or judicial practice. However, it is important to understand that the rhetoric of these commentaries, which claims for itself universal applicability, is situated in an empire of the imagination rather than in a bounded geographic area or judicial arena.

This religious practice of study for its own sake continues into the contemporary period. It is important for the academic community to realize that the traditional study of judicial process and legal interpretation and praxis has not necessarily happened in a context of actual litigation. At times it happens in a situation where there is no possibility for the specific religious court to take any action—as in Hameiri's Provence or the Muslim community in the contemporary United States. This does not deprive the study of its religious significance, nor does it minimize the stakes of the outcome for the scholar.

2

Guardianship of Women
in Islamic and Jewish Legal Texts

Rachel Adler and Ayesha S. Chaudhry

INTRODUCTION

What Is a Tradition?

When we talk about a tradition we are talking about the speech acts of
a web of transmitters: teachers to students, students to their students,
for as long as the tradition is in good order. The philosopher Alasdair
MacIntyre says that a tradition is not just a set of books or codes or
a body of ancient prescriptions.[1] A tradition is a conversation, even
a bit of a fight. Traditions in good order have conversations that are
fluid and vital, which embody ongoing disagreements. MacIntyre
provides a handy definition: "A living tradition then is a historically
extended, socially embodied argument, and an argument... about the
goods that constitute that tradition."[2]

Let's unpack that a little. A living tradition is historically extended.

---

[1] Alasdair MacIntyre, *After Virtue*, 2nd edn. (Notre Dame, Indiana: University of
Notre Dame Press, 1983), 222.
[2] Ibid., 222.

It stretches over many generations. It is socially embodied. There are real people living out the various positions in the argument. What MacIntyre means by "goods" is what the tradition cares about. When we talk about Jewish tradition or Islamic tradition, some arguments about goods will be about how to live a good life or how to act in accordance with God's will. In this chapter we look at how two traditions understand right relations between men and women, how they are enacted between father (or guardian) and daughter, and how marriage is correctly established. Who needs to do the arranging? Who needs to consent? How are financial resources to be distributed? Legal texts presume that discovering God's will is communal rather than individual. It has to do with actions and behavior, although intentions and motivations are also important. What we are looking at in our texts are examples of how participants at a particular stage of the conversation understood right relations in a gendered context and their legal impact on the lives of individuals, both at the time of their decision-making and later as their rulings become part of minority opinions or precedents for future generations.

Talking Our Way into the Conversation of a Tradition

Reading the texts of a tradition, especially the legal texts, is like walking into a conversation. Some people were invited into the conversation of a tradition, indeed educated and groomed to enter the conversation. But there are others of us whom the tradition never imagined as participants. How do newcomers, such as women or L.G.B.T. (lesbian, gay, bisexual, transgender) people, join the conversation of their own tradition when its past topics, language, and categories were framed by interests and experiences other than their own?[3] How will their

---

[3] Rachel Adler, "Talking Our Way in," *Sh'ma*, 23.441 (1992), 5–8; idem,

inclusion change future conversations? How does their inclusion change the meanings of old stories and old arguments? And what about talking across traditions? How can those of us who are not members of a particular tradition converse with the participants in that conversation?

Talking one's way in cannot be accomplished merely by gatecrashing or intrusion. It requires a reciprocal process. New participants need to learn the lingo. But veteran members need to do some learning too. Newcomers, whether within or across traditions, cannot be asked to shed their own unique perspectives and experiences and swap them for ones already reflected in the tradition. They must be welcomed as the people they really are. The tradition must allow itself to be challenged by the new categories and experiences the newcomers bring. This may require some serious rethinking of matters the tradition used to take for granted. It is not easy, and for a while both the decibel level and the anxiety level are high. The veterans think, "This is going to kill us and destroy the whole conversation." The new folks think, "What did I need this for? Why don't I just walk away?" But if they all persist they revitalize the conversation for all its participants. That is how traditions stay alive.

Conversations across traditions are particularly important because people have stakes in their traditions, stakes so high they may be willing to die for them or kill for them. All living conversations are capable of change, but changes must have integrity from within the tradition. You can't just invade a conversation and force upon it values, language, and behavior that it perceives as utterly foreign to it. The tradition has to appropriate the changes in its own distinctive process and vocabulary. So there are limits and boundaries to conversations across traditions

"Women and Tradition: Talking Our Way in," in *The Jewish Condition: Essays on Contemporary Judaism Honoring Rabbi Alexander Schindler*, ed. Alexander M. Schindler and Aron Hirt-Manheimer (New York: U.A.H.C. Press, 1995), 230–247.

and such conversations must be conducted respectfully. Yet it is possible to trust in the toughness of texts and the ability of religious traditions to absorb and respond to challenges.

The Text Is a Thou

In Jewish tradition the text is not a thing that you consume; it is an other with whom you converse. That is why after you learn a chapter of Talmud you say farewell to it: *Hadran alakh*—"We shall return to you chapter [whatever its name is]." Include the text as a participant. Ask where it is coming from. What is its logic? How is it understanding the problem being discussed? What are its assumptions? How does its sociohistorical context play into its definition of the problem? Whose voices does the text record? Whose voices are missing?

We recommend studying these texts in real conversation: read the texts aloud with at least one study partner. Reading together is an opportunity for discovery and growth. It necessitates believing that one does not already know everything, but, of course, that also makes us vulnerable. It is not only the text that has assumptions and a sociohistorical context. Think about what each of you is bringing to the conversation.

We the authors of this chapter, Ayesha and Rachel, are ourselves talking our way into conversations in which, as women, we would not have originally been included. We come to the texts with our own stakes, our own concerns, and our own challenges. We are interested in the lived experiences of religious women and in their welfare and dignity. We come with some training in ancient history and in gender theory. Probably, our conversation would be much different if we did not share this knowledge and these concerns. Through our learning together, we have come to see how these two traditions differ and what they have in common. We also come as religious people within our two traditions, and so as interested parties. "What we are interested in," Ayesha says, "is the space between submission and rejection." And that is the very space in which the conversation that constitutes traditions takes place.

READING AN ISLAMIC LEGAL TEXT TOGETHER

Background on the Islamic Legal Text

The Islamic legal text is drawn from a work called *al-Mukhtasar*, which was written by an eleventh-century Hanafi jurist. There are four major legal schools in Sunni Islam; the Hanafi school is one of them. The author of this text is Abu al-Husayn/Hasan Ahmad b. Muhammad b. Ahmad b. Ja'far b. Hamdan al-Baghdadi al-Quduri (d. 1037 c.e.). Al-Quduri was a well-respected jurist; he was the head of the Hanafi school in Iraq. *Al-Mukhtasar*, "The Abridgment," was a common name for concise legal manuals and contained the fundamentals of a particular legal school's jurisprudence. Al-Quduri's *al-Mukhtasar* is especially influential throughout the Muslim world, where it has been translated into several languages and been commented on by many scholars. Three names are mentioned throughout this text: Abu Hanifa, Abu Yusuf, and Muhammad al-Shaybani. Abu Hanifa (d. 767 c.e.) was the eponym of the Hanafi legal school. Though his own writings do not exist intact, his legal opinions are accessible through the writings of his students. His two most famous and influential students were Abu Yusuf (d. 798) and Muhammad al-Shaybani (d. 795). Abu Hanifa and his students disagreed politically as well as legally. For example, while Abu Hanifa refused the position of chief judge offered by the Abbasid ruler al-Mansur and subsequently died in prison, Abu Yusuf accepted this position.

Islamic Legal Text

The marriage of a free (*hurra*), adult (*baligha*), sane (*'aqila*) woman is/should be contracted with her consent (*rida'iha*), whether or not a guardian (*wali*) contracts her marriage. According to Abu Hanifa, [this is the case regardless of whether] she is a virgin (*bikran*) or deflowered but unmarried (*thayyib*). The two [Abu Yusuf and Muhammad] said, marriage cannot be contracted without a *wali*. It is not permissible for the *wali* to coerce (*ijbar*) an adult, sane virgin in marriage. If the *wali* asks for her permission (*ista'dhanaha*), and she is silent (*sakatat*), or laughs (*dahakat*), or cries without sound (*bakat bi-ghayr sawt*), that is [indicative of] her permission (*idhn*). But, if she refuses he cannot marry her. If he asks a *thayyib*, there is no question (*la budda*) that her consent must be verbal. If her virginity was removed (*zalat*) by jumping (*wathba*), or menstruation (*hayda*), or an injury (*jiraha*), or spinsterhood (*ta'nis*) then the law (*hukm*) of virgins [applies to her]. If her virginity was removed by fornication (*zina*), then according to Abu Hanifa she is in the same [category]. And the two, may God have mercy on them, said that she is under the ruling of the *thayyib*. If the husband says to the virgin, "The marriage [proposal] reached you, and you remained silent," and she says, "No, I refused it," her word takes precedence (*fa-l-qawl qawluha*) and there is no oath (*yamin*) due on her. There is no extraction of oath (*yastahlif*) in marriage according to Abu Hanifa. [But] Abu Yusuf and Muhammad said, oaths are extracted in it. The marriage is contracted in the language of betrothal (*lafz al-nikah*), marriage (*al-tazwij*), transference of ownership (*al-tamlik*), gifting (*al-wahba*) and charity (*al-sadaqa*). It is not contracted in the language of leasing (*ijara*), hiring (*i'ara*), and free contract (*ibaha*). The marriage of a minor male or female is valid if the *wali* marries them off, whether the minor girl is a virgin or not, so long as the *wali* is an agnate. If [two minors] were married off by the father or grandfather, then they do not have a choice after reaching maturity. But, if other than the father or grandfather married them off, then each of them has the choice when they reach adulthood: if they wish they may uphold the marriage [contract], and if they wish they may annul it. And the slave, the minor, insane (*majnun*) and the disbelievers (*kafir*) cannot be guardians to Muslim women.[4]

Explication and Reflection: Ayesha S. Chaudhry

This text is about the authority and power of guardianship in marriage. It raises and answers several issues with regard to the parties involved in contracting marriages. A helpful way to study this text is to unpack it by formulating the questions it raises along with the answers that it provides. By reflecting on how legal texts answer unasked questions, we can begin to discern the legal reasoning of a jurist. Inserting questions allows us to rephrase the text to uncover the issues that a jurist may be thinking about and trying to address through legal ruling. This exercise allows us to see, hear, and ask the questions the jurist is confronting but also the questions that remain unasked as well as questions that are left unanswered. The questions and answers raised by this text are listed on the next pages. My reflections are included following each Q&A in brackets.

---

[4] Abu al-Husayn b. Muhammad b. Ahmad b. Ja'far al-Quduri al-Hanafi al-Baghdadi, *Mukhtasar al-Quduri fi al-Fiqh al-Hanafi*, ed. Kamil Muhammad Muhammad 'Awaida (Beirut: Dar al-Kutub al-'Ilmiyya, 1997), 146.

Q. Can a woman represent herself and her interests when contracting a marriage, or must she be represented by her guardian?

A. On this point, there is disagreement. Abu Hanifa believed that a woman could marry herself, without a guardian. However, Abu Yusuf and Muhammad believed that a woman cannot marry herself and must be represented by a guardian.

[What conception of womanhood makes possible the question of a woman's legal capacity to represent herself? Why would her legal capacity to represent herself be questioned? Why isn't it assumed?]

Q. Can a woman be coerced into marriage?

A. It depends. She may not be coerced into marriage if she is a free, adult, and sane woman.

[This answer suggests that women who do not fit these categories—namely slaves, minors, and insane—may be coerced into marriage.]

Q. Must a free, adult, and sane woman consent to her marriage?

A. Yes, she must consent to her marriage.

Q. What are the ways in which a free, adult, and sane woman may express her consent to marriage?

A. It depends. If she is a virgin, then she may express her consent in three ways: (1) silence, (2) laughter, and (3) crying without sound. However, if she is deflowered but unmarried (*thayyib*), then she must express her consent verbally.

[Does this not suggest that refusal must be verbal? If so, it would require a great deal of courage and independence from a woman. The framing question of this text suggests that a woman would not have this independence to begin with, since her legal capacity to represent herself is contested. Also, it is counter-intuitive to argue that crying without sound counts as consent—in what world is this not seen as more likely a sign of distress or anguish? Laughter can express consent but also sarcasm. Finally, how do we know that someone is a virgin?]

Q. Can a guardian force a free, adult, sane woman into marriage if she refuses a marriage proposal?
A. No, she cannot be coerced into marriage; her guardian must accept her decision.

[Of course, if she refuses a marriage, then she has to go home with the guardian, who has a great deal of power over her and could make her life very difficult.]

Q. Speaking of the deflowered but unmarried woman, what are the ways in which a woman may lose her virginity?
A. A woman can lose her virginity in five ways: (1) jumping, (2) menstruation, (3) injury, (4) spinsterhood (*ta spi*), or (5) fornication.

[Is the deflowered, unmarried woman necessarily a divorcee or widow? It appears not, since the list of ways a woman can lose virginity does not include marriage, though it does include fornication. This casual mention of fornication is confounding and potentially helpful for women, who can claim loss of virginity through menstruation, jumping, or injury rather than fornication. In this case, they have a bit more power over the narrative of their virginity, which nevertheless remains a matter of public concern. In what ways can a woman lose her virginity before marriage? Fornication is listed casually as one of the ways in which a woman can lose virginity, alongside jumping, menstruation, injury, and spinsterhood. Why is there no discussion of the hadd punishment of a hundred lashes being applied to the woman who fornicates? Either the hadd is not relevant here (why not?), or it is expected that a woman will survive the punishment and be married. Why and how is spinsterhood a means of losing one's virginity? Is virginity restricted by age? Can older women not be virgins? What is the connection between age and virginity? While three activities on the list—jumping, injury, and fornication—are connected to the loss of a hymen, menstruation and spinsterhood are not hymen-related events. What connection does a hymen have to the concept of virginity here?]

Q. If a woman lost her virginity through fornication, does she have to verbally consent to her marriage?

A. On this point, there is disagreement. Abu Hanifa believed that, like the virgin, she does not have to verbally consent to her marriage. However, Abu Yusuf and Muhammad believed that fornication put her in the category of the *thayyib*, and therefore she must verbally consent to her marriage.

[So, according to Abu Hanifa the female fornicator is different from the deflowered but unmarried woman (*thayyib*) through lack of control over her person, such that she may be married without her consent. And Abu Yusuf and

Muhammad grant her greater control over herself because she is required to verbally consent to her marriage. It seems these scholars disagree with regard to the value of the experience gained through fornication. For Abu Hanifa, this experience does not put a woman in the category of the *thayyib*, but the question is "Why?" Is it because there is an assumption that her fornication may be a sign of her guilelessness and thus that she needs the protection of her male guardian to oversee her interests in arranging her marriage, or is it a punishment for the woman who fornicates that she still gets treated like a virgin? And why do Abu Yusuf and Muhammad grant the female fornicator agency in her marriage? Is it because her sexual experience makes her a capable agent in arranging her own marriage?]

Q. If there is a disagreement about the issue of consent after a couple has married, where a husband claims that his wife consented to the marriage proposal through silence, and the wife claims that she refused the marriage, then whose claim takes precedence?
A. In this case the wife's claim takes precedence.

[Interesting that here the discussion is limited to a contested claim about a woman's consent based on silence alone and not on whether she laughs or cries without sound.]

Q. Can there be extraction of oaths in marriage?
A. On this point, there is disagreement. Abu Hanifa believed that there could be no extraction of oaths in marriage, whereas Abu Yusuf and Muhammad [who seem to agree on everything!] believed that oaths could be extracted in marriage.

35

Q. What is the nature of a marriage contract? Is it more like a sale or a lease? What language is appropriate for it?

A. The language appropriate to use in a marriage contract is that of betrothal, marriage, transference of ownership, gifting, and charity. The language of leasing, hiring, and free contract is unsuitable for marriage contracts.

[So, marriage is more like the transference of ownership from the male guardian to the husband, rather than a loan or lease, where there is an expectation of profit for the original owner (father) after use?]

Q. Can a guardian marry off a virgin or *thayyib* minor?
A. Yes he can, so long as he is an agnate.

[What is it about an agnate that makes it less likely that he will take advantage of a minor? Or is there some other reason that an agnate guardian has more power over minors than other guardians do?]

Q. Can minors be married against their will and without their consent?
A. It depends.

Q. Can two minors who were forced into marriage seek to nullify their marriage once they come of age?
A. It depends on who the guardian was who arranged their marriage. If their marriage was arranged by their father or paternal grandfather (agnate), then minors cannot nullify their marriage. However, if anyone else contracted their marriage, then each party can choose to nullify or uphold the marriage contract.

[This does not mean that the couple cannot divorce, only that the marriage cannot be nullified. The husband is still allowed to divorce his wife, at all times.]

Q. What categories of people are unsuitable for guardianship of Muslim women?
A. Slaves, minors, the insane (*majnun*), and disbelievers (*kafir*).

[Women are implicitly included in this list, since they cannot be guardians. It is interesting to think of them in the category of slaves, minors, the insane, and disbelievers. What qualities do these people share that make them incapable of being guardians?]

Rachel Adler's Reflections on the Islamic Legal Text

In both traditions there seem to be questions about consent, namely, which categories of women have to consent to their marriage. That seems to suggest that women, when they are adults, are not like other kinds of property. They are more like people. The categories here are interesting. *The women must be free*, rather than slave women, who are perceived entirely as property and hence are not asked for consent about anything. *The women have to be adult*. If this were the Mishnah, I'd know that "adult" means a woman over the age of twelve-and-a-half. What does "adult" mean here? The text seems to assume the reader knows this legal definition. *They have to be sane*. That made me curious. Who wants to marry a crazy woman? Who marries off a crazy woman? I wish there were stories or legal examples.

I was intrigued by how the language delineating the nature of the marriage transaction is constructed. A marriage can be described as betrothal, marriage, transference of ownership, gifting, and charity, but apparently it cannot be validly contracted if the language of "leasing," "hiring," and "free contract" is used. But the latter three terms could describe a woman controlling her own sexuality and bestowing it under the terms she chooses. What seems similar to the Jewish texts about marriage is that the legal authority is explicitly rejecting those possibilities and making sure that this is a transfer from one man to another.

In both traditions an adult woman has to consent, but in Talmudic law a very thin kind of consent is sufficient. Silence constitutes consent. As long as she doesn't yell, "No, no. I absolutely refuse," she is assumed to have consented. In your text, a non-virgin has to consent specifically in words. As for the virgin, the *wali* has to study her non-verbal language to *discern* whether or not she actually consents, although, I must admit, the criteria sound as strange to me as they do to you. Couldn't she be crying because she is appalled or laughing because the whole idea is ludicrous? Could the difficulty about interpreting the young woman's non-verbal language mean that women were socialized not to speak much in the presence of men? Apparently, Jewish women were always rather mouthy, although the rabbis complain about it incessantly. I'm also curious about what kind of communication breakdown results in a husband thinking that his wife consented while the wife avers that she did not.

It is striking that virginity is a constructed category detached from the physical fact of whether or not the woman has a hymen. The Mishnah has an analogous category called *mukat etz*, a girl or woman whose hymen was perforated by a tree branch or something analogous. These women count as technical virgins, as long as the injury was disclosed before marriage. Both traditions seem to assume that hymens are delicate and easily injured. Here, according to Abu Hanifa, even if her hymen is missing because of fornication, she can be a virgin. That's a pretty liberal definition of "virgin"! I wonder what his reasoning was and how he justified it. I also wished I knew why Abu Yusuf and Mohammad disagreed with him. I wish we could reconstruct the argument. Abu Hanifa's opinion led me to wonder if an inclusive definition functioned to cover the tracks of a *wali* who had sexually abused his ward. I also wondered if a *wali* had to disclose that the woman was a technical virgin who lacked a hymen, or was the husband left to discover that for himself? What would that scenario have looked like? Would he have been angry or felt cheated? In the Talmudic tradition, if the husband did not see the proofs of virginity he was expecting, he was encouraged to go to court.[5] Even if he did not divorce her after the discovery, he still might be allowed to reduce the amount of her *ketubah* settlement. Was having a hymen less of a big deal for the writer of this text, and, if so, what social reality did that reflect?

One question the text left unanswered that I wondered about is what happens to the *wali* who has coerced his ward into marriage? The text says it is forbidden to do so, but there don't seem to be any consequences. Did that allow a *wali* to get away with coercion? Also, it struck me that, among the reasons for lacking a hymen, rape is not mentioned. Was rape uncommon in the writer's society or was it, as in many cultures, a secret the terrified girl kept, either because she was so sexually ignorant that she did not understand the significance of what had occurred or because it was his word against hers and her testimony was not considered as credible as a man's?

READING A JEWISH LEGAL TEXT TOGETHER

Background on the Jewish Legal Text

The Mishnah, originally transmitted orally, was written down about 200 C.E. under the supervision of Rabbi Yehudah Ha-Nasi in Roman

---

5 See Babylonian Talmud Tractate Ketubot, Chapter 1, for example.

Palestine. Our particular Mishnah is from Tractate *Ketubot* which deals with marriage arrangements and with the marriage document called a *ketubah* (plural: *ketubot*). In this document the economic contracts of the marriage are recorded and the husband must settle on a sum of money that the wife will receive at his death or in the event of divorce for any reason other than adultery. There is a lien on all the husband's property that funds this settlement. The *ketubah* makes it more difficult for the husband to divorce a woman, because it would be expensive for him. He can't just kick her out unprovided for.

During this period, all marriages of young girls were arranged by a father or a guardian. Our Mishnah applies to girls in the category of *qetanah*, a minor under the age of twelve, or in the category of *na'arah*, between twelve and twelve-and-a-half years, when they are presumed to be entering puberty. This period seems to have been when most girls were married.[6] A young woman over twelve-and-a-half, a *bogeret*, had to consent to the marriage and herself received the espousal money and the monetary settlement in her *ketubah* in the event of divorce or the husband's death. Because a *qetana* or a *na'arah* would, most likely, have returned to her father's house, he received the *ketubah* money. If married as a *qetana* or *na'arah*, but adult at the time of divorce or the husband's death, she received the sum herself.

---

[6] S. D. Goitein, *A Mediterranean Society: The Jewish Communties of the Arab World as Portrayed in the Documents of the Cairo Geniza*, 4 vols. (Berkeley: University of California Press, 1978), *Family*, vol. 3. From the sixth to thirteenth centuries in the Mediterranean area, according to the evidence of the Cairo Geniza, the girls were usually above the age of puberty, and would have been in the category of *bogeret* (adult). However, Goitein claims that their consent would have been *pro forma*: "There must have been countless cases in which a teenaged girl was shocked when her father communicated his choice to her, but I have searched the Geniza in vain for a complaint lodged by a daughter against a Jewish court, a Muslim authority, or even only a relative. A father's decision was like a decree of God" (3:79).

Jewish Legal Text

A father has rights over his daughter regarding her espousal (*kidusheiha*) whether by money, by deed, or by intercourse. He has a right to whatever she finds, to the work she produces, and to annul her vows, and he receives [the monetary settlement provided in] her bill of divorce, but he does not enjoy the usufruct [of property she owns] during her lifetime. When she is wed [and the marriage consummated] her husband has more entitlements than he [the father], for he can use the usufruct of her property during her lifetime, but he is liable for her maintenance, for her ransom, and for her burial. Rabbi Judah says, even the poorest man in Israel may not provide less than two flutes and one elegy-singer.

Explication and Reflection: Rachel

Our Mishnah is concerned with the comparative entitlements of fathers and husbands regarding daughters and wives. In the case of fathers, the Mishnah's emphasis is on economic rights over the daughter. Marriage at this time was a two-stage process. First the bridegroom must single the girl out as his chosen wife. This is what I have termed "espousal," in Hebrew, *erusin*, although another authority, Ze'ev Falk, uses two terms for it: "emption" and "inchoate marriage."[7] It is often inaccurately translated as "betrothal," but is more than betrothal, because if the bridegroom wants out he must give the girl a bill of divorce, even though the marriage has not yet been consummated. Consummation occurs in the second stage, *nesuin*, perhaps a year or

---

[7] Ze'ev Falk, *Jewish Matrimonial Law in the Middle Ages* (Oxford: Oxford University Press, 1966).

more after the espousal. This is when the girl leaves her family and resides with her husband.

Stage one, *erusin*, was given a new name by the rabbis. They called it *qiddushin*, from the root Q-D-SH, to be holy or set apart as holy. There were three ways of effecting first-stage marriage: (1) a transfer of money or something worth money from the bridegroom to the bride or, if she is a minor or *na'arah*, to her father; (2) a deed written by the bridegroom attesting that he is acquiring this woman, or (3) sexual intercourse for the sake of establishing marriage.

The father is entitled to any objects the daughter finds—in order, according to the rabbis, to avoid ill feeling in the home—and to whatever she produces as a minor or *na'arah*. At this time, children were involved from an early age in whatever the family produced. They helped farm, they wove or made rugs, and performed many other kinds of productive labor. The father also receives the monetary settlement in his daughter's divorce decree if she is still a minor or *na'arah* when divorced. However, if the daughter owns property that she inherited from one of her mother's relations, her father cannot use the usufruct during her lifetime.

The husband, however, has more entitlements than the father. Aside from having rights over what his wife produces and having the power to annul her vows, the husband is entitled to the usufruct from any property she owns. Of course, the property itself comes to him at her death. The Mishnah then begins to talk of the husband's obligations to his wife, all of which cost money. He must maintain her, providing food, clothing, lodging, even cosmetics. If she is taken captive, an exigency much discussed in Talmudic texts, he is obligated to ransom her at his own expense; and he must pay for her burial. In a Jewish society, burial is a universal right. A person with no one to bury him or her is called a *met mitzvah* because everyone has an obligation to bury that corpse. If no one else can be found to do it, a kohen/priest must incur ritual pollution and perform the burial. If there is family, but they are too poor to pay for the funeral, the community must pay for it. No one may be left to be devoured by animals or tossed in a ditch to rot. Apparently, there was a time when funerals were very expensive. When Gamliel II was the patriarch, between 80 and 110 c.e., he decreed that everyone should be buried in simple linen shrouds, which cut the costs somewhat. It was prohibited to bury people with valuables like gold or jewels. The corpse was carried to burial on a bier and deposited, *sans* coffin, in a cave which was then sealed with a stone. After decomposition, the bones were gathered and reburied in a small box called an ossuary.

Rabbi Yehudah seems to be enunciating minimum standards for that kind of burial. Even a very poor man must provide at least two flute players and one singer of funeral elegies. Flutes represent the breath and thus were common at ancient Jewish funerals. The elegy singers were *not* mere "wailing women," as the term *meqonenot* is often translated. They were paid officiants like rabbis today. They were performance artists who sang orally composed, often personalized, funeral poetry, both solos and call-and-response singing with the mourners. The purpose was to elicit the mourners' tears. What we learn here is that music and funeral poetry were so important that no one was to be deprived of them for economic reasons. The Gemara says that if there are questions about how elaborate or costly the funeral need be, the guiding criteria are the status and consequent economic habits of the woman's family of origin.

Q: Why can't the daughter contract her own marriage?
A: As a minor or *na'arah* she did not have that legal power. Indeed, she does not even have to consent.

Q: Why is it permissible to marry off little girls?
A: Today we would call it childhood sexual abuse, but it was common in that culture. In the later stratum

of the Talmud, the Gemara (300–550 c.e.), several influential authorities disapprove. "Rabbi Judah said in the name of Rav, one may not give up one's daughter for espousal as a minor. Rather, she should grow up and say, 'I want so-and-so.'" (Qiddushin 41a). Nevertheless, during the Middle Ages and even into the modern period, in some Jewish communities minors were married off.[8]

Q: If people could effect espousal through intercourse, a two-part process would not be necessary. Why not just do it that way for efficiency?

A: Although intercourse for the sake of espousal does effect marriage, it is much frowned upon by the rabbis. Their preferred method was a transfer of money, although the minimum sum was extremely small. They also wanted people to sanctify marriages rather than just making them monetary and sexual transactions. They developed blessings for both espousal and *nesuin*, which were celebrated with parties and feasting.

Q: What in the world is "usufruct"?

A: "Usufruct" means the profit earned by property. It could be interest or profits from business or from harvests on farmland. The father has to let those profits pile up. The husband can use them.

Q: Why would the husband get this right when the father does not have it?

---

[8] Avraham Grossman, "Age at Marriage," in *Pious and Rebellious: Jewish Women in Medieval Europe* (Waltham, Massachusetts: Brandeis University Press, 2004), 35–54.

A: The Mishnah seems to point us to an answer by listing the husband's obligations. In the Gemara on this Mishnah, they will quote a *baraita*, a teaching from the time of the Mishnah which did not get included in the Mishnah. According to the *baraita*, the entitlements to the products of the wife's labor, to what she finds, and to the usufruct of her property compensate the husband for his costly obligations to maintain her, ransom her, and bury her.

Q: Doesn't the father have to maintain her?

A: Only until age six. But, obviously, if he does not feed her he's not going to get a labor product out of her, much less her espousal money. There is an option, however, and that is to sell her as an (indentured) Hebrew slave.[9] She would work for a family, be fed and maintained by them, and at puberty was entitled to be married with a *ketubah* by either the master of the household or one of his sons. She was also empowered to refuse this marriage at puberty, a procedure called *miyyun*. The motivations for this sale may be either that the father is too poor to maintain her or to make an advantageous marriage for her, or, as Judith Wegner has suggested, that she has been raped and the sale allows the father to recoup his financial investment.[10]

Q: Does the father have to ransom her?

A: The Gemara argues about that. One view is that he would ransom her anyway without being obligated. The other argues that she could ransom herself using her property.

---

[9] The origins of this practice are in Exodus 21:7ff.

[10] Judith Wegner, *Chattel or Person? The Status of Women in the Mishnah* (Oxford: Oxford University Press, 1988), 25.

Q: What if the woman would rather maintain herself and retain her usufruct?

A: According to the Gemara, she can refuse maintenance, in which case she will keep her usufruct. This would work for a woman who was independently wealthy and a great businesswoman, but not for most wives of the time.

Q: What's all this about the power to annul her vows? Why would they care?

A: Vows are taken very seriously in this culture. They have to be fulfilled. A husband or father can annul her vows when they hear them, but otherwise only a Jewish court can annul vows. Vows could be a source of power and control for women. A woman could vow not to get any pleasure out of sex or to become a nazirite for a specified period of time and drink no wine and shave her head. These are mentioned by the Gemara as annoying vows that women could take. Apparently the men of that time did not find shaven heads attractive.

Ayesha S. Chaudhry's Reflections on the Jewish Legal Text

The question-and-answer method of reading the Islamic legal text and reading Rachel Adler's questions and answers on the Mishnah text helped me become aware of my own subjectivity and the ways that it was influencing my reading of each text. My own reading of the Islamic legal text helped me see what I thought was missing in the text, what disturbed me about the text, and also the things I wished the text discussed. These are captured in my reflections after each question–answer pair above. Rachel's questions and answers on the Mishnah text demonstrated to me that my reactions and the questions this text raised for me were distinct from hers. At times, I had basic questions about the text that might not arise for Rachel (with her extensive knowledge of Talmudic law), but at other times I wanted to push the text to yield answers that might not be as urgent for Rachel. We also remembered each other's traditions differently and also saw differing connections between our texts. This is captured in my questions–answers and reflections on the Mishnah text as follows.

Q. Does a father have authority to betroth his daughter?
A. Yes.

[In our study, Rachel tells me that "betrothal" here means "emption" (*erusin*), which is essentially a marriage without consummation (*nisuhic*). Is there a ritual marker for the transition of marriage from "emption" to a "consummated marriage"? And does a woman have any control over her person at that stage?]

Q. Can a father betroth his daughter without her consent?
A. It would appear so.

[The text does not say so explicitly. However, it completely ignores the question of consent, treating the daughter as an object who may be betrothed, rather than as a free, independent agent who might have a say in her betrothal.]

Q. What are the ways in which a father can betroth his daughter?
A. He can betroth her in three ways: (1) money, (2) document/deed, (3) sexual connection/intercourse.

47

[What does it mean to betroth a daughter through money? This reminds me of marriage as transference of ownership. Is the father paid for marrying his daughter in this scenario. How is marriage through deed/document different from marriage with money; is money involved in this transaction? Is this more like a lease or transfer of ownership? How does one marry his daughter through sexual connection/ intercourse, since presumably all marriages include sexual intercourse? Is this after the fact, i.e., once a girl has already had sex or been raped, can a father marry her to the man? This reminds me of the biblical story of Dina. Which of these three ways of betrothing is most empowering for a daughter? Which is most advantageous for the father? There seems to be an economic element to each scenario, even in the third case, where the father may be offloading an expensive and undesirable dependant.]

Q. In what ways does a father have control over his daughter, in addition to betrothal?

A. He has control over four things: (1) whatever she finds, (2) produce of her hands, (3) annulment of her vows, (4) receiving her bill of divorce.

[What are the things a daughter might find? Does this refer to something she picks up in the street, or to money she may earn from her labor? "Produce of her hands" sounds like it could be her earnings or anything else she might make, such as crafts, wool, cloth, etc. What is the difference between the things a daughter "finds" and the "produce" of her hands? In what ways does annulling vows signify a father's control over his daughter? Why would a woman make a vow, what sorts of vows might she make, and how does annulling a vow empower her father over her? Can a woman vow what she finds or the produce of her hands to someone else, and the father granted the right to annul such a vow? Can a father make a vow on his daughter's behalf? It appears that the answer is no, since this text speaks only of annulling vows. Another way to read this text is that controlling what a daughter finds and the produce of her hands is advantageous for a father, while the annulment of vows is a neutral right of the father, and receiving a daughter's bill of divorce is a liability. What does it mean, financially, to receive a daughter's bill of divorce? Is this something that empowers a father or is it a liability? Does he have to make a payment for her when she is divorced? Might a bill of divorce be comparable to returning merchandise?]

Q. Can the father eat of his daughter's produce in her lifetime?
A. No, he cannot.

[This introduces a contradiction: on the one hand, a father "controls" the produce of his daughter's hands; on the other, he cannot "eat" of it in her "lifetime." What then do "control," "eat," and "lifetime" mean? What is "produce"?]

Q. In what cases might a woman be freed from her father's control over her produce and things she finds?
A. If she were wed.

Q. Can a woman ever control her own produce or things she finds?
A. It appears not.

[This text does not consider the independent woman, without a father or husband controlling her assets.]

Q. Does the husband have the same authority over his wife as a father over his daughter?
A. No, his rights are greater than the father's.

Q. What advantages does a husband have over a father?
A. He can eat of a woman's "produce" during her lifetime.

[Once again this raises the question of what is the difference between "control" and "eating." Does either affect the control a woman has over her produce, or is she denied access to her produce in both cases, so it is all the same to her?]

Q. Does a woman have control over her produce?
A. No, her father or husband controls her produce.

Q. What are a husband's responsibilities/liabilities to his wife?
A. He is responsible for three things to his wife: (1) support, (2) ransom, and (3) burial.

["Support" sounds like maintenance. Does this mean basic food and shelter or is this requirement differentiated by social and economic class? Or is "support" left to the husband's discretion? What happens in the case of stingy husbands? Ransom is an interesting liability. It indicates a social context in which women were regularly abducted, at least as regularly as they might need support or die. Or, if they were rarely abducted, why is this responsibility included in the list? If a woman is unwed, who is responsible for

ransoming her? Why isn't this responsibility mentioned
for the father? The right to a burial is also a bit perplexing.
It seems intuitive that one would have to bury those in
one's care, such as one's wife, children, and slaves. It seems
like the basically decent thing to do, so why mention it? In
what sort of a social context does this responsibility need to
be emphasized? Were there instances in which a husband
refused to bury his wife properly?]

Q. What is the bare minimum a husband must do for his
wife's funeral?
A. According to Rabbi Judah, even the poorest must pur-
chase two flutes and one woman wailer/lament singer.

[Is R. Judah's position different from or the same as that of
the other rabbis? Why mention his position and not others'?
What do the others believe? Is he advocating for more or less
funeral rights for women? Just as the economic aspects of
marriage are highlighted in this text, the economic dimension
of death is also privileged here.]

FURTHER REFLECTIONS: RACHEL ADLER

This is a text that was designed to function in and to uphold a patriarchal
society. *Qiddushin*-marriage served to facilitate "the orderly transfer
of women and property from one patriarchal domain to another," as
Jacob Neusner puts it.[11] If this transfer was done when the girl was
young, she would move from her father's domain to her husband's

---

[11] Jacob Neusner, ed., *A History of the Mishnaic Law of Women: Part 5, The Mishnaic
System of Women* (Leiden: E. J. Brill, 1980), 268.

without being put at risk when not under anyone's control. The text reminds us that even in our own society, marriage is an economic arrangement. There are costs and there are obligations. In the world of the Mishnah these costs and obligations are distributed by gender. The major and all but universal career for a woman is being first a daughter and then a wife and mother, although she may earn money in fabric manufacture or as a baker or businesswoman, for example.[12]

Families are economic arrangements. In our society, children's labor and sexual activity are prohibited and regarded as morally wrong. Moreover, since our society is so technologically complex, children must study intensively before their labor will even be profitable. Gender is not absent from these arrangements, but women now have opportunities that Mishnaic women lacked. The Mishnah is explicit about entitlements and duties in a way few marrying couples are today. According to its terms, it is trying to be fair to all parties. It would be an interesting exercise to consider what we would regard as fair economic arrangements between parents and children or between husbands and wives.

In response to some of Ayesha's questions, what a wife or daughter finds is what she picks up on the road or digs up while gardening: a ring, a coin, an old tool. Finds are unexpected bonuses, whereas what is produced by a wife's or daughter's hands a father or husband can depend on as regular income. Ayesha wants to know which of the three ways of betrothing are most empowering for a daughter? This is a great question, and Talmud scholars love good questions. I'd have to say that none of the three ways sounds very good to me because they all confer possession or ownership on the husband. Ayesha also asks, "Which is most advantageous for the father? There seems to be an economic element to each scenario, even in the third case, where the

---

[12] See, for example, Miriam Peskowitz, *Spinning Fantasies: Rabbis, Gender, and History* (Berkeley: University of California Press, 1997).

father may be offloading an expensive and undesirable dependant." In the third case, designation through sexual intercourse, possibly both the bridegroom's family and the bride's saved some money. The feast was the financial responsibility of the bridegroom and his family, and if he acquired her through intercourse perhaps there wasn't one. In that case the father saved himself the cost of getting her dolled up for a feast. The Talmud assumes that her cosmetics and perfumes will be pricey, and, though the mother is the one who will know what to get and how to use it, the father will pay. But this may have been a socially unacceptable alternative, aside from incurring strong Rabbinic disapproval.

As for vows, fathers or husbands can only annul them if they hear them at the moment they are made. People can only make valid vows concerning what belongs to them, so a woman could not make a vow disposing of property or income that belonged to her father or husband, but she could dispose of what belonged to her, even gifts from a father or husband, in ways they might not have preferred. They can vow not to drink wine with their husbands, which Talmudic husbands seem to find exasperating, or not to eat certain foods. Vows give Talmudic women a measure of control they would otherwise lack.

The Talmud assumes that it is possible for women to have inherited or had allocated to them interest-earning property. In such cases, fathers are prohibited from using the interest, usufruct, for their own ends, but husbands do have the use of the interest on their wives' property, but not the principal, though they inherit the principal on the wife's demise. As for the financial arrangements of divorce, Ayesha asks what, financially, divorce means for the father if the divorced girl is still a minor or *na'arah*. It means the father would get her *ketubah* settlement. That money would come in handy, since presumably she'd be back on his hands. Ayesha also asks, "Might a bill of divorce be comparable to returning merchandise?" You could certainly make this analogy, and there is an excellent book about mercantile metaphors for *qiddushin*.[13] "Can a woman ever control her own produce or things she finds?" Ayesha inquires. Yes, if she's a widow or an unmarried adult (although this is very rare) or a divorcee. Ayesha is correct that this text does not deal with independent women. Its desire is, quite narrowly, to contrast the perquisites of fathers of non-adult females to the perquisites of husbands generally.

COMPARATIVE REFLECTIONS: AYESHA S. CHAUDHRY

Apart from the reflections that I have offered on the Islamic legal text at hand, what can be gained from feminists reading religious legal texts across the Islamic and Jewish legal traditions? Although both texts are inherently patriarchal, discussing the control that a father/guardian or a husband has over a woman, we have to ask if reading these texts side by side introduces new hermeneutical options for feminists. The concept of "emption," marriage pre-consummation, which is found in the Jewish legal text is not present in the Islamic legal text. What, though, if we were to think of *nikah* in this text as "emption" rather than "consummated marriage"? This may be a useful exercise because it significantly changes the tone of the passage, softening some of its harsher edges. If *nikah* is understood as emption alone, then this means that minors can be married off by non-agnate guardians only in emption. By the time they reach the age of maturity, though they are married, they can choose to annul the marriage. Seen in this light, the patriarchy in the law of minors is somewhat softened, because it does not involve unwanted sex on the part of the minor, if the marriage is only emption.

---

[13] Gail Labovitz, *Marriage and Metaphor: Constructions of Gender in Rabbinic Literature* (Lanham, Boulder: Rowman & Littlefield, 2009).

Of course, this does not solve the problem of the agnate guardian marrying the minor, since this marriage cannot be simply annulled.

Similarly, in the case of the disturbing ruling that a woman's silence counts as her consent, if *nikah* is emption rather than a consummated marriage, this reduces the power of the guardian over the virgin. Although he can coerce her into signing a contract, this contract does not necessarily result in unwanted sex (rape), nor can a guardian actually force the virgin to stay with her husband. Rather, a woman can deny that she was silent and her word takes precedence over her husband's claims to her consent through silence. So, although this text undeniably empowers male guardians over their female charges, it also grants women some measure of agency by allowing them to nullify their marriage if they were married by a non-agnate guardian or claim that they never consented to the marriage to begin with. Applying the concept of emption to *nikah* removes some of the negative consequences that would emerge for a minor or a virgin between the period of marriage and either her claim that her marriage should be nullified or her request for a divorce. This does not eliminate the problem of male guardianship over women and their ability to marry them off with or without their consent, but it does allow us to imagine a tangible improvement in the lives of women constrained by these laws, whether in the past or the present.

CONCLUSION

Ayesha to Rachel

We grounded our discussion of this paper in Alasdair MacIntyre's description of "tradition" as an embodiment of ongoing disagreements. During the workshopping of this paper, many of us were drawn to the metaphor of "play" to describe our engagement with our own and each other's texts. We felt like we were "playing" with these texts in the sense that "playing" denotes active engagement in a game with set rules, whereby we respect the rules of the game to engage in play. This play is meant to be well intentioned, meant to build on allegiances to similar goals and to build camaraderie in pursuit of those goals. The metaphor of play acknowledges that in the Jewish and Islamic traditions we use similar strategies in our relationships with the texts of our own traditions, and it creates a space for us to engage each other's texts. Play allows us to feel ownership of the process of interfaith reading and engagement with each other's sacred texts and traditions, recognizing them as at once different but familiar.

As we conclude this chapter of thoughtful and diligent reading of each other's and our own legal texts about the procedures of marriage, we have to ask ourselves some difficult questions. When feminists read patriarchal religious legal texts, are we playing the same game as key figures in our traditions, and, if so, do we want to be playing this game? Can new participants—who would be shunned by the tradition—enter the conversation and make constructive changes to the tradition? If tradition is the embodiment of ongoing disagreement, what are the limits of acceptable disagreement? At what point does a disagreement extend beyond the boundaries of tradition and become unsustainable? As women who enter the conversation of patriarchal religious traditions, we are already participating in a conversation in which we would have been unwelcome, undervalued, and in many instances forbidden from participating. As feminists, our central values about the equality of the genders are fundamentally at odds with the basic assumptions of the texts we read in this chapter, which build on and support the privileging of men over women. Given this fact, how exactly does our conversation add to the tradition? In taking the tradition apart, unearthing its assumptions, and stating clearly what was thinkable and unthinkable in its framework, how exactly do we impact the conversation of the tradition? Is it possible to change the tradition constructively from within or do we seek to replace this tradition with another? Can our patriarchal legal traditions be salvaged?

In this chapter, even as we break the confines of our traditions—by the very act of reading, speaking, and engaging with these traditions as feminists and the "other"—our readings remain committed to working within the logical constraints of our traditions. We diligently unpack texts in which women are defined by their sexual value and economic worth to men, where normative marriage is an economic transaction in which women have little to no agency. What does it mean to engage our traditions "respectfully" in this context? In our bid to "respect the integrity" of our traditions, do we also necessarily "disrespect" the integrity of living women, ourselves included? Does our respectfulness stop us from pushing further, demanding that women's humanity be recognized by these texts? And what does it do to us, and our worth in our own eyes, to try to figure out all the intricate details of a legal framework that ultimately denies our worth and disempowers us? Do we inherently disrespect ourselves when we respect the tradition? Two central questions this exercise raises are, first, can patriarchal legal traditions be "saved" so they can be read in gender-equal ways that no longer do violence and injustice to women, and, second, should we be trying to save these texts in the first place?

Rachel to Ayesha

Ayesha has raised powerful questions about the nature and legitimacy of feminists' engagement with traditions, and these deserve a careful response. Although it is possible to use MacIntyre's definition of a tradition to enforce a very conservative praxis, it is also possible to use it to explain how change can occur in traditions, and that is how I choose to use it. If traditions, unless moribund, are fluid, and if new participants in a conversation change the conversation as I have argued, then it becomes possible for women who join this conversation to do more than merely *understand* ancient legal texts about marriage. Instead, women, with their new narratives about marriage and their aspirations to gender justice, acquire the power to change law. Law is changeable, by definition. It governs the behavior of mutable human beings in mutable sociohistorical contexts. All legal systems contain mechanisms for change. That is why law needs to be interpreted. The question is who gets to engage in interpretation and who gets to make or amend the rules for interpretation? What I believe women can do when talking their way in is: (1) to appropriate the authority to become interpreters, (2) to challenge legal categories that were constructed without their input and that disadvantage them, and (3) to negotiate new rules of meta-discourse so it becomes possible to converse about and alter the existing rules of interpretation when necessary.[14]

In my opinion, *qiddushin* is not a viable way for an egalitarian Judaism to contract marriages. By definition, it is a way for men to acquire women as possessions. I would be glad to see the entire legal categories of *qiddushin* and *get*, de-acquisition and divorce as male prerogatives, uprooted or legislated into impracticability, as several other Jewish legal categories have been.[15] I have proposed a way of marrying that is rooted in Talmudic partnership law rather than Talmudic

---

[14] Meta-discourse to permit conversation and negotiation about the rules of interpretation has been proposed in Seyla Benhabib, "The Generalized and Concrete Other: The Kohlberg-Gilligan Controversy and Moral Theory," in *Women and Moral Theory*, ed. Eva Feder-Kittay and Diana T. Meyers (Totowa, New Jersey: Rowman & Littlefield, 1987), 162–163.

[15] See, for example, the law of the rebellious son who is to be executed in Deuteronomy 21:18–21; Mishnah Sanhedrin 8:1; Babylonian Talmud, Tractate Sanhedrin 69a–71b. The Talmud creates requirements that make the law totally impossible to enforce. Some authorities deny that there ever was a case.

property law, which I have called *B'rit Ahuvim*, Lovers' Covenant.[16] It relies on a minority legal opinion in the Talmud that maintains that there are permitted relationships that are neither *qiddushin*-marriage nor fornication and also uses precedents for customized contracts and ways for women to initiate divorce proceedings from Palestinian *ketubot* in the Cairo Geniza.[17] This ceremony and its contract can be customized for straight or L.G.B.T. couples and is widely available on the internet. Either partner has the power to dissolve the partnership. The innovation is not without dangers. Admittedly, what I've done creates status questions. Are these people going to be considered married by other legal decisors? What force do the conditions have to which the parties agreed by contracting the relationship? Will other Jewish legal decisors accept the way I have provided for undoing the relationship? These issues are, at this writing, still quite controversial. Nevertheless, the *B'rit Ahuvim* is an example of how women can use tradition to make their case and empower themselves. In doing so, they revitalize the tradition rather than reject and abandon it. I would maintain that *qiddushin* is part of our history and therefore ought to be remembered, but that does not mean that contemporary women should be condemned to its inequities. I hope that legal decisors wiser and more creative than I, both women and men, will devise alternative and more just ways for people to marry.

---

[16] Rachel Adler, *Engendering Judaism: An Inclusive Theology and Ethics* (New York: Beacon Press, 1999), Chapter 5. In fairness, there are a number of other proposals either reconstructing *qiddushin* or offering alternatives to it. For an account of these in English, see Melanie Malka Landau, *Tradition and Equality in Jewish Marriage: Beyond the Sanctification of Subordination* (London: Bloomsbury Academic Press, 2012).

[17] Babylonian Talmud, Tractate Sanhedrin 21a. Mordecai Friedman, *Jewish Marriage in Palestine*, 2 vols. (Tel Aviv: Jewish Theological Seminary, 1980). See also Adler, *Engendering Judaism*, 179–180, 203–205.

3

The Cowering Calf and the Thirsty Dog

Narrating and Legislating Kindness to Animals in Jewish and Islamic Texts

BETH BERKOWITZ (B.B.) AND MARION KATZ (M.K.)

INTRODUCTION

We would like to start by situating our discussion of Jewish and Islamic texts about animals within the relatively new field of animal studies. "Trying to give an overview of the burgeoning area known as animal studies is, if you'll permit me the expression, a bit like herding cats," says Cary Wolfe, a philosopher and leading proponent of animal studies.[1] Wolfe traces animal studies back to the 1970s and 1980s: Peter Singer's 1975 *Animal Liberation* had a galvanizing impact.[2] Many parallels can be drawn between animal studies and race and gender studies, which arose around the same time and were also associated with activist political movements. Scientific work going

---

[1] Cary Wolfe, "Human, All Too Human: 'Animal Studies' and the Humanities," *Proceedings of the Modern Language Association* 124L2 (2009), 564.
[2] Peter Singer, *Animal Liberation* (New York: HarperPerennial, 2009); see his recent follow-up anthology, *In Defense of Animals: The Second Wave* (Oxford: Blackwell, 2006).

back to Darwin has played a major role in animal studies, recent research showing other species to have emotion, cognition, and even culture comparable to that of human beings.[3] Some animal studies voices like that of Wolfe call for a reoriented, non-anthropocentric "posthumanities."[4] This tendency harks back less to Singer than to Derrida, in his lecture "The Animal that Therefore I Am," which was inspired by Derrida standing naked in front of his cat. In that essay, Derrida challenges the homogenizing vocabulary of the "animal" and the Cartesian philosophical tradition distinguishing human beings from all other creatures.[5]

Since the late 1960s, there has also been a lively debate in North America over the Jewish and Christian traditions' attitudes toward non-human animals, some scholars identifying these traditions' teachings as major contributors to exploitative and destructive Western attitudes to the natural world, and others attempting to vindicate them by reference to more inclusive and affirmative historical precedents.[6] Recently, Western Muslims and scholars of Islam have joined this dialogue.[7] In her 2012 book *Animals in the Qur'an*, Sarra Tlili

---

[3] See the many writings of Marc Bekoff and Frans de Waal arguing for forms of animal morality and culture. On animal emotion, see for example Barbara King, *How Animals Grieve* (Chicago: University of Chicago Press, 2013).

[4] See Cary Wolfe, *What Is Posthumanism?* (Minneapolis: University of Minnesota Press, 2010).

[5] Jacques Derrida, "The Animal that Therefore I Am (More to Follow)," trans. David Wills, *Critical Inquiry* 28:2 (2002), 369–418.

[6] See Carol Bakhos, "Jewish, Christian and Muslim Attitudes towards Animals," *Comparative Islamic Studies* 5:2 (2009), 177–179.

[7] See, for instance, Richard C. Foltz, *Animals in Islamic Tradition and Muslim Culture* (Oxford: Oneworld, 2006); Zayn Kassam, "The Case of Animals versus Man: Toward an Ecology of Being," in *A Communion of Subjects: Animals in Religion, Science and Ethics*, ed. Paul Waldau and Kimberley C. Patton (New York: Columbia University Press, 2006), 160–169. See also Kimberley Patton, who triangulates among Jewish, Christian, and Muslim traditions in "'He Who Sits in the Heavens Laughs': Recovering Animal Theology in the Abrahamic Traditions," *Harvard Theological Review* 93:4 (2000), 401–434.

THE COWERING CALF AND THE THIRSTY DOG

moves beyond arguments for human stewardship or compassion toward non-human animals to advocate a non-anthropocentric (or "ecocentric") reading of the Qur'an.[8] In this chapter we do not intend to intervene in the debate on the overall message or historical impact of either Judaism or Islam with respect to the treatment of non-human animals. We neither attempt a synthesis of each tradition's complex and contested teachings in this area, nor intend to offer (or enable) an ethical evaluation of their attitudes. The textual sampling offered here acknowledges and foregrounds the multivocality and diversity of each tradition without positing that its "non-monolithic nature" is in itself ethically exculpatory, as Tlili argues apologists have often done.[9] Rather than reifying each tradition (or simply celebrating its diversity), we seek to illustrate how texts from the two traditions drew us into conversation about many of the issues that still preoccupy us when thinking about non-human animals, and to draw our readers into this conversation. The questions raised by these texts include: What themes and contexts elicit discussion of non-human animals in our sources? How do the framing topics and structures shape the discussion? What human relationships (such as ownership, family, friendship, or enmity) inform and structure these texts' approach to non-human animals? How do inter-human relationships relate to human–animal relationships? What kinds of moral and legal obligations arise from our relations with non-human animals and our acknowledgment of their suffering?

In exploring the legal obligations formulated in our texts, we mean to join a growing conversation not only about animals and religion but also about animals and the law. Much debate has been stirred up in recent years by animal rights legal activists—Gary Francione and Steven Wise are leading voices—who argue that animals should be

---

[8] Sarra Tlili, *Animals in the Qur'an* (Cambridge: Cambridge University Press, 2012).
[9] Ibid., 6.

recategorized from property, as common law has long conceived of them, to "persons."[10] They recognize the radical shift this requires in cultural thinking, since "person" is almost if not entirely synonymous with "human" in our lexicon, and notions of legal standing, legal agency, and subjectivity in general would be challenged and transformed if other species were included within them. Francione has gone so far as to criticize the work of animal rights lawyers for their willingness to abide by the old paradigms as they argue their cases in the courts. He suggests that, along the lines of what has happened with other culture wars, the fight may need to be won first in people's private lives and in the popular media before it can be won in the law.[11] These debates point to the ways that law reflects and reinforces people's deepest assumptions and convictions about the nature of reality and about themselves. We hope that looking at animals in Rabbinic and Islamic law can help us to see some of the deep assumptions and convictions held by those who formulated these religious legal traditions and by those who continue today to study them and live by them. Whereas much of the current animal law discourse focuses on the present and on secular law for reasons that are understandable—there are millions of animals alive today whose survival and suffering are at stake—we wish to expand the discourse about animals and the law to include the religious traditions that have shaped our cultures and personal values in so many ways and that continue to do so.

This essay expands that discourse through a dialogue between the two of us about particular legal passages that each of us selected from the respective traditions that we study. (Our chapter does not have the same element of interfaith encounter as most contributions to this collection, since we both identify as Jewish.) Each of us originally

---

[10] See Gary Francione, *Animals as Persons: Essays on the Abolition of Animal Exploitation* (New York: Columbia University Press, 2008); Steven M. Wise, *Rattling the Cage: Towards Legal Rights for Animals* (New York: Basic Books, 2000).
[11] See Francione, *Animals as Persons*, Chapter 1.

brought a wide range of texts to the table; through a process of conversation about the overlaps and divergences among them, we came to
focus on a pair of texts from each tradition. For the Rabbinic tradition
that Beth studies, the first of those texts was from the Mishnah, the
second-century C.E. Hebrew-language legal collection from Palestine,
and from the Babylonian Talmud, a commentary on the Mishnah that
developed from the third through sixth or seventh centuries C.E. (the
period of canonization is a subject still debated) in what is now Iraq.
The selected passages from the Mishnah and Talmud expand upon
the Torah's obligation to help a person whose animal is struggling
under a heavy burden. The second Rabbinic text was a narrative from
the Babylonian Talmud about Rabbi Judah the Patriarch (Rabbi
Yehudah ha-Nasi, often called simply "Rabbi") in which he is first
punished for his cruelty toward animals and then rewarded for showing kindness. For the Islamic tradition that Marion studies, the first
text was a selection from the legal manual *al-Mughni* by Ibn Qudama
al-Maqdisi (d. 1223 C.E.), a prominent scholar of the Hanbali legal
school, addressing the question of whether the owner of a domestic
animal is legally obligated to feed it, and whether he can be compelled
to if he fails to do so. The second is a hadith (a statement traced
back to the Prophet Muhammad through a chain of transmission)
emphasizing the merit of kind actions toward non-human animals,
with a commentary by Muhyi al-Din al-Nawawi (d. 1277 C.E.), an
influential hadith scholar and jurist of the Shafi'i school. Although it
is drawn from a hadith commentary rather than a legal compilation,
it deploys legal categories to address the question of human obligation toward other living beings. Rabbinic and Islamic law both have
many passages about animals. We selected these two pairs of texts
because they stand out for their complexity and rich texture and speak
directly to the question of human obligations toward animals. Thus
they seemed to us to raise the key questions about animal standing
and subjectivity that we wished to explore, and they do so with the

65

multivalent, multivocal intertextuality that characterizes Islamic and Jewish legal traditions and that makes those traditions so intriguing and evocative. Because both sets of texts begin with and build on canonical sources rather than axiomatic principles, they invite us to explore how canonical texts shape and constrain discourse, as well as how the canonical texts are themselves developed, extended, and subverted by that discourse.

While seeking to draw attention to these shared patterns in our texts—the exegetical orientation, the use of technical terminology, the literary layers—we were also compelled to negotiate their many differences. Our texts come from very different contexts and time periods. The Mishnah and Babylonian Talmud were composed in Roman Palestine and Sassanid Persia in the second through sixth or seventh centuries C.E.; Ibn Qudama and al-Nawawi both wrote in Damascus in the thirteenth century. Whereas the Mishnah and Talmud are canonical for Rabbinic Judaism, Ibn Qudama and al-Nawawi have each been highly influential primarily (although not exclusively) within the specific Sunni schools of law (respectively, Hanbali and Shafi'i) in which each worked; followers of other Sunni schools, as well as members of non-Sunni streams in Islam, would look to other legal authorities. Furthermore, their work reflects a very mature stage of the Islamic legal tradition, rather than standing near the beginning of its development as do the Mishnah and Talmud. In part, the disparity of the sources arises from our personal areas of specialization; in part, it arises from the incomplete parallelism of the traditions, since no early Islamic legal text plays a role directly analogous to those of the Mishnah or Talmud in Jewish law. Nevertheless, the texts are parallel in some deeper and more structural ways. Each of them is built upon a set of intertexts (Bible, early Rabbinic traditions; Qur'an, hadith) that it invokes and manipulates, although the specifics of these intertexts vary. Each of them evokes and intervenes in what is understood as an ongoing, intergenerational legal debate among the authorities of its tradition. Each of them navigates multiple registers of legal argumentation and moral reasoning. In part because of their dialogic nature and multiple registers, each of them ultimately proves to be a very "open" text with respect to the issues that we are pursuing here.

We present the texts in two pairings. The Mishnah and Talmud discussing the obligation to help a burdened animal are paired with Ibn Qudama, since both discuss legal obligations to assist animals in need. The Talmudic narrative about Yehuda ha-Nasi is paired with al-Nawawi, since both discuss the merit that accrues from attending to animal suffering. In each pairing, we start with the Rabbinic text first, since it was composed earlier than the Islamic text. The primary text is presented first, followed by a commentary from the scholar who works in that tradition, followed by a dialogue between the two of us in which we explore themes and concerns that interested us. Because a dialogue by its nature is discursive and associative, we take the opportunity in our conclusion to draw out from our discussion prominent themes and to highlight significant strands. Our aim in the end is not to find coherence among our texts so much as to find shared thematics in their discourse about other species.

DIALOGUE 1: LEGAL OBLIGATIONS TOWARD ANIMALS

MISHNAH BAVA METZIA 2:10

[This passage of the Mishnah is based on Exodus 23:25 ("When you see the ass of your enemy lying under his burden and would refrain from raising it, you must nevertheless raise [it] with him") and Deuteronomy 22:4 ("If you see your fellow's ass or ox fallen on the road, do not ignore it; you must help him raise it").]

One unloaded [the animal] and reloaded, one unloaded and reloaded, even four or five times, one is [still] obligated [to help unload again], as it is said, "You must nevertheless raise [it]" (Exodus 23:5).

He (the animal owner) went and sat himself down [and] said to him, "Since the commandment is upon you, if you want to unload, unload"—one is exempt, as it is said, "with him" (Exodus 23:5). [If] he (the animal owner) was old or sick, one is obligated.

It is a commandment from the Torah to unload, but not to load.

Rabbi Shimon says: Even to load.

Rabbi Yosi the Galilean says: [If] there was upon him (the animal) more than his [appropriate] burden, one is not bound with respect to him—as it is said, "under his burden" (Exodus 23:5)—a burden that he is able to withstand.[12]

BABYLONIAN TALMUD BAVA METZIA 32A–B

Rava said: From the words of both of them (Rabbi Shimon and the anonymous position on the biblical requirement) it is learned that the suffering of animals (literally: "those who possess life") is [a concern of] scriptural status (literally: of the Torah).

... Say that [the following *baraita* (early Rabbinic teaching)] supports him (Rava): "One must care for the animal of a gentile in the same way that [one must care for] the animal of an Israelite."

---

[12] This translation is based on the version of the Mishnah found in the Kaufmann manuscript, which is viewable on the Online Treasury of Talmudic Manuscripts sponsored by Hebrew University.

If you say: That is all well and good if the suffering of animals is a concern of scriptural status, since that is why one must care for her (the gentile's animal) in the same way that [one must care for] the animal of an Israelite.

But if you say: The suffering of animals is not a concern of scriptural status, why must one care for her (the gentile's animal) in the same way that [one must care for] the animal of an Israelite?

There (in the case of the *baraita*, one must care for the gentile's animal) because of [a concern to prevent] enmity.

Commentary by B.B.

This Mishnah treats the biblical injunction to help unload an over-burdened animal found in Exodus 23:5 and Deuteronomy 22:4. The suffering animal is the "problem" that sets the scenario in motion, yet both the Bible and the Mishnah, as I will discuss, clearly privilege interpersonal relationships over interspecies relationships, the animal acting as the medium through which human relationships unfold. Nevertheless, this Mishnah, by a twist of fate wrought by the exegetical traditions built upon it in the Babylonian Talmud passage excerpted here, becomes the *locus classicus* in Jewish law for an obligation to prevent or alleviate animal suffering.

The biblical verses on which this material is based, Exodus 23:5 and Deuteronomy 22:4, are complicated texts, each one in itself and also in their relationship to each other. The Jewish Publication Society translation for Exodus 23:5 understands the verse to be instructing a person to assist his enemy if he should come across him on the road in need of assistance: "When you see the ass of your enemy lying under its burden and would refrain from raising it, you must nevertheless raise it with him." The original language of the verse is ambiguous

69

regarding the situation and what the addressee is being instructed to do: the verse can be read either as instructing a person to assist his enemy, or as instructing them to leave him alone.[13] Deuteronomy 22:4 clarifies the instruction in Exodus 23:5: "If you see your fellow's ass or ox fallen on the road, do not ignore it; you must help him raise it." The Deuteronomy formulation makes clear that the animal has fallen and requires help, unlike Exodus' formulation, where the animal can be understood to be merely resting. In Deuteronomy the addressee is clearly being directed to help a traveler stuck on his journey whose animal has fallen down under his burden, though Deuteronomy changes the addressee from enemy to friend, thereby lowering the interpersonal stakes.

As often when faced with biblical verses whose meanings overlap, Rabbinic interpreters associate one verse with one command and the other verse with another. In the Rabbinic reading reflected in the Mishnah, the Exodus verse requires a person to help unload an animal, and the Deuteronomy verse requires a person to help reload the animal after the animal has had a chance to rest. In the Rabbinic perspective the verses act as a tag-team, the Exodus verse describing the first obligation that falls upon the passer-by, and the Deuteronomy verse describing the chronological second obligation. Neither the biblical verses themselves nor the Mishnah, it should be noted, voice an independent concern for the suffering of the animal; in all of them

---

[13] According to Bible scholar Alan Cooper, the scenario is not, as this translation would indicate, that the animal is struggling and the addressee must overcome his dislike of his enemy to help him with his animal, but rather that the animal and enemy are resting and the addressee is being instructed to leave them alone. The crux of interpretation is the doubled verb at the end of the verse, *azov ta'azov imo*, which usually refers to departure, but if the traditional meaning of the verse is to be upheld it must be interpreted here as referring to assistance. In Deuteronomy's reformulation, the final verb becomes *haqem taqim*, which, unlike *azov ta'azov*, definitively refers to raising up the animal; see "The Plain Sense of Exodus 23:5," *Hebrew Union College Annual* 59 (1988), 1–22.

the animal is the vehicle, both literally and metaphorically, through which the human players interact. The animal's suffering appears to be a concern only in so far as it delays the human owner and creates an opportunity for one man to either exploit, abandon, or assist another.

The marginality if not complete absence of the animal's subjectivity is apparent in the exemptions that the Mishnah permits. These exemptions from the obligation to unload include when the animal owner does not himself make reasonable efforts and when the animal owner has overloaded the animal. As the Babylonian Talmud points out in a part of the passage not excerpted here, if animal suffering were the main motivating concern of the Mishnah, it would not grant these exemptions. If animal suffering were the concern, then the Mishnah would be more likely, not less, to obligate a passer-by in the case of the overloaded animal. The Mishnah offers these exemptions, it would appear, because the animal owner has violated the terms of the human social interaction by exploiting the other's assistance. The one moment in the Mishnah that potentially suggests otherwise is the consensus anonymous position that holds unloading—but not loading—to be a biblical commandment. One could construe the preference for unloading over loading to stem from a concern for the animal's comfort, though it seems equally if not more likely to be motivated by concerns that are exegetical (harmonizing Exodus with Deuteronomy) and/or practical from the owner's perspective (assistance with unloading is a more urgent need of the owner than assistance with loading).

We see in the excerpted section of the Babylonian Talmud that the prominent Babylonian *amora* Rava construes the Mishnah's preference for unloading as being motivated by a concern for alleviating animal suffering, even though the Mishnah passage as a whole does not seem to support this approach. Rava draws his inference about animal suffering from "the words of both of them," that is, from both the anonymous position and the position of Rabbi Shimon, even though Rabbi Shimon holds that loading the animal—returning to

71

the animal's back the burden that knocked him to the ground in the first place!—is an obligation equivalent in status to that of unloading. Perhaps Rava is picking up on Rabbi Shimon's language of "even" in his dissenting opinion that holds "even" loading to be obligatory. Though he holds both unloading and loading to be obligatory, his "even" seems to indicate that the more tenuous obligation is that of loading.

The Babylonian Talmud's extensive discussion of Rava's position, in my reading of it, calls Rava to task on his reading of the Mishnah. The Talmudic discussion juxtaposes Rava's pronouncement with a wide array of earlier Rabbinic teachings that seem to be at odds with it. In so doing, the Talmud seems to be highlighting Rava's radicalism. It is difficult to say just what the Talmudic editors think of Rava's radicalism: should we read the Talmudic passage as a celebration of Rava's legal creativity or as a critique of his departure from precedent? Either way, the Talmud surely wants us to notice it. The excerpted section brings gentiles into the discussion as the Talmudic editors seek textual support for Rava's claim. The assumption in this section is that a Jew can have no obligation to help the gentile. When the *baraita* teaches that a Jew must care for a gentile's animal, the Talmud infers that the concern must be for the animal, since it cannot be for the gentile. The passage implies that a Jew's obligation to animals is greater than his obligation to gentiles, drawing the lines of ethnicity or religion more sharply than it draws the lines of species.

The Talmud goes on to undo its own assumption, at least partly. The Talmudic editorial voice counters that, in fact, the *baraita*'s teaching does flow from a concern for the gentile and not the animal, but for different reasons than one might think. The Jew must care for the gentile's animal not because the animal deserves it, or because the gentile does, but rather for pragmatic reasons—if the Jew neglects to help, he will anger the gentile and risk a quarrel and, it is perhaps implied, persecution. This rationale—"because of enmity"—appears in a number of scenarios in Rabbinic law to explain Jewish behavioral obligations toward gentiles.[14] This passage, in sum, offers two ways of explaining the early Rabbinic instruction that a Jew must care for a gentile's animal: (1) concern for the well-being of the animal, and (2) concern for peaceful relations between Jews and gentiles. The passage appears to favor the second option, though the first remains as a step in the discourse of argument and therefore as a conceptual possibility.

We might call Rava the Peter Singer of the Talmud. Like Singer's animal rights classic *Animal Liberation*, Rava introduces into the culture a concern for animal suffering that had never before been fully articulated, and from there it takes on a life of its own. One contemporary iteration of this theme is in a *responsum* (*Yehaveh Da'at* 5:65 [64b]) by Rabbi Ovadiah Yosef (d. 2013, Israel) that addresses a question posed to him about whether one is obligated to pull over and help a person whose car has broken down by the side of the highway. Ovadiah Yosef suggests an analogy between the broken-down car and the Bible's case of the "broken-down" animal, but the analogy hinges on the same question that so occupies the Talmud—is it the animal, or the person, that the Torah is protecting? If the person, then the analogy to the hapless driver applies (what difference does it make whether his vehicle is a car or an animal?), but if it is the animal then the analogy to the car fails, since one has no moral obligation to a car. Ovadiah Yosef goes on, in his inimitably thorough style, to treat halakhic sources on animal suffering from the Talmud until today, giving special attention to the question of whether Maimonides accepts or rejects the principle that animal suffering is a scriptural concern. Ovadiah Yosef concludes that a person is indeed obligated to pull over and give roadside assistance, but along the way he shows just how complex are the Rabbinic legal traditions on animal suffering.

---

[14] Michael Pitkowsky, "Mipnei Darkhei Shalom (Because of the Paths of Peace) and Related Terms: A Case Study of How Early Concepts and Terminology Developed from Tannaitic to Talmudic Literature" (Ph.D. dissertation, Jewish Theological Seminary of America, 2011).

Exchange

M.K.: What is at stake in the debate about whether animal suffering is a biblical or a Rabbinic concern? Is a biblical principle more legally binding?

B.B.: Yes, a concern of biblical status has priority over a concern of Rabbinic status. It is curious how much energy this *sugya* expends on the distinction. The *sugya* seems to assume that animal suffering is a concern, and the only question is how much. But, in fact, when one reads the *sugya* closely, one gets the impression that the question of whether this is a biblical-status concern is really a question about whether this is a concern at all, at least in this case. For at the moments in the *sugya* when biblical status is denied the *sugya* really seems to be saying that animal suffering is simply not a problem that the early rabbis were concerned with. To me it appears to be an atypical application of the biblical/Rabbinic distinction; the denial of biblical status seems to be a way of denying any status whatsoever for this case.

M.K.: Would the rabbis have any other reasons to believe that the Bible is concerned with animal suffering? Why don't they cite any other biblical passages to address that point?

B.B.: One would think that a *sugya* whose central question is whether animal suffering has biblical status would discuss the Bible more, but it does so very little. We find that the *sugya's* real question is not whether animal suffering is a concern of biblical status, but whether the Tannaim (the earliest canonized rabbis) *think* animal suffering has biblical status. It's actually a great question whether the Bible is concerned with animal suffering, and it would seem to be the one the *sugya* is asking, but it's not. This *sugya* is fundamentally about the rabbis and whether there are resources in the earliest Rabbinic traditions for taking animal suffering seriously. In my reading, the *sugya* ends up showing that the earliest Rabbinic traditions do not in fact evince much concern for animal suffering and that it is only with the later rabbi named Rava—purported to have lived in the first half of the fourth century C.E., over a century after the Mishnah was edited—that this concern is raised. This is the classic *sugya* on animal suffering, and it is about that, but it's also about how new concerns are introduced into a tradition and the tensions that are produced as a consequence.

M.K.: Assuming the position that the animal does matter, is it relevant that the animal in this particular scenario is an economic asset of a human being—and a productive, working asset at that? The discussion of behavior vis-à-vis a gentile identifies a rationale (if only a pragmatic one) for consideration of an outsider to the community. Does the discussion of this *sugya* extend to the identification of rationales for the position that animal suffering counts, and, if so, does the animal's status as a human possession of economic worth (one whose value could presumably be reduced by injury or exhaustion) play any role? Relatedly, does the premise of "overloading" inherently limit the halakhic discussion around this *sugya* to beasts of burden, or is it ever related to non-human animals (including pets and wild animals) as a class?

B.B.: Your question points to an ambiguity that is at the heart of this *sugya*. The interests of an animal's owner often converge with the interests of the animal, since a healthy, vigorous, and well-exercised animal is a greater asset than a sickly and weak one. Conversely, the animal's suffering may cause a certain amount of economic "suffering" to the human owner. When the Bible requires a person to help someone whose animal is struggling under its burden, we may therefore justifiably ask, "Whose suffering is the Bible concerned with, the animal's

75

or the human owner's?" This uncertainty is what fuels the *sugya*. It's relatively clear, in my reading of the relevant sources, that for the Bible and the Mishnah it's the human owner's suffering, not the animal's, that is at stake, so in some sense there's not much ambiguity here. Yet Rava chooses to see the scenario as ambiguous. It's an interesting moment in which a legal interpreter finds ambiguity in texts that are actually rather clear-cut.

The entire Rabbinic discussion does stay limited to the case of beasts of burden. It's a typical case of the biblical texts constraining the terms of the Rabbinic ones: since the jumping-off point of the discussion is the Torah's obligation to help a person whose animal suffers under its burden, the discussion stays close to that model. The only departure from that model, and it's a noticeable one, is Rava, whose statement about the suffering of living creatures is formulated in very broad terms: literally, "the suffering of those who possess life is from the Torah." Rava is not speaking only about carrying burdens, and he is not speaking only of donkeys. It's owing to Rava's global formulation that this *sugya* came to be the *locus classicus* for Jewish law's stance on animal suffering. Without Rava, this *sugya* would consist of a handful of traditions about donkeys who are too tired to keep walking.

M.K.: What is the thematic context of this *sugya* within the text of the Mishnah? Is there a specific topic that elicits the question of the overloaded animal, and if so, how should it contribute to our understanding of the passage?

B.B.: The larger set of interests in this section of the Mishnah has very little to do with animals and further points to animal subjectivity not being much of a concern for the Mishnah. The legal topic of Mishnah Bava Metzia Chapter 2 is lost objects. What is a person's obligation when they find an object that was lost by someone else? What should they do if they can't find the owner? What are their obligations for maintaining the object while they look for the owner? Exodus 23:4 and Deuteronomy 22:1–3 are the starting point for these questions, and the primary example of lost property that they furnish is an animal who has wandered off. The verses we have been discussing that require assistance for the burdened animal appear immediately after the verses dealing with lost animals; it is this juxtaposition within the Torah that causes the Mishnah to speak of our topic where it does. I recently read a dissertation on this chapter of Mishnah that looks at it from the perspective of political theory, since this material is fundamentally about how property mediates human relationships. The animal is more or less just an example of property, along with coins, food, clothing, utensils, or books, which also appear in this chapter.

IBN QUDAMA, AL-MUGHNI,[15] "BOOK OF MAINTENANCE," CHAPTER ON THE MAINTENANCE OF SLAVES

Whoever owns an animal (*bahima*) must take care of it and pay for what it needs, including fodder and the employment of someone to tend to it, because of the report that Ibn 'Umar transmitted from the Prophet that he said: "A woman was tormented (*'udhdhibat*, i.e., in the afterlife) for the sake of a cat that she shut in until it died of hunger; she neither fed it, nor let it out to eat the vermin of the land"—agreed upon [that is, the report is transmitted in the authoritative hadith collections of both al-Bukhari and Muslim]. If he fails to provide for it, he is compelled to do that. If he [still] refuses or is unable to do so, he is compelled to sell it or to slaughter it if it is something that is slaughtered

---

[15] Ibn Qudama, *al-Mughni* (Beirut: Dar al-Kutub al-'Ilmiya, n.d.), 9:317–318.

[i.e., if it is a pure animal that is licit to eat]. Abu Hanifa said: The ruler does not compel him, but commands him to do so as he commands him to do right and forbids him to do wrong, because an animal has no rights with respect to legal rulings. Do you not see that it has no standing to make a claim and no claim can be made against it? Thus, it is like a crop or a tree. In support of our [opinion—that is, the position of the Hanbali school to which Ibn Qudama belongs—it can be argued] that it is the maintenance of a living being (hayawan) that is incumbent upon him; thus, the ruler is entitled to compel him to pay it, like the maintenance of slaves; it differs from the maintenance of trees or crops, which is not obligatory. If he is incapable of paying [the maintenance of his animal] and refuses to sell, it is sold on his behalf, as a slave is sold if he demands to be sold when his owner does not have sufficient resources to maintain him, and as [a man's] marriage is annulled if he does not have sufficient resources to maintain his wife... If [the animal] is licit to eat, he is given a choice between slaughtering it and maintaining it; if it is not licit to eat, he is compelled to provide for it, like a chronically ill slave, as we have mentioned before. It is not permissible to make an animal carry more than it can bear, because it is equivalent to a slave, and the Prophet (peace be upon him!) prohibited burdening a slave with more than he can bear, [and also] because it involves tormenting and harming a living creature (hayawan) that has a sanctity (hurma) of its own, and that is not permissible. One may take no more of its milk than is left after fulfilling the needs of its baby, because fulfilling the needs of [the animal's baby] is incumbent on its owner, and its mother's milk is created for it, so it resembles the baby of a female slave.

Commentary by M.K.

This passage opens with what appears to be a broad rule about the obligation to feed domestic animals, supported by a statement in which the Prophet asserts the sinfulness of starving animals in one's care. However, the fact that this action is morally reprehensible does not establish whether it is legally sanctionable. Following the doctrine of his own Hanbali school, Ibn Qudama states that a delinquent owner must be compelled by the authorities to provide for the needs of his livestock. Strikingly, however, it is equally acceptable for him to slaughter them if they can legally be slaughtered and eaten; the animals' status as living beings (which must not be tormented) is cross-cut by their status as economic assets and sources of food. The eponymous founder of the Hanafi school of law, in contrast, argues that the delinquent owner must merely be morally exhorted; an animal is not a legal person and does not possess any legal rights. The Hanafi position could be understood as a tacit invocation of the exclusively human possession of *dhimma* (sometimes rendered as "legal personality"[16]), the notional locus in which both obligations and entitlements inhere. Muslim legal theorists defined the *dhimma* as being inseparable from human personhood, a principle that made it possible to posit the existence of obligations toward human beings who were not legally responsible (*mukallaf*), such as infants and the insane. Unlike legal responsibility (*taklif*), possession of a *dhimma* was not contingent upon being intellectually or physically capable of understanding and complying with commands and prohibitions. As Sarra Tlili has discussed in detail, there is abundant material in the Qur'an that would support the attribution of personhood and even legal responsibility to non-human animals. Animals are depicted as worshipers of God (Qur'an 17:44) and recipients of divine inspiration

[16] See Chehata, Chafik, "Dhimma." *Encyclopaedia of Islam*, 2nd edn, ed. P. Bearman, Th. Bianquis, C.E. Bosworth, E. van Donzel, and W.P. Heinrichs (Leiden: Brill, 2015).

(16:68). Animals also appear at times to bear moral accountability; the prophet Sulayman (Solomon) holds the hoopoe responsible for a misdeed by threatening it with punishment (27:20–26), and verse 81:5 speaks of beasts being "gathered" on the Day of Resurrection. Commentaries on the Qur'an—particularly, although not exclusively, in exegetical narratives—sometimes reflect the assumption that animals have moral and spiritual lives. However, classical legal theorists consistently denied their possession of both *dhimma* and *taklif*; Hanafi jurists in particular linked the *dhimma* to God's primordial covenant with the children of Adam (Qur'an 7:172), thus making it coextensive with humanity. Although these concepts are tacitly invoked through the denial that animals can be the subjects of legal claims, it is typical of classical Islamic legal argumentation that the point is more overtly made in terms of a choice of legal analogy, rather than of a deduction from axiomatic principles. An animal, in this view, is more like a fruit tree than like a member of the owner's household. The reader is assumed to understand that a person's trees and crops are at his or her disposal. Ibn Qudama counters by pointing to the domestic animal's status as a living and sentient being, which differentiates it from inanimate crops and associates it with dependent human beings.

The remainder of the argumentation is based on an analogy between domestic beasts and slaves, with a secondary parallel to wives. This passage appears in Ibn Qudama's "Book of Maintenance," which immediately follows the section on divorce in his legal manual; the placement of the "Book of Maintenance" and the preponderance of material on the maintenance of wives and ex-wives both suggest that the subject of maintenance is structurally elicited by the larger theme of marital obligations, to which Ibn Qudama appends discussions of children and slaves. In our passage (and in the legal tradition more broadly), however, the most direct analogy is between domestic animals and slaves, rather than between animals and wives or children. Although the underlying logic is not fully articulated, this is probably because domestic animals and slaves both have the dual status of economic assets at the owner's disposal and household members entitled to his or her care. It is significant that in this model the obligation to maintain—and, conversely, the prohibition on allowing starvation—is a direct function of the ownership and/or authority one exercises over the members of one's household; care is the obligation of a hierarchical superior to his or her dependent subordinate. This is not a question of noblesse oblige; the obligation to feed and care for a wife, child, slave, or animal is one that may (according to most scholars) be imposed on an unwilling husband, father, or owner, thereby depriving him of some of his autonomy.

Exchange

B.B.: The quoted hadith seems to set a low bar for animal protection in that the woman appears to be sadistically starving her cat; she prevents it from feeding itself. Ibn Qudama, on the other hand, takes animal protection quite a bit further (especially in the end of the passage where the animal's parenting role is respected, though as a function of the human owner's obligation). Is there a tension between the orientation of the hadith and that of the legislations being built upon it?

M.K.: It's interesting to ask why Ibn Qudama chose this particular hadith, which is not the only relevant text that would have been available to him. The hadith about the thirsty dog (see p. 97) seems to set a higher bar: the person there is not simply refraining from sadistic detention or starvation of an animal, but going to considerable personal trouble in order to ease an animal's discomfort out of empathy with its thirst. One possibility would be that Ibn Qudama doesn't want to suggest that the authorities could intervene to enforce more expansive forms of kindness toward animals. (He—or his legal school—is less protective of private property rights than Abu Hanifa and his followers, but still doesn't envision the authorities intervening to make sure your barn is cozy.) Another reason for choosing the hadith about the imprisoned cat would be that it addresses the situation of a domestic animal who is completely at the mercy of a human being. Because Ibn Qudama is specifically interested in the responsibilities that householders have toward their dependents, he needs a precedent in which the person is in control of the animal.

B.B.: Your first suggestion—that Ibn Qudama chose this hadith rather than another to exclude more expansive requirements—points to a silent or subtle outer limit of the law when it comes to animal care. If so, is it because you think Ibn Qudama wouldn't have had a robust standard of animal welfare (don't starve the animal to death, but not too much beyond that), or because you think he wouldn't have had a robust standard of legal intervention (the law prevents you from killing creatures, but not too much beyond that)?

M.K.: I think what's really at stake here is the question of legal intervention. My sense is that all of the jurists involved would have agreed that one shouldn't starve or torment animals, and probably also that ideally one should treat them with a high degree of kindness. They differ primarily on the question of whether the authorities can do anything about it if somebody treats animals poorly. In this sense, "Islamic law" as it's being articulated here straddles the line between "law" and "ethics" in a modern Western sense. Ibn Qudama is interested in different kinds and levels of obligation, including many that can't be enforced by the authorities—but he (and his interlocutors) is quite aware of an important distinction between things one simply should do and things one can be made to do (or punished for doing) by the powers that be.

B.B.: Your second suggestion above has your author seeing cattle as more similar to cats than to dogs (at least for these purposes), which raises historical questions about how this author would have thought about various domestic animal species. My guess is that if you asked people today whether dogs or cats are more controlled by their owner and less able to fend for themselves (which is the paradigm our author would be seeking for his legal purposes, as you point out), I think most people would say dogs. Your suggestion invites us to think not only about how cultural constructions of animals vary by context, but also about how cultural constructions fuel legal interpretation, and vice versa.

M.K.: I don't think that the species of the animal is the key factor here. The basic parameters of Islamic law relating to animals suggest that dogs are both more problematic than cats (because they are ritually polluting and one is forbidden to keep them without a specific legitimate objective such as hunting) and more thoroughly domesticated (because they are envisioned as being trained for hunting, herding, and other functions). The issue of tormenting animals, though, seems to be independent of these considerations. I think the key thing here is the role the woman has taken on vis-a-vis the cat—she has shut it in (*habasatha*). The act of *habs* ("detaining," the same verb is used to denote the woman's imprisonment of the cat) is widely used by jurists (particularly Hanafi jurists) to identify just what it is that makes a husband responsible for the care and sustenance of his wife. Earlier in his discussion of maintenance (*nafaqa*), Ibn Qudama explains that a woman is detained (*mahbusa*, that is, subjected to *habs*) for her husband, "which prevents her from acting and earning on her own behalf; thus, he must necessarily support her, as is the case of a slave with his master."[17] The term *habs* points to the balance of prerogatives

---

[17] Ibn Qudama, *al-Mughni*, 9:230.

and obligations that Ibn Qudama sees in each of these relationships—human and animal, husband and wife, owner and slave.

B.B.: Ibn Qudama seems to get a lot of mileage out of the concept of *hayawan*. How does that concept allow him to bypass the problem of legal standing? Or is it the analogy to slaves and wives that gets him around this problem?

M.K.: I think it's really the analogy with slaves and wives that does most of the work here; the concept of *hawayan* offers a piece of supporting evidence for a series of points Ibn Qudama has already made. However, it's also an interesting interpretive move because, in one word, it establishes an over-arching category that includes both human and non-human animals. (Classical Arabic legal texts sometimes use the phrase *hayawan ghayr adami*—literally, "non-Adamic animal"—to mean non-human animal, so it's explicit that *hawayan* potentially includes both "descendants of Adam"—i.e., humans—and those who are not.) This is not a term that he's attributing to the Prophet or to any specific legal authority; he apparently believes that non-harm of living things will be sufficiently obvious as an underlying principle of sharia.

B.B.: Plant life acts as a foil for Ibn Qudama in his argument against Abu Hanifa. Ibn Qudama establishes a commonality between human beings and animals at the expense of plants, and the cultural cost is that plant life seems to be denied as somehow a real mode of living. Legal protection of plants, by the logic of this passage, becomes unthinkable.

M.K.: There's certainly a sense in which the protection of plant life is thinkable for a jurist like Ibn Qudama. For instance, in the context of the law of war there are serious limitations on the destruction of the enemy's trees and crops (see 10:509–510). However, the main concern there seems to be wanton or needless destruction (*itlaf*), rather than the rights of the plant as a living being. The text does a lot of its interpretive work implicitly, through the choice of analogies and the assumption that its audience will share certain understandings. Ibn Qudama apparently doesn't need to tell us why a "crop" is a compelling example of something toward which its human owner has no enforceable obligation of care—either because he believes his readers all share a basic understanding of the concrete legal rules, or because he believes they share basic sensibilities that don't need to be articulated, at least in this context.

B.B.: There seem to be three main legal topics for Ibn Qudama that fall under the rubric of care for animals: basic provisions (and what happens if these aren't supplied), bearing burdens, and milking. Basic provisions are his focus, and bearing burdens and milking come up as spinoff or secondary topics. Bearing burdens, as we saw, is the starting point for the Talmudic discussion of animal suffering, if only because the Torah speaks of it. Can you address how you see these subtopics fitting together for Ibn Qudama?

M.K.: The reason Ibn Qudama leads with the obligation to feed the animal is that this whole discussion is elicited by the broader topic of the "provisions" (*nafaqa*) that someone needs to supply for his dependents. Having considered the case of failure to feed, he then looks at other scenarios of harm or duress. This probably doesn't reflect a hierarchy of values and is primarily an artifact of the structure of the text.

B.B.: Then it's similar, structurally speaking, to the Mishnah that deals with animal suffering, since its focus on bearing burdens is a function of the biblical verses that are its scaffolding and cannot be shown to reflect some kind of cultural preoccupation on the rabbis' part with burden-bearing. But where do Ibn Qudama's structuring principles come from? Do they come from earlier canonical texts or are they a product of his own devising? Provisions for dependents seem to be a basic category in any legal system, but where does his particular version of this category come from?

M.K.: Ibn Qudama's text is a commentary, so to a large extent its structure is dictated by that of its source text—which in turn is based on an older textual tradition. Where and how individual issues (particularly ones that aren't themselves traditionally central to the legal discussion) get worked into these frameworks can be quite revealing of the authors' mentalities, although they can themselves also become conventional.

B.B.: Is the word for tormenting that comes up with respect to bearing burdens the same word used in the hadith about the cat? If so, is Ibn Qudama's use of that word meant to hark back to the hadith? Is he developing a vocabulary of suffering here? How is the word *hurma* being employed in the rhetoric of the passage? Is this "religious" (for lack of a better word) language meant to be a kind of moral window-dressing, or do you see it as fundamental to the legislative activity?

M.K.: The same word (*ta'dhib*) does indeed occur both in the hadith about the cat and in the statement toward the end about "tormenting" a living creature. Interestingly, in the hadith it's used to describe not the woman's actions toward the cat, but the woman's punishment after death; it's possible, though, that we're supposed to infer a "measure for measure" punishment where she suffers broadly the same kind of treatment (i.e., "torment") that she meted out in this life. I think the word *hurma* could be taken in a couple of different ways, and its translation could be changed accordingly. The most limited, nuts-and-bolts literal translation of the word would be "forbiddenness." Thus, the statement could simply mean that living things have a status that gives them the protection of legal prohibitions. Something that didn't have *hurma* would then be "free game," like (say) a dangerous animal that one can kill on sight without legal liability. "Having *hurma*" would then be the same as being *muhtarama* (protected) in the passage from al-Nawawi (see pp. 97–8). A more expansive interpretation of the word *hurma* would be "sanctity," which supplements the idea of being protected by prohibitions (as in "the sanctity of the human body") with a positive sense of dignity or numinousness that might be understood to underlie that protection. "Inviolability" might combine both of these aspects.

B.B.: The reference in the hadith to the woman's punishment after death makes me curious about the play of genres in the larger passage. On the one hand, we have moments in this passage that feel non-legal or even anti-legal, including the hadith about the woman's punishment and Abu Hanifa's position that animal care is a matter of moral consciousness rather than legal compulsion. Then we have Ibn Qudama pushing us squarely into the realm of law with his analogy to slaves and his talk of permissibility and prohibition and licit and illicit. Yet even within Ibn Qudama's own legal arguments there are appeals, if only implicitly, to what seem like "soft" principles of right and wrong.

Your double reading of the word *hurma* speaks to this doubleness of genre, where on the one hand you have a more legalistic notion and on the other hand something more expansive that we today might call religious. It's striking to me how Ibn Qudama seems to mobilize in his discourse both legal and moral authority and, instead of setting them up as a binary, as Abu Hanifa reportedly does, he weaves them together in his rhetoric and in his legal thinking. You said earlier that "he apparently believes that non-harm of living things will be sufficiently obvious as an underlying principle of the sharia," but I wonder if it's a creative act on his part to make it seem obvious in a way it may not actually be.

M.K.: Your points here suggest the extent to which "law" may more generally be a misnomer when dealing with classical sharia (and, I suspect, perhaps also with halakha). Even aside from issues of thematic scope (for instance, the inclusion of issues of ritual), the sharia as a set of discourses corresponds only poorly to our modern Western understanding of the categories of "law" and "ethics." For one thing, Muslim jurists place actions within a five-level schema ranging from "forbidden" through "undesirable," "neutral," and "recommended," to "obligatory." In general, modern Western law doesn't deal with what is undesirable or recommended; we're never told that it is forbidden to park within twenty-five feet of a street crossing, blameworthy to park within thirty feet, and commendable to park even further away. Sharia thus deals with issues of moral aspiration and other-worldly reward (some actions, for example, being meritorious but not mandatory) in a way that modern "law" doesn't. Of course, the distinction between aspiration and obligation has a lot to do with the issue of this-worldly enforceability, which is at stake in this passage. Even when enforceability is affirmed, there isn't necessarily the same assumption of a state monopoly on coercion as often associated with modern law. Neither the Hanbalis nor the Hanafis completely meld or conflate what we would think of as "ethics" and "law" (the question of whether something is an enforceable obligation or not is a coherent and significant one for both of them), but neither does either of them exclude the "ethical" from their area of expertise as scholars of the sharia (both of them assume that this question is a proper one for them to discuss as jurists, regardless of whether they affirm the enforceability of the owner's obligation to feed the animal or not). Rather, the relationship between what we'd call the "legal" and the "ethical" is something that they're actively working out within the domain of sharia discourse.

DIALOGUE 2: COMPASSION TOWARD ANIMALS

BABYLONIAN TALMUD BAVA METZIA 85A

The sufferings of Rabbi Elazar ben Rabbi Shimon were preferable to those of Rabbi, for those of Rabbi Elazar ben Rabbi Shimon came through love and left through love, [while those] of Rabbi came through an incident and left through an incident.

"Came through an incident"—what was it?

There was a calf[18] that was being brought to slaughter. He went and hanged[19] his head in Rabbi's lap and cried.

He said to him, "Go![20] For this you were created."

They say: Since he had no compassion, let sufferings come upon him.[21]

"And left through an incident"—[22]

One day Rabbi's slavewoman was sweeping the house. She cast aside[23] the children of a weasel[24] and was sweeping them.

He said to her, "Leave them alone! It is written,[25] 'His compassion is over all his creatures' (Psalms 145:9)."

---

[18] In some manuscripts: "There was a calf *in the house of Rabbi* that was being brought to slaughter."

[19] In one manuscript: "He went and folded his head into Rabbi's lap and cried." Another manuscript: "He went before him and buried his head in Rabbi's lap" (the crying is omitted).

[20] "Go" is missing in one version.

[21] In some versions this sentence is abridged, and "They say: 'Since he had no compassion...'" is absent. This telling does not thematize compassion and also does not feature the anonymous "they" pronouncing Rabbi's fate.

[22] In some manuscripts the symmetry is complete, the Gemara asking, as before, "What was it?"

[23] Some manuscripts: "There were some children of a weasel living there [*shari* instead of *shadi*), and she was sweeping them."

[24] *Bnei karkushta.* One version uses the more familiar Hebrew *huldah.*

[25] "It is written" is absent in some versions.

They say: Since he had compassion, let us be[26] compassionate to him."[27]

Commentary by B.B.

This story about Rabbi Yehuda ha-Nasi appears in an elaborate narrative cycle about the founding fathers of the Rabbinic movement. Yehuda ha-Nasi is known as perhaps the most prominent of these founding fathers because of his status, wealth, and influence as a patriarch representing the Jews of Palestine to their Roman rulers. Scholars interested in animal ethics tend to focus on this story and not give much attention to the larger cycle (e.g., Aaron Gross in "Jewish Animal Ethics;" Kimberley Patton in "'He Who Sits in the Heavens Laughs'"), while scholars interested in Rabbinic culture's self-perceptions are less interested in this particular narrative (Daniel Boyarin skips over it in his now classic treatment of this story cycle in Chapter 7 of *Carnal Israel*).[28] It is useful, however, to consider the story in terms simultaneously of its animal ethics and its role in Talmudic culture.

Boyarin describes the story cycle as a carnivalesque, riotous exploration of gender, sexuality, reproduction, and Rabbinic ideology. In Boyarin's reading, the central tension across the stories is generated by the rabbis' interest in replacing genealogical filiation (father produces son) with pedagogical filiation (rabbi produces disciple), to thus achieve eternal life through Torah study rather than through sex and family. Boyarin proposes that "this is a text about male bodies, sexuality, and

---

[26] Most other versions have *rahamu* ("be compassionate").

[27] In some versions this last line is absent, and instead it says, "His sufferings left him." One manuscript uses the same verb, "leave alone," to describe Rabbi's sufferings that Rabbi used beforehand in his comment to the slavewoman.

[28] In line with my interest in considering the context, I included the beginning of the story, which the scholars oriented towards animal ethics tend to omit.

reproduction and, moreover, that it is a text that manifests enormous anxiety about the reproduction of men in rabbinic culture."[29] But if we read more carefully and with an eye toward animals, we may see that this is also a text about animal bodies and animal reproduction. Animals are scattered throughout the story cycle and play significant parts in the Rabbinic drama. The animals in our story, we may notice, are "children" (the calf, the young weasels) whose lives are threatened; that threat seems to mirror the one to human lineages that runs through the story cycle. In an earlier scene the same Rabbi Elazar with whom Rabbi is compared at the beginning of our story cries in remorse over a man whose execution he has engineered; in our story the calf crying on his way to his own execution recalls the crying Rabbi of that scene. In both of these episodes Rabbi suffers because he does not initially show appropriate compassion. Rabbi's suffering is dramatized in the preceding episode by describing his howls of pain as louder than those of his many animals during their feeding hour, thus representing Rabbi as a kind of howling animal himself. The entire story cycle begins by making the comparison explicit: when Rabbi Elazar is asked by a Roman officer how to catch criminals, Rabbi Elazar offers a hunting strategy, saying, "Aren't they to be compared to animals?" These parallels and connections between our episode and the larger story cycle—and we could no doubt find more—suggest to us that animal ethics are not an isolable theme here but are interwoven into a much broader set of Rabbinic interests and concerns.[30]

---

[29] See Aaron Gross, "Jewish Animal Ethics," in *The Oxford Handbook of Jewish Ethics and Morality*, ed. Elliot Dorff and Jonathan Crane (Oxford: Oxford University Press, 2013), 419–432; Patton, "'He Who Sits in the Heavens Laughs';" Daniel Boyarin, *Carnal Israel: Reading Sex in Talmudic Culture*, (Berkeley: University of California Press, 1993), 198.

[30] Other lines of animal inquiry in the story cycle include: a worm coming out of Rabbi Elazar's ear; his father in a dream comparing him to a chick; his corpse being described as protecting his town from wild animals; a snake wrapping around the opening of his tomb; and the imagery of lions and foxes.

Boyarin at one point describes the concern of the story cycle as "the imbrication of death in the production of life," and that seems a helpful approach for interpreting our story.[31] The routines of animal destruction and disruption that characterize human life are problematized by this story, and compassion is introduced as the antidote to suffering, the suffering both of the animals and of Rabbi himself. Rabbi, like the thirsty man in the story told by the Prophet in the text below, learns through his own suffering to identify with the suffering of animals. Only once Rabbi learns the importance of attending to animal suffering is his own suffering relieved, just as the man who gives water to the dog is forgiven by God in the hadith we will next discuss.

The story invites us to contrast its two halves, the first where Rabbi doesn't show mercy, and the second half where he does. In the first half, Rabbi comes across as heartless when he ignores the cries of the calf who seeks refuge in the folds of his clothing; in the second half, Rabbi takes pity on animals who are basically pests that any good exterminator—like the slavewoman doing her job—would remove. In the first half, Rabbi quotes a teaching in Mishnah Avot 2:9: "If you have learned much Torah, do not take it as merit for yourself, since *for this you were created*." Although Mishnah Avot 2:8 teaches humility for the Torah scholar, Rabbi twists its meaning so that it becomes a justification for his own cruelty. In the second half, Rabbi cites a biblical verse, Psalm 145:9, dedicated to the praise of God's kingship, now acknowledging the true source of power—God—and showing appropriate humility. Later that same psalm describes "all flesh" (verse 21) praising God. These various contrasts between the first half and the second half of the story all serve to dramatize the character change that Rabbi undergoes in his relationship to animals.

As indicated by my footnotes on the text, the Talmudic tale comes with much manuscript variation, so it's tricky to read into the precise

---

[31] *Carnal Israel*, 209.

wording. I'll offer some comments, nevertheless, on the literary features of the version in the standard printed edition. The calf is described as "hanging" his head in Rabbi's lap, which gives a human, execution-like quality to the slaughter, since hanging is one of the elements of Rabbinic judicial execution. Rabbi's lap is described as *kanfe de-Rabbi*, which evokes the Talmudic expression *kanfe ha-Shekhinah*, "the wings of the divine presence," likening Rabbi to God in his power to let the calf live or die. When the calf seeks protection in Rabbi's lap, it also evokes a child seeking protection in his parent's lap, which is another common way in which the noun *kanfa* is used. The *kanfa* or lap of Rabbi is literarily echoed in the sweeping activity of the slavewoman in the second half of the story, which is described by the similar-sounding verb *kansha* (an unusual usage). Finally, the themes of reproduction, filiation, and the body to which Boyarin points are picked up in the multiple associations of the repeating root *r-h-m*, which refers to compassion but also often to love and is sometimes used to refer to a mother giving suck to her young, frequently within the animal world.

The story about Yehuda ha-Nasi appears in an earlier iteration in the Palestinian Talmud, with some striking differences:

> One time he (Rabbi) was passing and saw a certain calf going to be slaughtered.
>
> He (the calf) lowed and said to him, "Rabbi, save me!"
> He (Rabbi) said to him, "For this you were created."
>
> And in the end, how was he (Rabbi) cured? He saw them killing a nest of mice. He said, "Leave them alone! 'His compassion is over all his creatures,' it is written."

In this version the calf speaks instead of nuzzling in Rabbi's lap, the slavewoman does not appear, and the nest of mice about to be killed replaces the weasel children being swept away. Talmud scholars tend to presume that the Babylonian redactors used the Palestinian version as a base text and made creative changes to it. If that is the case here, then it's worth contemplating the concerns that prompted these small but significant narrative shifts from the Palestinian Talmud to the Babylonian Talmud.

Exchange

M.K.: Should we assume (or does the Jewish interpretive tradition assume) that Judah ha-Nasi infers from this sequence of events that animals should not be slaughtered or eaten? I'm assuming not, given the continuing overall acceptance of the legitimacy of kosher slaughter. If not, what are the elements in the story (or external to the story) that avert this obvious implication?

B.B.: I agree that the story leaves us with a lingering question about animal slaughter. Is the story a critique of animal slaughter? Is the slavewoman being criticized for her treatment of the young weasels? Are we meant to become vegetarian and to stop calling the exterminator after we've read this story? This conclusion seems doubtful, since animal slaughter and consumption are so central to Jewish law and culture and I can't imagine the storytellers liked having pests in their houses any more than people today seem to. So your question stands: what are the elements that avert this conclusion? Perhaps it would be helpful to bring Boyarin back into the discussion, since he concludes his chapter on the story cycle this way: "In a culture in which the body is the very center of the sense of being human, the problem of the body—male and female—remains unsolved."[32] I would say that the problem of the animal body remains unsolved

---

[32] *Carnal Israel,* 219.

as well, as does the question of just what it should mean to exercise compassion toward other species. That's a major difference between narrative and law: law has to be conclusive, but narrative doesn't. In fact, the power of narrative lies in the fact that it explores tensions without explaining them away or resolving them, and that seems to be the case here.

M.K.: The incident with the nest of baby weasels is an interesting sequel to Rabbi's encounter with the calf, because his relationship to these animals is very different. Rather than a domestic animal that is being led to a death for which we may presume it was intentionally bred, he is faced with wild animals whose mother has presumably sought refuge in the warmth of his home. Do we assume that the maid was going to kill the weasels—or that she was going to toss them out of the house, perhaps causing their death as a side effect? Do we infer that Rabbi is now going to harbor a happy family of weasels in his home? All of the animals in this story appear to function as props for good or bad human sentiments; it's hard to imagine an ongoing role for them after they serve as object lessons for Rabbi.

B.B.: The Palestinian Talmud and Babylonian Talmud form an interesting contrast to each other with respect to this plot point, since it's clear in the Palestinian Talmud that the mice are about to be killed, whereas in the Babylonian Talmud the verbs are a little irregular, and the manuscripts vary for some of them, so it remains fuzzy just what the fate of the weasels is. I wish I knew more about the Babylonian Talmud's cultural associations with weasels so that I had a better sense of what it means to shoo them out of one's house, if that is in fact what the slavewoman is trying to do.

Maybe it's because I'm primed to read it this way, but I see a certain pathos in the animals' lives being described here which allows them to transcend their role as teaching tools for humans. The calf seeking protection in Rabbi's lap and the weasel family being swept away seem to exert a pull on one's emotions that feels different from, for instance, the way animals work in Aesop's fables. Animal suffering, the reality of it, does seem to reach the surface of the text.

M.K.: What significance, if any, does the maidservant have here? Is it simply that we can't imagine a high-ranking rabbi of royal descent sweeping out his own vermin? This silent woman, who seems like a mere instrument of Rabbi's good or bad moral choices, seems to offer a bit of a counterpoint to the other major power relationships here (between Rabbi and the calf and between him and the weasels).

B.B.: It's worth thinking twice about the narrative role of the slave-woman, since she doesn't appear in the Palestinian Talmud version and seems to be a narrative device inserted by the Babylonian redactors. It makes sense to ask what narrative power or payoff they get from her. Since Rabbi is a figure in Rabbinic history associated with power and wealth (as well as Torah learning), he stands in stark contrast to the slavewoman. One interpretive possibility I'm drawn to is that she functions as a kind of everyman with an everyman's relationship to animals, neither particularly cruel nor particularly kind, just doing her job and trying to get by, in some ways similar to the weasels she comes across looking for a spot to call home. Rabbi, on the other hand, illustrates the extremes, first repellently cruel, then absurdly kind. The story thus lays out a spectrum of relationships between humans and animals.

If we shift the story's perspective and look at the incident instead from the slavewoman's perspective, we find that she faces a lose–lose situation: if she doesn't sweep the weasels away she can expect to be reprimanded or punished for not doing her job, but when she does sweep them away she is criticized by her master for being cruel. Isn't there an irony in a slavewoman being criticized for not respecting the dignity of the weasels and their freedom to roost where they would like? Is the slavewoman able to "roost" where she would like? Of course not, yet this irony doesn't reach the surface of the text.

AL-NAWAWI, *SHARH SAHIH MUSLIM*, BOOK ON KILLING SERPENTS AND OTHER [DANGEROUS ANIMALS], CHAPTER ON THE MERIT OF ONE WHO GIVES WATER AND FOOD TO PROTECTED ANIMALS[33]

[Hadith:] Qutayba ibn Sa'id reported to us from Malik ibn Anas in what was read to him from Sumayy the freedman of Abu Bakr from Salih al-Samman from Abu Hurayra that the Messenger of God (peace be upon him!) said: "Once when a man was walking on a path he became very thirsty; he found a well, climbed down into it and drank. Then he came out and saw a dog that was panting and eating damp earth out of thirst. The man said [to himself], 'This dog is just as thirsty as I was,' so he went down into the well and filled his shoe with water, then held it in his mouth until he climbed back up and gave the dog water to drink. So God thanked him and forgave him." They said, "O Messenger of God, do we really receive a reward for [our good actions toward] these animals (*baha'im*)?" He said, "There is a reward for every [being with a] moist liver."

Commentary: His statement "There is a reward for every [being with a] moist liver," means that there is a reward for

[33] Yahya ibn Sharaf al-Nawawi, *Sharh Sahih Muslim*, ed. Khalil al-Mays (Beirut: Dar al-Qalam, 1407/1987), 14:492–3.

good actions toward every living being to which one gives
water or the like. A living being is called "the possessor of a
moist liver," because the body and the liver of someone who
is dead dry out.[34] This hadith contains encouragement to
act kindly to animals that are legally protected (al-hayawan
al-muhtaram), which are those that one is not commanded
to kill. As for those that one is commanded to kill, one must
obey the command of the [divine] law to kill it. The [animal]
that one is commanded to kill is like the non-believer in a
state of war (al-kafir al-harbi), the apostate, the vicious dog,
and the five "sinful" (fawasiq) animals that are mentioned
in the hadith and their likes. As for animals that are legally
protected, reward results from giving them water and also
behaving kindly to them by feeding them and other things,
regardless of whether they are owned or have no owner
(mubah), and [if they are owned] regardless of whether they
belong to [the person who is kind to them] or to someone
else; and God knows best.

Commentary by M.K.

In this hadith the man's benevolent action toward the dog is motivated
by empathy: recognizing the dog's symptoms of distress, he concludes
that it is suffering the same agonies of thirst that he has himself just
experienced. The Prophet's Companions, hearing this story, question
whether non-human animals are really within the circle of ethical
concern; he then affirms that every living being can be the object of
ethical action and thus the source of divine reward. The distinctive

---

[34] Although al-Nawawī does not say this, the phrase may also imply sentience; the
liver was traditionally regarded as the seat of feelings and passions, so in this context
it may imply the ability to suffer.

phrase "every [being with a] moist liver," which is an unusual and oblique way of referring to living things, evokes the theme of wetness and dryness that weaves through the anecdote—and perhaps contains a distant echo of the Qur'anic declaration that "We [God] made of water every living thing" (Qur'an 21:30). The link between moisture and life is both fundamental and embracing, although the phrase "every [being with a] moist liver" presumably refers to animals rather than plants, which don't have livers—and ultimately what is at stake is the shared experience of suffering, which narrows the circle to sentient beings.

In his commentary al-Nawawi immediately introduces another limitation that is not stated in the hadith: the animal in question must be *muhtaram*—that is, it must possess the status of sanctity or inviolability (*hurma*) that renders it impermissible to kill it without proper cause. (In the case of an animal that one is allowed to eat, slaughter for the purpose of consumption would be a proper cause.) Al-Nawawi then offers a list of living beings that are not *muhtaram*, including both human beings (non-believers in a state of war with the Muslim polity and apostates from Islam) and non-human animals (vicious dogs and the five "sinful" animals). The five "sinful" animals are rats, scorpions, vicious dogs, crows (*al-ghurab*), and kites (*al-hida'a*); according to a statement attributed to the Prophet, although it is generally forbidden to kill animals in the sanctuaries of Mecca and Medina, all of these animals should be killed on sight even by a pilgrim.[35] Although their name suggests malevolence, Muslim commentators generally agreed (based on animals' lack of *taklif*) that their defining feature was not moral turpitude, but inherent harmfulness to humans. Whereas the non-*muhtaram* human beings cited by al-Nawawi are understood to have forfeited their inherent ethico-legal sanctity by their own

---

[35] See Bukhari, *Sahih*, *Bad' al-khalq*, *Bab Khams min al-dawabb fawasiq yuqtal fi'l-haram*.

wrongdoing, animals fall on one side or the other of this divide based purely on the divine decree.[36] It is notable that not all Muslim scholars agreed that non-vicious dogs were *muhtaram* (i.e., protected by law). Based on hadith reports, some scholars (including Malik) held that it was obligatory to kill any harmful dog, and permissible to kill any dog regardless of harm, unless it was a dog licitly used for herding or the like. Others held (also based on hadith) that only pure black dogs should be killed.[37]

The distinction between *muhtaram* and non-*muhtaram* animals that al-Nawawi brings to bear on the interpretation of this story appeared to some commentators to conflict with the general principle of benevolence toward sentient animals expressed in this hadith, which represents the dog as a living and suffering being worthy of moral consideration. Ibn Rushd notes that "many scholars" reasoned, based on this text, that "If there is reward for kindness [toward dogs], then there must be moral odium (*al-wizr*) for unkindness; and there is nothing more unkind toward [the dog] than killing him." According to this logic, the command to kill dogs must be abrogated (*mansukh*) by the Prophet's statement in favor of kindness to dogs. Thus they argued that "no dog should be killed, whether black or otherwise, unless it is vicious and harmful."[38] Drawing on another hadith that advocates

---

[36] The early Hanafi defender of hadith Ibn Qutayba (d. *ca.* 889 C.E.) notes the objection that animals cannot be *fawasiq* in the sense of being sinful or disobedient because they are not like devils, jinns, or human beings that can be sinful or rightly guided. Ibn Qutayba responds that this contention (that animals lack *taklif*) is in conflict with the word of the Qur'an, which recounts that the prophet Sulayman threatened to punish the hoopoe for its infraction. However, Ibn Qutayba's view was not the one that prevailed in legal discourse over time. Ibn Qutayba, *Ta'wil mukhtalif al-hadith*, ed.'Abd al-Qadir 'Ata' (Cairo: Dar al-Kutub al-Islamiya, 1981), 134–135.

[37] For a survey of juristic opinions, see *al-Mawsu'a al-fiqhiya*, s.v. "kalb," para. 26 (*qatl al-kalb*), 35:132–134. For al-Nawawi's own views on this issue, see al-Nawawi, *Sharh Sahih Muslim*, 10:493–497.

[38] Ibn Rushd, *Bayan*, 9:354–355.

kindness in all things, including in slaughtering,[39] other scholars saw killing animals as an action that might not be incompatible with a mandate to be kind to them—one is permitted to kill them, but not to torment them in the process.

By foregrounding the distinction between *muhtaram* and non-*muhtaram*, which cuts across the human/non-human divide, al-Nawawi asserts that there are limits to the inclusive scope of moral concern (all animals) suggested by the hadith. As a jurist, he seeks to reconcile apparently conflicting ethico-legal rules by invoking a distinguishing factor. While limiting the mandate of benevolence to animals that are *muhtaram*, in another respect he broadens the scope of moral concern; although the reference to ownership seems ungrounded in the text of the hadith, al-Nawawi is clearly familiar with the logic (see p. 79) according to which the obligation for care arises from the prerogatives of ownership. Al-Nawawi asserts, based on the hadith, that it is meritorious to provide succor to animals whether or not one owns them and, indeed, whether or not they are owned at all. Perhaps because this passage appears in a hadith commentary rather than a legal manual, he does not address the question of compulsion by the authorities.[40]

Exchange

B.B.: Is there any particular symbolism in the hadith to the man using his shoe to bring water to the dog? Is that simply the only thing he had available to carry the water? Does it signify poverty? Does it signify some degree of humiliation he is willing to suffer in order to relieve the suffering of the dog?

[39] See Muslim, *Sahih, Kitab al-Sayd wa'l-dhabā'ih wa-ma yu'kal min al-hayawan, Bab al-Amr bi-ihsan al-dhabh wa'l-qatl, wa-tahdid al-shafra.*
[40] Al-Nawawi, *Sharh Sahih Muslim,* 10:493–497.

I'm assuming it's common for a hadith to be structured in this way, as a story (about the man) within a story (told by the Prophet) within a story (the tradents of the hadith). Would it be more powerful, or less so, if the Prophet himself had acted the way that the man did? I have in mind the Yehuda ha-Nasi narrative, where the central character is Yehuda ha-Nasi himself. The hadith feels more like a parable, since it's about a generic man and generic dog, and I'd imagine the parable form is used in this context, as it is in other cultures, to teach universal-type ethics. Can you say something about the use of a parable to teach this lesson about compassion for animals?

M.K.: I think the most obvious interpretation of the shoe (which is occasionally made explicit by classical commentators) is simply that the man really went to a lot of trouble to bring the water out of the well. The detail about carrying it in his mouth dramatizes the ingenuity and effort involved. Another resonance (although not, to the best of my knowledge, one that's made explicit in the interpretive tradition on this hadith) is that using the mouth to carry things is something that's usually typical of animals (like dogs) rather than of people. This reinforces the point that the man is momentarily put in a place where he can experience things a bit more like a dog. As some commentators point out, the man himself seems to be traveling through an unpeopled area with no provisions—but whether this is out of poverty, imprudence, or extreme trust in God is not something the story seems concerned to clarify. Regardless, I think the man's empathy with the dog arises from the fact that the situation puts the two of them on a much more even footing. Of course, the man has some advantages over the dog (and, implicitly, some responsibilities arising from those advantages)—he has the ability to climb into and out of the well, and footwear that can be repurposed as a vessel. Ultimately, though, it doesn't matter if, as a human being, you have greater intellect, the power of speech, or a higher rank in the cosmic scheme of things—if you have a "moist liver," you can die of thirst.

The story-within-a-story structure is distinctive but certainly not unique. One very specific thing that the Prophet's use of a story or parable is doing here is, as you suggest, universalizing the point of the anecdote. Not only is the Prophet's story timeless (in the sense that it deals with "a man" with no defined identity in an unspecified setting), but the fact that the animal involved is specifically a dog led some scholars to infer that it reflects a previous religious dispensation (that is, that it harks back to a time before the Prophet Muhammad promulgated the specifically Islamic strictures relating to dogs). It's also significant that this story from the timeless past depicts someone following a basic moral intuition rather than formal prophetic guidance: even a guy alone in the desert can figure out that it's good to alleviate the suffering of fellow living beings. It's the relationship between this universalistic human intuition and the concrete rules associated with one's own religious dispensation (which, among other things, distinguish among different forms of non-human animals) that then becomes the challenge for legally minded commentators like al-Nawawi.

B.B.: Could you say more about what it means to read the hadith as reflecting a previous religious dispensation? Does that mean that its application would be limited (that was then, this is now—or, perhaps, that was them, this is us)? Does that mean the universalistic feel of the story ironically restricts its relevance? The story-within-a-story structure seems possibly to remedy a tension that could arise between basic moral intuition and formal prophetic guidance, since the story itself represents the former but, as it's the Prophet who tells the story, we also have the latter. Do any commentators see the literary structure that way, or is the tension unavoidable between the approach to dogs in this hadith and that of other traditions?

M.K.: In general, the status of commandments originating from previous prophetic dispensations (*shar' man qablana*, "the laws of those who went before us") is ambiguous, both in terms of epistemology (that is, how one can reliably know about the revelations of previous prophets, given the corruption that Muslims believed to have affected the transmission of their scriptures) and in terms of authority (that is, whether the default assumption was that such rules remained valid unless countermanded by the revelation to the Prophet Muhammad, or whether they required explicit reconfirmation). These two questions sometimes (although not always) canceled each other out, since the only unimpeachable way to know about the commandments of previous prophets was if they appeared in the Qur'an or hadith (which could be taken as divine reaffirmation for the current religious dispensation). In this case, there is no real problem, since the whole thing is on the authority of the Prophet Muhammad; it's him who is vouching (presumably on the basis of his own prophetic knowledge) for the fact that God rewarded the man for his action, and the culminating statement that God rewards good deeds toward all animals is in his voice. However, I do think that the timeless story-within-a-story changes—and enhances—the force of the Prophet's statements. In this respect the hadith somewhat resembles another in which the Prophet identifies the principle "If you don't feel ashamed, then do what you like" as deriving from the "first revelation." Muslim scholars consistently treat this as a statement of the Prophet (that is, it carries his authority regardless of its attribution to an earlier revelation). However, as in the case of the hadith we're examining here, an expression of basic intuitive common sense is also implied by this device to be primal or timeless. "Don't do things that you'd feel ashamed of!" and "Recognize the suffering of other living beings!" are implied to be universal human principles, rather than the specific legislation of the Muslim community.

B.B.: As you point out in your commentary, al-Nawawi restricts the scope of the hadith by excluding animals who are not protected, and he expands it in other ways, by requiring a person to help protected species not only by giving water but also by other actions, and by discarding ownership as a relevant criterion. He thus presents a highly polarized treatment of animals, it seems to me, calling on people to treat some animals with compassion and to exterminate others on sight. I wonder if implicitly he is also presenting a highly polarized treatment of people, since certain categories of people appear on the unprotected animals list. How essential are the human categories here, or are they tangential to the topic? Do you think it may be important to him to "animalize" apostates and non-believers and if so in what way?

M.K.: In the context of this particular hadith, "animalizing" a category of human beings doesn't seem to be a distancing or stigmatizing move; "animal" (in the sense of "sentient, vulnerable living thing") is functioning in this anecdote as a quite positive and inclusive category. For his part, al-Nawawi qualifies and limits this inclusive category by "humanizing" certain categories of animals in a negative sense— that is, just as some humans may forfeit their right to ethico-legal consideration, so do some animals (although the reasons for this are less clear in the case of the non-human animals, who aren't obviously morally culpable). Even so, I don't find this move very visceral or emotive; in this passage al-Nawawi is writing primarily as a jurist, trying to square the lesson of the story (which seems to exclude the possibility of harming any living thing) with the categories and rules of the legal tradition (which allow or even demand this under certain circumstances, regardless of whether we're dealing with a human or a non-human animal). For at least one other commentator, rather than serving to "animalize" hostile non-Muslims (or former Muslims), the parallel with non-human animals is actually used to draw excluded

ISLAMIC AND JEWISH LEGAL REASONING

humans back into the circle of moral concern. The eleventh-century Andalusian exegete Ibn Battal comments on the hadiths about the woman and the cat and the traveler and the dog: "These hadiths encourage people to employ compassion toward all created beings (*khalq*), both unbelievers and believers, and towards all mute animals, and to be kind to them. [They demonstrate] that that is something for which God forgives errors and expiates sins, so every rational believer should desire to obtain his share of compassion and use it towards the members of his species and towards every animal, for God did not create them in vain."

B.B.: What I think you're suggesting is that the term "animalization" doesn't work to describe what's happening in this text because the categories of animal and human are being shaken up. The active dividing line for al-Nawawi is not between animal and human but between some animals and humans, who are said to share a "moist liver," and other animals and humans, who seem to share some quality of sin, danger, or destructiveness. We should be clear, though, that all these creatures, good and bad, are in the circle of moral concern in the sense that some moral charge is attributed to them, whether it be positive or negative, and some action with respect to them is dictated, whether it be nourishing or killing.

You represent Nawawi's concern as trying to reconcile the story in the hadith with the legal tradition, but I wonder if you could see it as reconciling certain stories, those oriented toward empathy, inclusiveness, or universalism, with other kinds of stories that may be more invested in category construction and consolidation. Our case at hand could leave the impression that story is a kinder genre than law, but I think we all know stories that are cruel and laws that are compassionate. There's no doubt that this hadith leans in the direction of identification and empathy, however, which seems to be the spirit in which Ibn Battal read it.

When legal or ethical texts require people to show compassion for animals, often the requirement is based on an argument that it is good ethical training for human beings. Showing compassion toward animals gets humans into the habit so that they'll be more likely to show it to each other. That doesn't seem to be the argument here. If it's not, what is? In other words, according to this text, why exactly is it important to show compassion toward animals? Does the narrative genre within the hadith leave this implicit and at the level of intuition and emotion? Is it less implicit for al-Nawawi?

M.K.: Basically, it's important to be kind to animals because God likes it. In al-Nawawi's worldview there is no criterion more final or more consequential than being pleasing to God, so here I think it would be hard to see the value of acts of compassion to non-human animals as being instrumental in the service of some other ultimate aim, such as human self-cultivation. Certainly one could raise theological questions about the relationship between God's preferences and the basic moral reasoning brought to bear by the thirsty man. Why does God like this? Specifically, does God reward things that are identifiable as ethically good by the unaided intellect, or could God have chosen to endorse actions that to us seem irrational or repugnant? As a member of the Ash'ari school, al-Nawawi presumably had an opinion on this (very roughly, that God could have chosen to reward anything—including acts that appear bad to us), but it's not a direction he's interested in pursuing here. It suffices to say that God approves of and rewards this type of action, and it certainly helps that it "feels right" intuitively.

B.B.: Your answer points to just how essential are the questions about law and morality that these texts raise. We seem to be rehearsing the classical question of whether the good is loved by the gods because it is good, or is good because it is loved by the gods; according to this text, is showing compassion to animals loved by God because it is good, or is it good because it is loved by God? It seems that al-Nawawi, if asked the question, would likely say the latter, but the hadith points more in the direction of the former. Perhaps the question itself—"Why should we show compassion to animals? What makes such a stance good?"—is foreign to the text, which assumes either that this will be clear to its audience or that its audience won't ask the question to begin with. But the fact that the Prophet's Companions show some surprise upon hearing the story suggests that, at least for the audience within the hadith, the reasons were not that obvious.

CONCLUSION

We began our discussion by considering some of the structural similarities between our texts; we conclude by considering thematic similarities in their treatment of animals. At the most basic level, we observe that all our texts are interested in other species, especially in the capacity of other species to suffer and in what the implications of that suffering are for people. Both sets of texts define responsibilities toward animals: the first Mishnah and Talmud passages require a person to assist in the unloading of a burdened animal, while Ibn Qudama likens animals to wives and slaves and requires the householder to care for them in a comparable way. The second set of texts, the Talmudic story about Rabbi Yehudah ha-Nasi and al-Nawawi, both dramatize animal suffering by linking it to human suffering and promising reward to the person who attends to that suffering.

At the same time, the texts start with the assumption that animals do not possess major elements of legal personhood and are defined by their value and utility—or lack thereof, like the young weasels of the Talmudic story—to human beings. Even though animal suffering is recognized and problematized, animal labor and slaughter are left intact. One could argue that curbing extremes of exploitation serves only to reinforce and to routinize everyday suffering. We were not surprised to see our texts treat animals as commodities, but we are interested in the role this commodification plays in the larger legal discourses. Why and when does it become legally pressing or productive to disenfranchise other species? When does defining legal personhood as coextensive with humanity—and thus denying it to animals—serve to grant protection to certain categories of persons that may not otherwise be thought to possess it, like fetuses, children, women, slaves, people with disabilities, or non-Jews/non-Muslims? Are taxonomies or analogies that pair certain kinds of animals with certain kinds of human beings (whether slaves, wives, or outsiders to the religious community) simply "dehumanizing" with respect to the humans in question, or do they (despite genuine tensions with the ethics of many modern members of these religions) also in some ways helpfully destabilize our assumptions about the bright line between humans and all other animals? The particular texts we chose, we suggest, do not simply deny legal personhood to animals; they rethink legal personhood itself as they consider how much and what kind to attribute to animals.

We can look for legal personhood not only in the legal substance but also in the rhetoric of the texts. Although we have been speaking of "the animal," our texts often speak of particular species and individual animals—think of the cowering calf of the Yehudah ha-Nasi story and the thirsty dog of the hadith. These animals may not have names but they have narrative presence. Even when our texts do speak in more abstract and homogenizing terms, those terms—like Rava's "possessors of life," Ibn Qudama's *hayawan*, and the "moist liver" in the hadith in al-Nawawi—can seem to shift the frame of discussion through their literary associations and conceptual power. Almost subliminally, the language makes a case for animal personhood. Other terminology—like the term *bahima* (used to refer to edible domestic quadrupeds such as the cow), or al-Nawawi's class of non-*muhtaram* animals—defines specific groups of animals in terms of their utility or danger to humans and emphasizes the limits of their personhood, or—like the rabbis' generic *behemah*, similar to our own "animal"—relegates all animals to an inferior category in opposition to humans.

This play of terminology, which occurs largely below the level of overt analysis in the texts, significantly complicates the surface conclusions that they reach. Both sets of texts invoke the kind of axiomatic principle—the impermissibility of harming or tormenting living things—that we tend to seek when struggling with questions of animal rights. However, in our sample texts from both traditions these broad statements of principle occur almost parenthetically and play a surprisingly marginal role in the course of the argumentation (or, in the case of the Talmudic discourse about animal suffering, are presented as deductions from prior traditions and not as free-standing claims to be argued on their merits). Our authors build "up" from complex examinations of human–human and human–animal relationships, not "down" from first principles. Both sets of texts are deeply entwined in the authority structures of their own religious traditions, the Talmud showing as much interest in whether the ancient rabbis cared about animal suffering as in animal suffering itself, and Ibn Qudama fully invested in the scholarly politics of the Sunni legal schools. The hero of the Talmud's story about compassion for animals is none other than Yehuda ha-Nasi, the Rabbinic authority figure par excellence, and Nawawi is in part concerned to demonstrate that a very broad prophetic mandate for compassion toward animals does not conflict with other elements of the legal tradition.

Most importantly, however, both in terms of the thematic arrangement of the larger texts from which these passages are excerpted and in terms of the logics they deploy, concerns about the value and well-being of animals are deeply informed by concerns about human beings in terms of which they are structured and framed. Although sensitivity to animal suffering is intermittently recognized as a genuine and independent concern, even the texts that do so are often placed in contexts generated by human agendas and implicitly or explicitly made conditional on what is "necessary" in terms of human objectives (whether these be the slaughter and consumption of animals or their use for transportation or agricultural work). One might even say that the texts see compassion itself in instrumental terms, as a means of pleasing God and gaining divine rewards.

These texts about animals thus raise broad questions about the relationship between law and ethics in classical Judaism and Islam, about the relationship between what is required and what is right, why either or both of these must be pursued, and what role compulsion and coercion, both moral and physical, should play in that pursuit. They offer us both a maximal and a minimal model of our moral commitments toward animals, painting a world where it is understandable both to overload beasts of burden and to harbor household pests, to kill rats on sight and to identify with wild dogs. In the world of these texts, it may be that a largely taken-for-granted framework of hierarchical relationships between people and animals is only colored and modulated by exhortations to compassion; nevertheless both sets of texts potentially genuinely destabilize this framework. The specifics of their scenarios are outmoded—few Jews today transport merchandise on beasts of burden, and no modern Muslim would model the treatment of animals on rules relating to slavery—and yet the questions they raise remain relevant.

4

Policing Women

Virginity Checkers and the
Sotah Ordeal as Sites of Women's Agency

AYESHA S. CHAUDHRY AND SHARI GOLBERG

WOMEN POLICING WOMEN:
FROM MONTREAL TO JERUSALEM

Montreal

In Montreal, Canada, on June 20, 2010, a nineteen-year-old girl named Bahar Ebrahim was punished by her mother for spending an entire night out and behaving like a "prostitute" and a "whore." Bahar's parents, Ebrahim Ebrahimi and Johra Kaleki, are Afghan nationals who migrated to Canada via Pakistan. Horrified by Bahar's behavior, which included smoking, drinking, and having boyfriends, her mother tried to "fix" her by stabbing Bahar in the face, neck, shoulder, and arms. Thanks to the knife's bluntness, a fact that Johra later lamented, Bahar survived this attack. She was saved by her father, who, upon hearing the screams, pulled his wife off his daughter, who then called the police. When the police arrived, Johra reportedly screamed, "I want to kill her, I want to kill her," adding, "She's my daughter; I can do whatever I want." Johra told the sergeant-detective who interviewed her in custody that she had tried to raise her daughter as a "Muslim," monitoring her behavior as well as making sure her outfits were not "too short and skimpy." Upon hearing that her daughter would survive the attack, Johra is recorded as saying that this experience would make her daughter "strong and give her wisdom…it means she will give up her ways of living." She portrayed the stabbing as a "price" that both she and Bahar were paying as a consequence of Bahar's behavior. When interviewed in the hospital, Bahar said that she had been trying to break free from the strict rules with which she was raised. However, she worried about how this incident would affect the reputation of her family in her community, specifically the fact that it would damage the marriageability of her younger sisters. In a troubling twist, three years later, Bahar is a defense witness in Johra's trial, where the defense is pleading insanity. She has testified that her mother is "merciful" and would not "hurt a fly." Since the stabbing, Bahar has married in a wedding that she says—in a laudatory manner—was "organized" by her mother. She now accepts some of the blame for the incident, saying she made a "mistake," "should have come home a little earlier." Considering herself at fault, she said that she "should not have treated [her] mother that way" and that, although "I don't blame myself," "it's maybe one percent my fault."[1]

This story is worthy of our attention for many reasons, but we are most interested in the ways in which it demonstrates perfectly the roles that women play in policing their own and each other's sexual

---

[1] See various stages of this story develop at: http://news.nationalpost.com/2012/09/26/its-for-your-good-let-me-finish-afghan-canadian-told-police-she-stabbed-daughter-with-kitchen-knife/; http://news.nationalpost.com/2012/09/25/if-she-survives-she-will-become-more-wise-afghan-woman-accused-of-stabbing-daughter-at-montreal-home/; http://news.nationalpost.com/2012/10/01/stabbed-daughter-defends-mother-she-could-not-hurt-a-fly/, http://www.dailymail.co.uk/news/article-2210688/Its-good-Let-finish-Mother-confesses-stabbing-daughter-19-neck-stayed-late.html#ixzz2ecu2xF7X

behavior in the service of preserving patriarchal religious and cultural norms. There is no male character in this story who regulates the sexual conduct of his daughters and leads the charge in punishing her when she violates her sexual boundaries. On the contrary, the Muslim male in this story—Bahar's father—is the one who saves Bahar from her mother's attack. It is unlikely that Bahar would still be alive if Ebrahim had not been home when the attack occurred. The role of sexual regulator and disciplinarian was inhabited by Johra, a mother of four daughters, who confesses that she was motivated by her religious convictions to regulate and punish Bahar's transgressions.[2] Despite the fact that mental health issues may have influenced the extreme nature of Johra's behavior—as was argued by the defense— sexual management and accompanying distress at the violation of sexual norms is fairly commonplace in many religious, and in this case Muslim, communities. This story highlights that the line between sexual management and punishment is fine; social supervision of sexual behavior necessarily contains elements of vigilantism and the difference in policing social behavior through verbal or physical violence is a difference in degree rather than kind. This story also illustrates how women regularly perform such social vigilantism by supervising each other's behavior.

Jerusalem

Expressions of sexual management within communities—religious or otherwise—are not always this extreme. Often a vague threat of violence or public shaming is sufficient to inscribe modesty codes in

---

[2] As we can see, religion plays a complicated role in this story, since Johra first stated that she stabbed her daughter because she was violating religious norms relating to appropriate female behavior. However, in her trial she also said that in stabbing her daughter she "went against" her "religion and God" and that she expects to be "punished in this world and the day of Judgement."

one's consciousness. Once these norms are internalized, people begin regulating their own behavior as well as that of others. Although separated by geography and tradition, Bahar Ebrahim probably could have easily related to the fictional story of Dina Reich and the real-life culture of surveillance and spectacle that would hound her creator, American-Israeli novelist Naomi Ragen.

> "It isn't easy for girls like us to get married at all."
>
> "What! Why not?" Chaya Leah bellowed…
>
> "There was a woman. A great-great-great-great aunt." The eyes of the other two sisters widened.
>
> "I don't know when she lived exactly. Fifty or seventy-five years ago. In Poland. Her name was Sruyele…She ran away with another man!"
>
> "Was it on Mother's side or Father's?"
>
> Devora exploded, "What difference does it make? She was like a *sotah*! She ran off with another man! She ran away and left her fiancé, her parents, behind."
>
> The girls held their breath in hearing the horrible term. The *sotah*, a married woman suspected of adultery, was held up to public ridicule whether or not she was guilty."[3]

Thus begins Ragen's 1992 novel *Sotah*, a story that follows the Reich sisters' efforts to find love and happiness within the strictures of the ultra-Orthodox community of Jerusalem. As the opening pages reveal, the sisters' marriage prospects are threatened because of a historical family scandal in which a distant female relative ran off with a man while she was betrothed to someone else. The eldest sister likens this situation to the case of a *sotah*, a suspected adulteress, despite the fact that the young woman in question was not yet married, since from the

---

[3] Naomi Ragen, *Sotah: A Novel* (New York: St. Martin's Griffin, 1992), 11.

perspective of Jewish law a betrothed girl, though not yet co-habiting with her husband-to-be, is still off-limits to other men. As the story evolves, the cautionary tale about their disgraced ancestress comes back to haunt the middle sister, Dina, when she too is accused of having an improper relationship with a man who is not her husband. Exiled from her community by the Modesty Patrol, a group of self-styled thugs who enforce rigid notions of appropriate behavior, Dina longs to find her way back to her family. "I wish there was a holy Temple, that I could drink the bitter waters in front of the whole town and they would see that I am innocent," she moans.[4]

In describing Dina's predicament, Ragen has to use a phrase such as "like a *sotah*" because the concept has no real application today, even in ultra-Orthodox communities.[5] Although the Hebrew Bible and Talmud provide us with the details of an elaborate and violent ordeal implemented to expose publicly the suspected adulteress' transgressions, as we shall see, the Talmud suggests that even by the first century c.e. the ritual was no longer carried out. Nonetheless, the strict modesty code dictating appropriate behavior between the sexes—governing whom a woman may talk to and what spaces she may occupy, and delineating what constitutes sexual brazenness in females—is still very much in play. Ironically, in a strange twist of life imitating art, Naomi Ragen in recent years found herself a victim of the very modesty patrols she critiques in her novels when she refused to sit at the back of a Jerusalem bus.

In 2004, at the request of some ultra-Orthodox communities, certain public buses in Jerusalem were designated *mehadrin*, or scrupulous

---

[4] Ibid., 462.
[5] Despite the fact that Numbers 5, the text that describes the *sotah* ordeal, is read aloud in the synagogue each year as part of the annual Torah cycle, the concept of the *sotah* is not widely known outside of more traditional Jewish circles. In fact, the term *sotah* is so obscure in modern Hebrew that when Ragen's novel was translated for a Hebrew-speaking audience the title was changed to *And to Your Husband Shall Be Your Desire*, referencing Eve's punishment in the book of Genesis. See Ragen, *Sotah*, ix.

in terms of "kosher standards," to enable men and women to sit separately.[6] Men were expected to enter through the front door and sit at the front, and women were to enter through the rear door and sit at the back. Women were required to be modestly dressed on these buses, advertisements were censored, and secular music was prohibited.[7] However, people in ultra-Orthodox neighborhoods also began to comply with these standards on public buses that were not specially designated as *mehadrin*.[8] In two well-publicized cases, in 2004 and

---

[6] Although the term "kosher" is most often applied to food products, the word is usually defined as "fit" or "proper for use" and hence can refer more generally to the status of an object (e.g., a Torah scroll, mezuzah, etc.). In this respect, it is quite similar to the notion of "halal," which simply means "lawful" and may likewise be applied to a whole range of objects and activities.

[7] In 2011, a court ruling struck down the legality of these buses. See Dan Izenberg and Jonah Mandel, "Court Scraps 'Mehadrin' Buses," *Jerusalem Post*, January 6, 2011, http://www.jpost.com/National-News/Court-scraps-mehadrin-buses

[8] The practice of women sitting at the back and men at the front is also commonplace on a public bus operating out of Brooklyn, New York. The bus, which runs from one high-density ultra-Orthodox Jewish area of the city to another, is operated as a franchise: although the bus itself is the property of the New York City Department of Transportation, a private company pays the city for the right to offer a public service to its customers. The private company's board is said to consist of several rabbis, who established the seating guidelines. See Christine Haughney, "At Front of Brooklyn Bus, Clash of Religious and Women's Rights," *New York Times*, October 19, 2011, http://www.nytimes.com/2011/10/20/nyregion/bus-segregation-of-jewish-women-prompts-review.html; "NYC Bus Makes Woman Ride in the Back," *NYC News*, October 19, 2011, http://crownheights.info/nyc-news/38367/nyc-bus-makes-women-ride-in-back/. In 2011, after a local female journalist exposed the gender segregation, there was a public outcry coupled with condemnation from city officials that the bus was in violation of municipal laws. Rather than lose their rights to the service, the bus company agreed to publicize new guidelines indicating that discrimination was against the law and that customers could sit wherever they wished. However, the blogger Shmarya Rosenberg reported that as of 2013 the previous seating arrangement was still in place and that Yiddish-language guidelines posted on the buses still reinforced the segregation. See Shmarya Rosenberg, "Hasidic Bus Company Still Illegally Gender Segregating Public Buses," failedmessiah.com, October 13, 2013, http://failedmessiah.typepad.com/failed_messiahcom/2013/10/hasidic-bus-company-still-illegally-gender-segregating-public-buses-123.html

2006, women who sat at the front of the bus on regular public buses were verbally harassed, spat on, and even physically assaulted by male passengers. One of those women was Naomi Ragen. In both cases, no one came to the help of the women being attacked. The bus driver did not stop the vehicle to try to intervene and, most significantly, other women simply continued to get on at the back of the bus. As Ragen explained in her recollections of the attack, the women were "dutifully crowded at the back. Many of them were engrossed in reciting Psalms."[9] In both these cases, other women were silent. On the one hand, their silence is about modeling what they perceive to be modest behavior. On the other hand, their silence is also accusatory: "Pious women don't behave *that* way," they say wordlessly, both to the women who have dared to sit at the front and to one another. Although they themselves did not throw any punches, they too were witnesses to the abuse and hence were passively complicit in it. In that moment, their gazes become one with the male gaze. They watched, they catalogued compliance, and in the process demarcated which women were part of their community and which women were not. As we shall see, this is precisely the role that all women are asked to play in the spectacle

---

Given the long history of African-American segregation in the U.S., a segregated bus in Brooklyn touches a cultural nerve in a way that a segregated bus in Jerusalem may not, given that bus routes in Israel have often informally been divided along religious, ethnic, and national lines and in 2013 some efforts were even made to do so more formally. See Chaim Levinson, "Israel Introduces Palestinian-Only Bus Lines Following Complaints from Jewish Settlers," *Ha'aretz*, March 3, 2013, http://www.haaretz.com/news/national/israel-introduces-palestinian-only-bus-lines-following-complaints-from-jewish-settlers-1.506869. But what is common to the ultra-Orthodox-operated services in both Brooklyn and Jerusalem is the ongoing compliance of female passengers whose buy-in is needed to reinforce standards of modesty. Although one woman passenger acknowledged that other bus lines in the community have a divider in the bus to prevent the mingling of the sexes, she felt that a reverse of the policy, with women in the front and men in the back would not work, because "[the men] are not allowed to see the women."

[9] See Naomi Ragen, "Egged and the Taliban," August 1, 2004, http://www.naomiragen.com/israel/egged-and-the-taliban/

of the *sotah* ritual. Women are invited to witness the humiliation of another woman who has dared to transgress acceptable social boundaries. As a result, the spectacle is not merely about the accused. It is a warning to other women to know their proper place—whether at the back of the bus or in their interactions with males—lest they too be subject to the same humiliations.

Although, at first glance, the case of attempted murder in a Montreal suburb looks different from a series of altercations on a Jerusalem bus line, both these episodes are characterized by explosions of violence and also by more subtle, pernicious forms of social coercion. In both circumstances, the women have internalized certain modesty norms that they believe they must act on and enforce to prove their piety. Both situations give rise to the following question. How are individuals empowered to police each other's behavior in informal social contexts? Where do they derive this authority?

There are many reasons—political, social, cultural, and religious—that may empower members of a community to supervise each other's bodies and sexual conduct. Insofar as religion and culture are inextricably bound, religious texts bear some responsibility for cultural norms that encourage people to police their own sexual behavior. And religious texts provide sufficient examples to authorize women to carry out social vigilantism in formal and informal ways, empowering them to be agents of patriarchy. In this essay we will examine two religious legal texts, one Islamic and the other Jewish, that recruit women to supervise and report back on each other's behavior. Since these texts are fundamentally patriarchal, they play an interesting game simultaneously empowering and restricting women's role in policing their own behavior. Women are granted a great degree of power in witnessing against each other, but minimal power in influencing the legal outcome of their testimony. Since these legal texts are also religious and therefore normative texts, they bear a great burden of responsibility, because they influence cultural norms and social practice. Even if we might argue that these texts do not exactly represent the social history in which they were written, they are considered authoritative texts by various communities of Muslims and Jews and, as such, continue to bear tangible impact on Muslim and Jewish women's lives.

THE *HIDAYA*: TESTIMONY IN CASES OF *ZINA*

The first text we will examine is the Islamic legal text that appears in the section on corporal punishments (*hudud*). It was written by al-Marghinani (d. 593/1197), who was a leading Central Asian Hanafi jurist. His *Hidaya* (*The Guide*) was and continues to be an influential compendium of Islamic law. According to classical Islamic law, fornication and/or adultery, hereafter referred to as *zina*, is a punishable offense. Jurists disagreed about the exact punishment for a couple convicted of *zina*, but they agreed that the punishment is either a hundred lashes or death by stoning. Many scholars argued that if the fornicator is married the punishment is death by stoning, but if he or she is unmarried then they are to be lashed a hundred times. This is complicated by the fact that the word *zina* does not distinguish marital status; it describes both the adulterous act of the married person and the fornication of the single male or female. A couple cannot be convicted of *zina* unless four witnesses testify against them, each bearing witness that they have seen the act of intercourse. If for some reason the testimony of the witnesses turns out to be false, the witnesses are liable for punishment comparable to the punishment for *zina* itself. Each witness is to be lashed eighty times. Hence, the act of accusing someone of *zina* is rather weighty and can make the accuser eligible for punishment himself. I say "himself" rather than "himself or herself" here because something else that is relevant to this discussion is that in general the witness of men and women in Islamic law is unequal. The witness of two women is equivalent to the witness of one man. In this context we begin to see the relevance of the Islamic legal passage, in the chapter on corporal punishments (*hudud*), that theorizes about the case of a virgin accused of *zina*. The text reads,

> If four men bear witness against a woman, accusing her of *zina* but she is a virgin, the *hadd* penalty is averted from the couple and the [four witnesses] (*'an-huma wa 'an-hum*) since *zina* cannot co-exist with virginity. This problem requires the women to check [the girl accused of adultery] (*nazarna ilayha*) and declare that she is a virgin. The witness of [the women] is a [sufficient] proof (*hujja*) for overturning (*isqat*) the *hadd* penalty but it is in[sufficient] proof for the obligation/liability (*ijabihi*) of [the *hadd* penalty]. Therefore, the *hadd* penalty is overturned from the couple but it is not made incumbent on [the four witnesses].[10]

This text grants women power as active agents in maintaining patriarchal sexual norms among women while simultaneously limiting their agency and power over men. To explore the contours of this text, it is helpful to consider the details of the scene this text evokes. In this vivid scene, four men stand in a courtroom having accused a couple of *zina*, and the female charged with *zina* turns out to be a virgin. The main question the text seeks to answer is this: should the four male witnesses be lashed eighty times for false testimony when a girl accused of *zina* turns out to be a virgin? A secondary question the text addresses is: what is the weight of women's testimony—can it nullify the *zina* penalty against a couple who are accused of *zina* by four men and can it make a penalty of eighty lashes incumbent on men who bear false witness?

---

[10] Abu Bakr b. 'Abd al-Jalil al-Rashidani al-Marghinani, *Al-Hidaya Sharh Bidaya al-Mubtadi* (Lebanon: Dar al-Kutub al-'Ilmiyya, 2000), 395.

Although the text is narrowly concerned with these questions, it also assumes a great deal of background. Several things have happened before we arrive at this courtroom scene, where a judge must decide whether to lash four men who have borne false witness against a couple where the girl is a virgin. Before this scene, four men arrived in court to accuse a couple of *zina*. The girl defended herself (or was defended) by the claim that she was still a virgin and therefore could not have committed *zina*. At this point, the couple and the witnesses are at an impasse. Who is telling the truth and who is lying? The obvious thing to do appears to be to verify the girl's claim: is she really a virgin? How can one verify this claim? The text assumes that there are "women"— let's call them "virginity testers"—who can be mobilized to "check" a woman's virginity. The text does not tell us who these women are, who they are employed by, and whose interests they serve. It seems to assume their existence as a matter of fact. Although the text does not say so explicitly, Charles Hamilton, in this translation of this passage, describes these women as "females employed to examine the woman accused."[11] These women check the girl's virginity and then report back to the court.

But let us linger with the virginity testers. Are they already present in court or do they have to be summoned? How many women check a girl's virginity? How did they become virginity testers? How is one trained for such a task? And how do they check this girl's virginity? Is this test physical, checking for the hymen, or verbal, checking for knowledge of sexual acts? If the test is verbal, is it carried out in public or in private and what sorts of questions are asked, what answers are acceptable? If the test is physical, where is this examination carried out? Is there a room, off to the side perhaps, that is used for this purpose? And what exactly does the examination look like? What tools are

[11] Charles Hamilton, trans., *The Hedaya, or Guide: A Commentary on the Mussulman Laws* (Delhi: Islamic Book Trust, 1982), 190.

used? Does the room have a table with stirrups? How do they "check" a girl's virginity? Is the examination visual or does it involve prodding with a finger? Since Islamic legal texts distinguish the existence of the hymen from virginity, acknowledging that the hymen can be lost through non-sexual acts like jumping, menstruation, and spinster-hood (see Chapter 2), one has to wonder if the test is physical at all. Thinking about the details of the precise nature of the virginity test reveals its nebulous nature, exposing the considerable power vested in the virginity testers. These women basically make a subjective call as to whether the girl is a virgin or not. Since the virginity testers are not necessarily reporting back with a hundred percent certainty, what set of interests influence and inform their report? This seems to be a position of great power over a couple—they can have the couple lashed or exonerated—and puts the virginity testers at the intersection of divergent interests. Their personal relationship with either accused person, as well as with the four witnesses, the judge, and/or the state, etc., will likely influence whatever decision they reach about the girl's virginity.

In our scenario, for whatever reason, these women testify that the girl's claim to virginity is "true." She is a virgin. This makes it unneces-sary to lash the couple, and the virginity testers' testimony exonerates both individuals accused of adultery. Their extraordinary power over the fate of both individuals—male and female—is, however, restricted to the couple. Because they are women, their testimony is not weighty enough to subject the male witnesses to corporal punishment. As we shall see, there are similar limits to the powers of women's testimony in Jewish legal texts as well. In our text the trustworthiness of both the virginity checkers and the virginity test are inextricably bound; there is a deep distrust of both. The text does not trust the results of this test enough to punish the four witnesses based on its results, but it does trust the test results enough to convict or exonerate the couple accused of adultery. The testimony of the female virginity testers can be relied upon to determine the fate of the accused couple, but it cannot be relied upon to condemn the four male witnesses, who are the real trouble-makers in this scenario. After all, the whole point of lashing false witnesses eighty times—a punishment comparable to the punishment of *zina*—is to discourage wanton accusations of *zina* and the accompanying social unrest. Removing the punishment for false testimony expands the purview of the male witnesses. The male witnesses in this case may well be encouraged to continue supervising their community's sexual behavior, casually accusing couples of *zina*, without any worry of getting punished. If the accused girl is deemed to have been deflowered, then she will be lashed or stoned. If the accused girl turns out to be a virgin, there are no repercussions for the four male witnesses; they walk free. The most disempowered characters in this story are the accused couple. Between the two of them, the girl accused of *zina* carries their fate on her person—the examination of her virginity will determine what happens.

It is important to emphasize here that the virginity test is not strictly a medical examination of the existence of a woman's hymen. Muslim legal discussions about virginity and how one may lose her virginity attest to this fact. Chapter 2 in this volume discusses al-Quduri's (d. 1037 c.e.) list of five ways in which a woman may lose her virginity, namely, jumping, injury, menstruation, fornication, and spinsterhood. If virginity itself is a nebulous, non-physical category, then the methods for testing for it are also vague and ambiguous. The vagueness of the test means that it can be used at the discretion of those in power to either protect or punish women accused of adultery. Very much like the test of bitter water that we will encounter below, this test is meant more as a regulator of women's sexuality than to establish clear proof of virginity by a foolproof method. This fact was recently brought to light when a pregnant fifteen-year-old girl accused of fornication in Dubai was subjected to a virginity test by the state authorities and was deemed to be a virgin. The virginity test is "medicalized" in Dubai, so a medical report was produced verifying the virginity of the girl. The "medical" nature of the test maintains the ambiguity of virginity testing in our text, since this medical report testified to the virginity of a woman who was 29 weeks pregnant. Nevertheless, the test results allowed the authorities to protect the girl and her boyfriend by putting them under Dubai's judicial department's supervision. To protect the couple from family members who might hurt them, this supervision provided the couple with housing and family mediation.[12] In this instance the virginity test worked in the favor of the couple by shielding them from harm. Still, the existence of the test indicates an acceptance of social mores that prescribe strict regulations on individual sexual choices and punish those who break the rules. Further, the test transforms the female body into a test site. As the test site, the female body literally bears the burden of proof for the innocence or guilt of the couple. Violating the body of the accused determines whether bodily harms ends with that violation or continues through lashing or stoning.

This text, insofar as it is viewed as a religious, legal, and normative text, influences the attitudes of those Muslims who consider it authoritative. For such believers, this text encourages the social supervision of individual sexual practices either at a state or a personal level. Where believers live in a society that has had opportunity to "establish Islamic law," as in Taliban-ruled Afghanistan (the Taliban

---

[12] The report reads, "On August 8, [2013] authorities subjected a pregnant 15-year-old girl, who was charged with having premarital sex, to a virginity test. According to the authorities' medical report, the girl was still a virgin despite being 29 weeks pregnant at the time of the test. Authorities placed the girl and her 17-year-old boyfriend under the supervision of Dubai's judicial department. No further information was available at year's end. Judicial supervision typically included housing individuals to ensure their well-being, providing for family mediation and reconciliation, and preventing relatives from harming individuals or committing honor crimes." See more at: http://www.state.gov/j/drl/rls/hrrpt/humanrightsreport/index.htm?year=2012&dlid=204387#wrapper

happened to be Hanafi), we have seen the literal (mis)application of these laws. The law is applied to varying effects in countries like Dubai, where virginity tests are part of the state apparatus used to regulate sexual practice. Where believers live in a society in which "Islamic law" is not formally applied, these legal, religious texts continue to wield a great deal of normative influence in setting the standard for acceptable sexual norms. They encourage individuals to judge and influence the sexual practices of members of their families and communities, particularly those over whom they have power. In some cases, families even pressure individual doctors to perform virginity tests on their daughters.[13] It is in these contexts, where individuals informally undertake social surveillance based on religious texts that encourage formal social supervision of the sexual choices of individuals, that the slippage from verbal to physical violence is facilitated. In this religious legal text, women do the work of patriarchy in a manner that is entirely gendered. In their service of patriarchy virginity testers wield a great deal of power over and against other women, influencing the course of their lives in extremely tangible ways. However, their power is simultaneously restricted on grounds of their gender, their testimony is insufficient to convict the four male witnesses to receive any punishment; the four male witnesses are free to continue their own social vigilantism, perhaps even to accuse a virginity tester of adultery. The unequal weight of the testimony of men and women ultimately puts the virginity testers in a disempowered position relative to male witnesses who bear false witness.

But the limited ability of women to testify against or on behalf of one another, either formally or informally, is not limited to Islamic law. We will now consider a Jewish legal text in which women's social

---

[13] In Quebec, the Quebec College of Physicians had to issue a warning to doctors to stop performing virginity tests, after several cases in which patients or their families had demanded them. For more on this story: http://news.nationalpost.com/2013/10/12/degrading-virginity-tests-on-women-must-stop-quebec-doctors-group-urges/

supervision of and gossip about one another may have limited testimonial weight in determining the marital, economic, and social fate of the female subject of their gossip.

MISHNAH *SOTAH*: TESTIMONY IN THE CASE OF SUSPECTED ADULTERY

Like the virginity checkers in the *Hidaya* text, early Rabbinic texts also recruit women to participate in the monitoring, policing, and rebuking of the behavior of other women. The first Mishnah in Chapter 6 of the Talmudic Tractate *Sotah* features four different categories of women: the *sotah*, the "Women Spinners," the *sotah*'s female kin, and the female slave. Although elsewhere the Talmud lumps all women together as a "separate people,"[14] here the rabbis are attempting to demarcate those who are part of the Rabbinic project and those who are operating against Rabbinic interests. As we shall see, though, even when the rabbis portray women as agents of their system they retain vestiges of suspicion about women's motives and competencies and their potential for unruly behavior. At the end of the day, the *sotah* is actually a stand-in for every woman, and that is why every woman is compelled to participate in her shaming.

In order to understand how the *sotah* becomes a stand-in for all women, we need to gain a more thorough understanding of what a *sotah* is. Although the word *sotah* is derived from a Hebrew word meaning "to stray, turn aside or deviate," the entirety of Tractate *Sotah* deals with the subject of the suspected adulteress. As hinted at earlier, this pertains to a case where there is no proof of adultery, only a suspicion. Since, biblically, a man can marry as many women as he wants, it is entirely licit for a married man to have relations with an unattached

---

14 See *b. Shabbat* 62a.

woman.[15] Consequently, in Jewish law, adultery, or *ni'uf*, is defined as sexual relations between a man and a married woman.[16] In cases of proven adultery, where at least two witnesses attest to the crime[17]— the biblical punishment was death,[18] but what if a man suspected his wife but had no proof?

The Sotah Ordeal

The biblical resolution to this problem was the *sotah* ordeal described in Numbers 5:21–31. The ordeal required that a man who had been "moved by a spirit of jealousy" should bring his wife to the High Priest, who would then loosen her hair, rend her garments, and prepare for her a concoction of water mixed with dust from the floor of the Temple. She was then to recite an oath/curse that included God's

---

[15] By the Talmudic period, the rabbis would suggest that a man should not marry more women than he could support and the ideal number was reduced to four. See *b. Yevamot* 44a. An ordinance around the year 1000 c.e. attributed to Rabbi Gershom banned polygyny entirely for Jews living in Ashkenaz, while at the same time making divorce contingent upon a wife's consent.

[16] The biblical and modern Hebrew word for "whoring" or "harlotry" is *zenut*, which has a congate in the Arabic word *zinah*.

[17] As per Deuteronomy 19:15, two or three witnesses are needed to establish evidentiary certainty.

[18] The punishment for adultery mandated in the Bible was execution (by stoning or choking) for both the man and the woman (Deuteronomy 22:21–22; Leviticus 20:10). In the case of a woman who is proven to have not been a virgin at the time of her marriage, the punishment is stoning, whereas one who falsely accuses her and besmirches her reputation only pays a fine (Deuteronomy 22:13–21). In other cases of adultery the accused are executed by strangulation, since the rabbis understood any death sentence where the mode of death was not specified to be referring to strangulation (b. Sanhedrin 52b). Later the consequences became less grave: a man was compelled to divorce his adulterous wife and she was not permitted to marry her lover. Different communities came up with other punitive measures over time, ranging from flogging, excommunicating the couple, or publicly shaming them by shaving their heads and parading them through the streets. See Rachel Biale, *Women and Jewish Law* (New York: Schocken Books, 1995), 189.

name and detailed what would happen to her if she was guilty. The oath was then blotted out from the scroll in the bitter waters and she was compelled to drink this liquid. Her inquisitors would then wait to see the waters take effect. If she was innocent, the waters had no impact, but if she was guilty "her belly would swell and her thigh would rupture" (Numbers 5:27). Many traditional interpreters, including Maimonides, understood this to mean that the woman would die.[19] However, since the innocent woman is not only allowed to resume regular marital relations with her husband, but is also promised that "she shall conceive seed" (Numbers 5:28), several contemporary exegetes have understood the effects of the water as referring to the suspected adulteress miscarrying the child of her paramour or suffering a prolapsed uterus that will render her infertile.[20]

The rabbis of the Mishnah added to the details of the ordeal, suggesting that a man first had to warn his wife of his suspicions in front of two witnesses and declare that she was not to be alone with such-and-such man and should even refrain from talking to him (b. Sotah 2a). If she persisted in having contact with the man in question, despite the warning, her husband could formally accuse her of adultery. As Ishay Rosen-Zvi and others have pointed out, the significant departure from the Bible in the Mishnah is that, suddenly, the notion of the woman's innocence has disappeared.[21] While the biblical account of the sotah ritual contains no references to rules of evidence, the Mishnaic discussion starts by describing the evidence that is necessary to kick the ritual into action. The biblical text refers to the jealousy of the

---

[19] See Maimonides, *Mishneh Torah, Sefer Nashim, Sotah*, 3:16–17.

[20] Biale, *Women in Jewish Law*, 186 Tikva Frymer-Kensky, "The Strange Case of the Suspected Sotah (Numbers V 11–31)," in *Women in the Hebrew Bible: A Reader*, ed. Alice Bach (London: Routledge, 1998), 463–474; Baruch A. Levine, *Numbers 1–20: A New Translation with Introduction and Commentary* (New Haven: Doubleday, 1993), 201–204.

[21] See Ishay Rosen-Zvi, *The Mishnaic Sotah Ritual: Temple, Gender and Midrash*, trans. Orr Scharf (Leiden: Brill, 2012), 3.

husband (*ve-qana*) and to the wife's indiscretion being "undetected" (*ve-nistera*). However, the rabbis understood these two terms as referring not simply to baseless suspicion on the part of the husband, but rather to "formal rules and stages of evidence": first "warning" (*qana*) and then hiding or seclusion (*nistera*).[22] Although some scholars have suggested that the biblical ritual actually served to protect a woman from baseless accusations, by constructing a socially acceptable outlet for a man's wild suspicions that would exonerate his wife and restore marital harmony between them, the rabbis' anxieties about the lack of evidence in the biblical scenario led to a formalization of this process which all but ensures that the *sotah* ends up being guilty.[23]

This focus on the woman's culpability is underscored throughout the Mishnah; if witnesses came forward to testify she had "committed misconduct" (*she-nitmaet*, from the root *t-m-a*, connoting defilement), she was considered guilty, was divorced from her husband, lost the monetary compensation due to her as part of her marriage settlement (known as her *ketubah*), and was forbidden from reuniting with either her husband or her lover (*b. Sotah* 27a). However, if she maintained her innocence the *sotah* ordeal was put into action, as a means of humiliating her and forcing a confession out of her. As described by the rabbis, the woman was now brought to the local court so that two

---

[22] As Rosen-Zvi has noted, even before the rabbis both Philo and Josephus were troubled that the ritual seems to be entirely motivated by a husband's jealousy, requiring no real basis for his suspicion. Philo in particular suggested that the accusation is "not made in wanton spite, but with honest intentions and is founded on reasonable doubt." See Rosen-Zvi, *Mishnaic Sotah Ritual*, 23; Philo, *The Special Laws*, III:53–55; Josephus, *Antiquities of the Jews*, III:271.

[23] See for example, Biale, *Women and Jewish Law*, 187. "The insignificance of the actual physical ordeal is intended in order to practically guarantee that a woman could prove her innocence. This means that the real purpose of the ordeal is not to convict adulterous women who have been skilful enough to hide their transgression, but primarily to afford a way for women to clear themselves of suspicion." A similar idea already is at play in the midrashic commentary on the book of Numbers, Sifre (*ca.* fourth or fifth century), which understands the ritual as designed to "make peace between husband and wife." See Sifre 16:21, 42:61.

sages could be assigned to the case; then, together with the jealous husband, they would bring her to the high court in Jerusalem for the ordeal to be administered. At this point, they would still appeal to her to confess and thwart the implementation of the ordeal, "for the sake of His great name which is written in holiness so that it may not be obliterated by the water" (*b. Sotah* 7a). If she confessed at this late stage, the consequences were the same: automatic divorce, no *ketubah* payment, and she was forbidden to both her husband and her lover.

But if she still held that she did nothing wrong she would be taken to the East Gate of the Temple, and before they compelled her to recite the oath and drink they would loosen her hair, remove her ornaments, tie her clothes with a common rope just under her chest, and bare her breasts for all to see. She was only spared the gaze of her male and female slaves. The explicit, almost pornographic account of her exposure has been noted by many authors, including Judith Hauptman. "Ripping off her clothes to partially expose her body is both strange and suggestive. It feeds the sexual fantasies of the bystanders, in particular the young priests."[24] The revealing of her body in this way was understood as a measure-for-measure punishment: "She exposed herself for a transgression; the holy one blessed be He held her up for exposure" (*b. Sotah* 8b).[25] The Mishnah in Tractate *Sotah* goes on to describe the content of the oath, the materials that could be used to write it down, who is automatically disqualified from drinking the bitter waters, what effects the water will have (her eyes bulge out, her face turns green, and her eyes swell—*b. Sotah* 20a), in which circumstances the waters may have no effect (if she has merit from past good deeds and learning, if her husband cohabited with her

---

[24] See Hauptman, *Rereading the Rabbis*, 21.

[25] Rosen-Zvi points out that this measure for measure is used differently than in most other places, where it is seen as a divine justice within scripture; here it is a reenactment of punitive measures triggered by sinful behavior. See Rosen-Zvi, *Mishnaic Sotah Ritual*.

just prior, or if he too has committed sexual transgressions—*b. Sotah* 23a, 7b, 47b), and how the effects of the water will also extend to her paramour (*b. Sotah* 28a). After this long analysis, and almost play-by-play description of the ordeal, we are told that the ritual fell out of use in the aftermath of the destruction of the Temple because the number of suspected adulterers became too high, so it was no longer considered efficacious: "when adulterers multiplied the ceremony of the bitter water was discontinued and it was discontinued by Rabbi Jonathan ben Zakkai" (*b. Sotah* 47a).[26] Given that the rabbis were writing in a period when the ordeal was no longer carried out, their discussions should be seen as an attempt to manage and attend to suspicions of adultery in a post-ordeal universe.[27]

The Text: *m. Sotah* 6.1

The section of Tractate *Sotah* we will be looking at concerns incomplete or substandard sources of evidence that a woman has committed

---

[26] Although the second folio of the Tractate already contains the suggestion that the rabbis no longer have access to the mechanisms for carrying out the ordeal: "R. Hanina of Sura said: Nowadays a man should not say to his wife, 'Do not be secluded with So-and-so', lest we decide according to R. Jose son of R. Judah who said: A warning [is effective] if given on [the husband's] personal testimony. If she then secluded herself with the man, since we have not now the water for a suspected woman to test her, the husband forbids her to himself for all time." See *b. Sotah* 2b.

[27] Of course, we have no evidence that the ordeal was carried out to begin with. There are perhaps parallels to the rite in the Hammurabi code which suggests that "If the wife of a man her husband has accused her, and she had not been caught in lying with another male, she shall swear by God and shall return to her house. If a wife of a man on account of another male has had the finger pointed at her, and has not been caught in lying with another male, for her husband she shall plunge into the holy river." See "The Code of Hammurabi," 131–132, trans. L. W. King, *The Avalon Project*, http://avalon.law.yale.edu/ancient/hamframe.asp. There are also echoes of the use of ordeal-like measures in Exodus 32:20, where Moses melts down the Golden Calf, grinds it into dust, and makes the idol-worshipping Israelites drink it. See *Introduction to Tractate Sotah*, trans. A. Cohen, ed. Isidore Epstein (London: Soncino Press, 1952).

misconduct. In particular, different kinds of women's testimonies are examined, including gossip and the testimonies of female kin. Not only are women divided into those who are virtuous and those who are not, but even women living in the same household are positioned as rivals to one another. As we shall see, the imagined culture of surveillance is quite strong here.

> If a man warned his wife (*kine lah*) and she secluded herself [with another man] (*ve-nisterah*), even if he heard [that she had done so] from a flying bird (*off ha-poreach*), he divorces her and gives her the marriage settlement. Such is the statement of R. Eliezer. R. Joshua says: [He does not do this] until women who spin by moonlight (*mezorot be-levana*) discuss her.

> If one witness said, I saw that she committed misconduct (*she-nitmaet*), she does not drink the water. Not only that, but even a slave, male or female, is believed also to disqualify her for the marriage settlement. Her mother-in-law, her mother-in-law's daughter, her associate-wife, her sister-in-law, and her step-daughter are believed, not to disqualify her for the marriage settlement, but that she should not drink.

The "Offenses"

Two different levels of "offenses" are described in this text. In the first paragraph of the Mishnah, a woman is suspected of having "secluded" herself with another man despite having been warned not to do so. In the second paragraph of the Mishnah, on the other hand, a woman is suspected of having "committed misconduct" with a man who is not her husband. How are these different? We shall discuss the implications of these actions but, for now, it will suffice for us to consider that the Mishnah is discussing two different scenarios.

The Consequences

In terms of the consequences of these suspected activities, three major issues are at play in this text:

1. Does she need to submit to the ordeal?

2. Must she be divorced from her husband?

3. Does she lose her *ketubah* payment?

The ordeal kicks in to remedy situations where there is a suspicion of wrongdoing, but no "proof." As Tikva Frymer-Kensky has described, the ritual is performed "in answer to a crisis in the legal system...it is impossible to 'solve' the case by normal legal means...there is a suspect (the wife) but no knowledge of whether a crime has been committed... [so] special quasi-legal procedures are prescribed to resolve the situation by religious means."[28] Consequently, the issue of divorce comes up almost as soon as there is some foundation—however flimsy—to suggest the woman has been unfaithful. For, as we have already seen, if she has been with another man she is prohibited to both her husband and her lover. But, since her eyebrow-raising behavior goes against the "practice of the Jews," she is not only divorced but also loses her rights to her marriage settlement.[29] In most of the Tractate, the rabbis seems to be evaluating (a) "Does she drink?"—i.e., is there enough proof to transform a suspicion into evidence and thereby forgo the ordeal of the bitter waters?—and (b) "Does she lose her *ketubah*?"—is

---

[28] Frymer-Kensky, "The Strange Case of the Suspected Sotah," 463.
[29] See *b. Ketubot* 72a, where any woman who goes out with her head uncovered, spins wool in the street, or converses with any man is divorced and deprived of her *ketubah* payment. All these actions are deemed to be going against "the practices of the Jews" or *dat Yehudit*. This is distinguished from practices that are very clearly for the rabbis transgressions according to the law of Moses, such as having sex while in a state of ritual purity or being negligent about separating dough for the priests.

the evidence against her sufficient for her to lose her *ketubah* upon divorce?[30]

The Limits of Evidence: Gossip

The larger debate here seems to be about testing the limits of evidence, and what constitutes evidence to begin with. Whereas in the Bible slandering a woman's virtue results in payment of a fine,[31] here gossip, and the gossip of women in particular, is regarded as hard evidence, sufficient for a man to divorce his wife. That the rabbis are willing to entertain such sources as legitimate illustrates how desperate they are to manage and control *sotah*-like behavior. Two types of "gossip" are discussed here, each deriving from a different source: the "Flying Bird" and the "Women Who Spin by Moonlight" (Women Spinners).

To understand the significance of these sources and how they differ, we must return to an earlier debate between the two sages referenced in our text: Rabbi Eliezer and Rabbi Joshua. Earlier in Tractate *Sotah*, in the very first Mishnah, Rabbi Eliezer suggested that whereas two

---

[30] Since a man may divorce his wife for any reason—let alone if he has suspicions that she has been unfaithful—the question of whether or not she is divorced is less salient than whether she must still submit to the ordeal or whether she is denied her marriage settlement.

[31] See Deuteronomy 22:13–20. In the biblical case, a man accuses his new bride of not having been a virgin prior to their marriage. If his charge proves to be false after her parents display the "tokens of her virginity" for all to see, the man is publicly "chastised" by the elders of the city, he must pay a hundred shekels of silver, and he is never permitted to divorce her. Of course, if her parents cannot produce the evidence that she was a virgin, she is to be stoned at the door of her father's house. However, if their own texts are to be believed, by the Mishnaic period the rabbis seem to lack both the will and the resources to enforce capital crimes. See for example *b. Sanhedrin* 40a and *m. Makkot* 1:10: "A Sanhedrin which decides a verdict of death once in seven years is called murderous. Rabbi Elazar ben Azariah said, even if only once in seven years. Rabbi Tarphon and Rabbi Akiba said: 'If we were members of the Sanhedrin, there would never be a verdict of death.'"

witnesses are required to warn a woman to stay away from a particular man, only one witness or the husband's own testimony is needed to confirm that she secluded herself with the man she was warned about, and that this second set of testimony after the seclusion was sufficient to compel her to undergo the ordeal. Rabbi Joshua was recorded as disagreeing with him and insisting on a higher degree of certainty: just as two witnesses are required at the time of warning, two witnesses are also required to attest to the woman having disregarded the warning and secluded herself with the man. Here, the text brings the dispute of the two sages back into focus and examines how their rulings apply to other related scenarios: Rabbi Eliezer suggests that the Flying Bird is sufficient as evidence, whereas Rabbi Joshua suggests that the Women Spinners are sufficient evidence. But sufficient evidence for what?

According to the text, if a husband gets word that his wife, "the suspected adulteress," has disregarded warnings and secluded herself with a particular man, she no longer needs to drink the bitter waters. In other words, this transient source—whether it be the Flying Bird or the Women Spinners—is enough evidence to move suspicion into some sort of confirmation. The ordeal is only for cases where "there be no witness against her" (Numbers 5:13), so the Flying Bird or Women Spinners qualify as some degree of "witness." Yet, these are not the same as actual "witnesses" to the seclusion which the first Mishnah required to compel the woman to undergo the ordeal.[32]

---

[32] Medieval commentators are divided on their understanding of the precise topic under discussion. Rashi understands that, according to Rabbi Eliezer, the rumor would have been sufficient evidence to compel her to undergo the ordeal, since he holds that even the husband's own testimony is sufficient to kick-start the ordeal process. Because of this, Rashi believes that Rabbi Eliezer's comments here refer to a situation where the husband was unwilling to have her drink the waters and instead preferred to divorce her. Rashbam and Maimonides disagree, suggesting that even for Rabbi Eliezer a vague rumor is not the same as one witness. Although Maimonides also suggests that the scenario being described here is a rumor of actual misconduct, rather than simply seclusion, the rumor is still not weighty enough for the woman to forfeit her *ketubah*. See *b. Sotah* 31b; *Tractate Sotah*, ed. Isidor Epstein (London: Soncino Press, 1934), 31b, note 15.

These ambiguous sources cast enough suspicion for her to be divorced from her husband. However, neither of them is considered to be a weighty enough source for her also to go penniless. She is divorced from her husband based on these "testimonies," but, perhaps because the information cannot be accurately and independently verified, she does not lose her *ketubah* payment.

But are the Flying Bird and the Women Spinners equal in terms of the way they are regarded or is a hierarchy of evidence being described here? Is the Flying Bird a more ethereal source than the Women Spinners? By suggesting that one requires the "testimony" of the Women Spinners about a suspected adulteress having violated her husband's warning before a man can divorce his wife, is Rabbi Joshua requiring a sounder source than Rabbi Eliezer?[33]

First let us examine the implications of these two types of "testimony."

The Flying Bird

This seems to refer to a vague rumor that came to the husband's ears through the grapevine. Although the eleventh-century commentator Rashi suggests that it refers to information provided by a male or female slave, others, including Maimonides, suggest that "Flying Bird" may refer to a talking bird, such as a parrot that repeats what it has heard.[34] Either way, this source is seen as not quite baseless, but as flimsy at best, a lone voice not necessarily attributable to any particular person.

---

[33] This debate between the two sages actually goes back to the first Mishnah in Tractate Sotah, where R. Eliezer is similarly more lenient regarding the testimony required to make the woman submit to the ordeal and R. Joshua is more strict, requiring two witnesses after the husband's jealousy is ignited. See *m. Sotah* 1.1.

[34] See I. Epstein, "Notes." *Tractate Sotah* (London: Soncino Press, 1952).

The Women Spinners

The Women Spinners, on the other hand, seem to have a different sort of symbolic meaning in the world of the Mishnah. Rabbi Joshua seems to hold out for a slightly stronger confirmation than a rumor from an unknown source. Miriam Peskowitz has examined images of spinning thread in Roman Palestine and has illustrated the way the loom becomes synonymous with women's labor in a Rabbinic context. Accordingly, in her book *Spinning Fantasies*, she suggests that the spinning woman is not an idle one. She is industrious, supports her family with "the work of her hands," just like the "Women of Valour" in Proverbs 31:13. Indeed, she works so hard that she even makes use of the last light of the day—the moonlight—to finish her work. As Peskowitz explains, "Spinning displays their loyalty and respectability, their domesticity and thrift. It establishes them as reliable witnesses against another woman's transgression."[35] These pious, hard-working women are implicitly contrasted to the suspected adulteress, who uses her time to deceive her husband instead of working hard for her family. Because of its source, these women's gossip has legs. In the imaginary world constructed in the text, the group of women gossip about their neighbors as they spin, and eventually this gossip finds its way to the husband of the suspected adulteress. How it reaches him we do not know. Significantly, the text does not imagine a similar gathering of men in the market, the bathhouse, or the study house, passing on the town tales they have heard from their wives. But the plurality of voices condemning the man's wife seems to add credence to the rumor. As opposed to the hard-to-trace, singular, and accusatory message of the Flying Bird, the Women Spinners are a group, working as part of a community and

---

[35] Miriam Peskowitz, *Spinning Fantasies: Rabbis, Gender and History* (Berkeley: University of California Press, 1997), 135.

speaking on behalf of the community. As Peskowitz remarks, in the world of the text, the Women Spinners' interests are Rabbinic interests—they are complicit in preserving Rabbinic notions of marriage, chastity, and piety. The suspected adulteress, on the other hand, is not part of their virtuous clique. She is an outsider. The motives of the Women Spinners are not evaluated here; we do not know if their chatter arises out of spite, a sense of duty, empathy for the husband, or as a way to break up the monotony of their mind-numbing task. However, although their claims are enough to break up the woman's marriage, they are not weighty enough to deprive her of her *ketubah*. Despite being a laudable group, they are, after all, just women. And women are generally not considered to be competent as witnesses.[36] Their disqualification as witnesses in a court of law was generally understood as having to do with their inexperience in the public sphere (see *b. Gittin* 46a).[37]

Women as Witnesses

However, this does not apply in all cases. Women were considered reliable witnesses in matters that were particular to their expertise, such as their first-hand knowledge of women's customs and/or places frequented only by women. For instance, women were, for the most

---

[36] Women were considered reliable witnesses in matters that were particular to their expertise, e.g., issues of menstrual status/purity, or to speak to women's customs and/or places only frequented by women. Their disqualification as witnesses in a court of law was generally understood as having to do with their inexperience in the public sphere (see *b. Gittin* 46a).

[37] As a result, some contemporary rabbis, especially in the conservative movement, question the ongoing validity of this restriction in the modern age where women's roles have changed. See for instance Rabbi Aaron Mackler, "The Testimony of Women Is as the Testimony of Man," Committee on Jewish Law and Standards, November 2004.

part, trusted to speak to matters of menstrual status and purity,[38] and a midwife's testimony was accepted pertaining to which twin was born first.[39] But the ability to stand as a reliable witness was not limited to matters of female biology and reproduction. Women were able to provide testimony in the case of the death of their own husband or other women's husbands,[40] they could attest to the signing of a divorce document in their presence,[41] and they could affirm that another woman had not been raped in captivity and could resume marital relations with her husband if he was of the priestly class.[42] In all these cases, women are providing information about the marital status of another woman, and the women featured in our text fill in the gaps in that same arena. The uncertain nature of a woman's personal status was considered enough of a danger to the sexual boundaries of the community to allow a woman's testimony to be considered credible, provided that there were no male witnesses who could corroborate the

---

[38] See b. Niddah 56b. Although even here the rabbis describe trying to control the process themselves by examining samples of bloodstains provided to them by women. See b. Niddah 20b. For more on this practice, see Charlotte FonRobert, "Yalta's Ruse: Resistance against Rabbinic Menstrual Authority in Talmudic Literature," in Women and Water: Menstruation in Jewish Life and Law, ed. Rahel Wasserfall (Waltham, Massachusetts: Brandeis University Press, 1999), 60–81.

[39] b. Qidd 73b.

[40] m. Yevamot 15:1–3. Notable exceptions in this case are female relatives including her mother-in-law, her mother-in-law's daughter, her associate-wife, her sister-in-law, and her step-daughter. See m. Yevamot 15:4. As we shall see, it is these same women whose testimony is accepted in the case of the sotah but has similarly limited application.

[41] See m. Gittin 2:7. Although, arguably, the document itself serves as weightier proof than their testimony.

[42] According to the Halakha, a woman taken captive was presumed to have been raped unless there were proof to the contrary. Although having been sexually violated would generally not have any impact on her marital status, if she were married to a kohen, a man of the priestly class, she would be unable to resume relations with him. Because of their historical role in carrying out the rites of the Temple, the kohen must remain in a state of ritual purity. This means they must not be exposed to sources of pollution, such as a corpse, and may not marry a divorcee, a harlot, or a woman who has been "profaned." See Leviticus 21:6–8.

matter.[43] In the case of female captives, the woman is believed when she speaks of her own ritual status, unless male witnesses are present. However, when women are taken as captives together, a woman is believed when she testifies to the status of her female co-captive, even if a male witness disagrees with her testimony.[44] As we shall see, when it came to the status of a female captive, someone who was taken against her will, there was a concerted effort to give a woman the benefit of the doubt and treat her leniently so that she might resume relations with her husband. But such sympathy disappears in a case of a woman who is suspected to have acted amorally on purpose. In the case of the *sotah*, every effort seems to be made to indict her, by widening the definition of what is considered acceptable testimony, extending reliability to the gossip of women and the Flying Bird.

But though these unconventional sources seem rather a low bar to accept when dealing with testimony, it was not all that unusual for the

---

[43] Although adultery was understood to be polluting and was frequently used as a metaphor for the breach of loyalty between God and the Jewish people, from a legal standpoint a greater concern was that the ritual status of any potential offspring ensuing from an adulterous union would be considered illegitimate, a *mamzer*, and would not be allowed to marry within the Jewish people. So determining to whom a woman "belonged" caused quite a bit of anxiety and took up a considerable amount of Rabbinic thought. On women as sources of anxiety and danger in the Rabbinic system, see Jacob Neusner, *A History of the Mishnaic Law of Women*, Parts 1–5 (Leiden: Brill, 1980); Judith Romney-Wegner, *Chattel or Person? The Status of Women in the Mishnah* (Oxford: Oxford University Press, 1988). For texts that equate adultery with pollution of the land, see for example Jeremiah 3:1–9 and Ezekiel 23:48; also Eve Levavi Feinstein, "Sexual Pollution in the Hebrew Bible: A New Perspective," in *Bodies, Embodiment and Theology of the Hebrew Bible*, ed. S. Tamar Kamionkowski and Wonil Kim (London: Bloomsbury Academic, 2010). On the problematic nature of adultery as a metaphor for the broken relationship between God and Israel, see Adler, *Engendering Judaism*, 156–167; also Plaskow, *Standing Again at Sinai*, 128–134; Naomi Graetz, *Silence Is Deadly: Judaism Confronts Wifebeating* (Jerusalem: J. Aronson, 1998), 36–51. On the centrality of the *mamzer* issue in contemporary Jewish law, see Marty Lockshin, "Orthodox 'Intolerance' a Blessing?" *Shma* 17:321 (1986), 3–4.

[44] See *m. Ket.* 2:6

rabbis to seek out different kinds of "evidence" in particular scenarios. When it came to the case of a husband whose death was unconfirmed, even a disembodied voice was accepted in order to allow a woman to remarry. According to *m. Yevamot* 16:6, "It once happened, that a man, on the top of a mountain, called out, 'A.B., son of C.D., of the place E. is dead.' They ascended the mountain without finding the person from whom the voice had proceeded, yet the wife [of A.B.] was permitted to marry again." Just as leniency was exercise in the case of a woman captive, the rabbis also sought to ease the burden on a woman whose marital status was in doubt because of a missing spouse.[45] When it came to testimony for capital crimes, on the other hand, the rabbis emphasized the gravity of the situation to witnesses, telling them to consider their words very carefully. As Rosen-Zvi has noted, the *sotah* is warned in a similar fashion before her ordeal, but whereas the witnesses in capital cases are reminded neither to perjure themselves nor to withhold valid testimony, the *sotah* is not allowed to argue her innocence. The aim is to get her to confess and acknowledge her guilt so that the ordeal need not be put into motion.[46]

The Limits of Evidence: Incomplete Testimony

Part of the goal of Mishnah *Sotah* 6.1 seems to be to determine which forms of testimony are acceptable enough to thwart the need

---

[45] Contemporary rabbis continue to make every effort to resolve these situations when men go missing (on the battlefield, due to acts of terror, etc.) and may lower the burden of proof so that women are allowed to remarry. See, for example, Rabbi Chaim Jachter, "The Bet Din of America's Handling of the World Trade Center Agunot: Methodology of Agunah Crisis Management," *Rabbi Jachter's Halacha Files*, May 10, 2003, koltorah.org

[46] See Rosen-Zvi, *Mishnaic Sotah Ritual*, 49–53, where he compares the phrasing of the warning in the Mishnah to similar passages in Sifre and in the Tosefta and illustrates how the Mishnaic text removes all possibility of innocence.

for the ordeal. In the second part of the Mishnah we are presented with some other categories of sketchy or incomplete testimony: a single witness, a male or female slave, and a female relative of the Sotah. These people all come forward with serious charges. They do not merely suspect that the Sotah secluded herself with a man she was specifically warned about, but they claim that the Sotah "committed misconduct." How are these two acts different? Has the woman who has committed misconduct actually gone further than just being alone in a room with a man? Indeed, the rabbis understand misconduct to imply contact of a sexual nature. While seclusion on its own does not constitute adultery, the rabbis illustrate that this is a slippery slope. They debate precisely how much time would need to elapse before one could assume that sexual contact had occurred between a man and woman who were secluded in a room together:

> ...sufficient for a person to walk round a date-palm. Such is the view of R. Ishmael; R. Eliezer says: Sufficient for preparing a cup of wine; R. Joshua says: Sufficient to drink it; Ben Azzai says: Sufficient to roast an egg; R. Akiba says: Sufficient to swallow it; R. Judah b. Bathyra says: Sufficient to swallow three eggs one after the other; R. Eleazar b. Jeremiah says: Sufficient for a weaver to knot a thread; Hanin b. Phineas says: Sufficient for a woman to extend her hand to her mouth to remove a chip of wood [from between the teeth]; Pelemo says: Sufficient for her to extend her hand to a basket and take a loaf therefrom. (b. Sotah 4a)

Still, seclusion is not quite yet misconduct. While a vague rumor is enough to substantiate a claim of seclusion, something more solid is required if the issue is actual sexual contact. And, since the offense is so serious, if someone makes a claim about misconduct such a claim cannot so easily be dismissed. However, the consequences are entirely different depending on who lays the charges. In other words, not all testimonies are created equal.

When one male witness comes forward with a charge that the *sotah* committed misconduct, the text explicitly states she does not need to drink the waters. Even though this does not constitute proof of adultery, since that would require two male witnesses, the one testimony turns "suspicion" into a higher degree of confirmation. It is not entirely clear from the Mishnah if the woman also loses her *ketubah* on the grounds of this single testimony. As we shall see, one may be able to infer this from the comments regarding the testimony of a male or female slave. Either way, in the case of the suspected adulteress who is thought to have committed misconduct, the evidentiary burden is reduced and even one single witness is believed.

The lowering of the evidentiary standard seems to be a common trope when it comes to the *sotah*. Several sources, which are not generally trusted, are deployed here strategically by the rabbis of the Mishnah. The testimonies of the *sotah*'s mother-in-law, sister-in-law, step-daughter, or sister-wife—in other words, the *sotah*'s female kin—or those who live in the same household as her are believed sufficiently to confirm misconduct, so they remove any need for her to undergo the ordeal. However, the testimony of these women is not weighty enough for her to lose her *ketubah*. Their proximity to the woman, living in the same home or in close quarters with the suspected adulteress, makes them ideally situated to know if she has committed misconduct. They have access to information that others may not have, so their testimony is believed enough to remove suspicion and eliminate any need for the ordeal. However, as relatives of the *sotah*'s husband, they have a vested interest in finances that would come her way, since money for her *ketubah* comes out of the family estate and has an impact on the money available for their own maintenance. It is for this very reason that in *Yevamot* 15:4 these same female relatives are prohibited from testifying to confirm the death of a woman's missing husband. That their testimony has any effect in the case of the *sotah* given their exclusion elsewhere is quite surprising. Fully aware of the ulterior motives at play, the rabbis are here inviting women to spy on other women, setting them up as rivals, manipulating and capitalizing on what they perceive to be naturally occurring tensions between women. Whether or not these female kin or the Women Spinners are correct in their testimonies, the *sotah* can end up divorced from her spouse and stuck with the label of *sotah*. She may never overcome the public shaming associated with the accusations they have levelled against her. Nonetheless, she may still receive monetary compensation in the event of divorce, because these female testimonies come, after all, from suspicious sources and are not weighty enough to qualify as substantiated truth.

The Peculiar Case of the Female Slave

The testimony of the female slave is most interesting among the female witnesses whose testimonies are accepted in the case of the *sotah*. Whereas the testimony of the Women Spinners and female kin are sufficient to suggest the *sotah* is guilty and stave off the ordeal, the female slave who claims the *sotah* committed misconduct is believed "also" to disqualify the *sotah* from her marriage settlement. It is not clear what the word "also" refers to here. Is the male/female slave believed "also," like the one male witness? Or believed "also" to eliminate the possibility of the *sotah* drinking the bitter waters *and* to disqualify her from the marriage settlement? If the *sotah* loses her *ketubah*, she obviously does not have to drink, for she is already assumed to be guilty; so in this case one consequence contains or seems to imply the other. Slaves are generally not witnesses, since to be considered a witness one is supposed to be an adult, free male (see *b. BQam*

14b–15a). Why is the slave, including the female slave, trusted in this matter?

The assumption seems to be that the female slave has nothing to gain or lose from sharing this information. But is that truly the case? The rabbis here do not see the slave as having nefarious motives, wanting to get even with a person who has possibly mistreated her. It is interesting to consider that, according to *b. Gittin* 40a, if a man wants to make a female slave his wife he first has to manumit her. If a female slave had caught the eye of her master and wanted to do away with his wife, she would have several motives for bringing a false testimony against the lady of the house for having committed misconduct with another man. Apparently, the rabbis do not seriously consider this option, certainly not enough to limit the scope of the female slave's testimony.

Perhaps more significant in deciphering the surprising acceptance of a female slave's testimony is the fact that the *sotah* in the ordeal is spared from having her slaves witness her with her chest bared. This was, according to *b. Sotah* 7b, because her "heart was prideful toward them" (*mipnei she-libah gas ba-hen*), a strange phrase variously understood as being connected to pride, being bold, familiarity, or intimacy.[47] A brief examination of this phrase and where else it is used will help us understood why the testimony of the female slave holds so much weight here.

The same phrase appears in *m. Gittin* 7:4 in a situation where a man has given his wife a divorce in the event that he dies. Since the status of this divorce is unclear, and any subsequent sexual relations between the man and woman may affect the status of her potential remarriage, the couple may not be secluded in a room together unless there are witnesses present. However, a woman's own maid is not regarded

---

[47] See entry for *gus* in Marcus Jastrow, *Dictionary of Targumim, Talmud and Midrashic Literature* (London: Luzac, 1926), 224.

as an appropriate witness, since *libah gas be-shifhatah*, the woman is "familiar" with her and is not embarrassed to have sexual relations in front of her. Hence, her presence would not act as a deterrent. This familiarity is connected to the maid's appropriate or inappropriate status as a witness.

We see a similar use of this phrase in *Ketubot* 27b in another scenario where a woman captive is discussed. We are told that if a whole town is taken siege it is assumed that all the women will be violated, which will make all the priests' wives unable to resume relations with their husbands. However, if there are witnesses to indicate otherwise, these witnesses are believed; even a woman's own slave is trusted in this matter. When the *gmara* raises the scenario of the unclear divorce from *Gittin* 7:4 above and suggests that allowing one's own maid to testify here, in the case of a female captive, seems like a contradiction, several explanations are offered to resolve the apparent discrepancy. One rabbi suggests that perhaps the *Gittin* scenario refers to the woman's own maid not being able to testify but that in the case of the female captive the Mishnah is referring to the husband's handmaid. This explanation is dismissed because the Mishnah is clear that only testifying on behalf of oneself is prohibited, implying that the testimony of anyone else—even one's own handmaid—is allowed. The *gmara* then explores the possibility that a woman's own handmaid "is like herself," meaning that the level of intimacy and loyalty between them is so strong that that it is as if they are the same person—their motives and desires are indistinguishable from one another's—so the handmaid cannot be trusted in the same way that a person cannot be trusted to speak truthfully about themself in such a situation. Although this explanation is also dismissed by the *gmara*, it speaks to the connection between a woman and her handmaid from the perspective of the rabbis and makes it seem even stranger that in the case of the *sotah* a woman's handmaid is indeed trusted to testify that her mistress has committed misconduct.

In *Ketubot* 27b, it is ultimately Rav Ashi who explains that there is no contradiction because the two situations in which the testimonies of a woman's handmaid are being assessed are quite different from one another. In the case of the unclear divorce described in *Gittin* 7:4 the maid may remain silent about what she saw, thereby allowing the woman of the house to carry on as before with no consequences to any of her relationships. As a result, her silent presence is not regarded as an act of witnessing. However, in the case of a woman who was taken captive, if the maid remains silent her mistress is assumed to have been violated and is prohibited to her husband. Since the maid is compelled to speak up and testify, which is a much greater degree of responsibility than passively remaining silent, she is believed in the case of the female captive, but not in the case of the doubtful divorce, where her silence simply benefits her mistress. In the case of the *sotah*, though, the maid's testimony is believed. One would think that her silence here would also benefit her mistress, just as in the case of the doubtful divorce, where her testimony is not allowed, *mipnei she-libah gas me-hen*—because her presence is not a deterrent to sexual transgression.

The phrase *mipnei she-libah gas me-hen* does not come up when the Mishnah is discussing why a handmaid may not be able to testify that her mistress has committed misconduct. It is the very intimacy and familiarity between them, the fact that the maid's presence would not act as a deterrent to her mistress engaging in sexual relations, that the rabbis are relying upon in order to confirm the *sotah*'s guilt. Although it would be very easy for the handmaid to remain silent, if she chose to speak up against her mistress' indiscretion her mistress would be prohibited to her husband and her lover, and the rabbis do not want to stand in the way of testimony of that nature.

Still, it is telling where the phrase *mipnei she-libah gas me-hen* does come up in Tractate *Sotah*. It is not in relation to the maid being able to testify; rather, as mentioned earlier, it is offered to explain why she is unable to be part of the audience when her mistress is publicly exposed during the ordeal. In *Sotah* 7b, in a detailed explanation of how her humiliation should be played out, we are told "whoever wishes to look upon her comes to look, with the exception of her male and female slaves, *mipnei she-libah gas me-hen*." Rashi understands the term *mipnei she-libah gas ba-hen* to mean that the maidservant is like a member of the woman's household, whose presence would strengthen her resolve, and here the goal is to make the woman feel vulnerable and afraid in order that she will confess.[48] Rosen-Zvi, on the other hand, understands *mipnei she-libah gas ba-hen* to mean "she has no shame from them," just as it was understood in *m. Gittin* 7:4. Whereas Rashi understands the goal of the ordeal to be the eliciting of a confession, Rosen-Zvi sees the ritual as having the express purpose of humiliating the *sotah*. This could explain why someone in front of whom the *sotah* has no shame would be barred from the ordeal.[49] However, it seems odd to exclude them for this reason alone, since their presence in the crowd would not detract from her more general humiliation. Perhaps the key lies in understanding how the female slave is different from some of the other female testifiers we have examined thus far. Let us return to *Sotah* 7b, where we are told,

> Whoever wishes to look upon her [the *sotah*] comes to look, with the exception of her male and female slaves *mipnei she-libah gas ba-hen*. All women are permitted to look upon her, as it is said, "that all women may be taught not to do after your lewdness." [Ezekiel 23:48]

The rabbis of the Gemara later understand from this Mishnah that although anyone can come to gaze upon the exposed body of the *sotah*

---

[48] See Rashi, *b. Sotah* 7b.
[49] See Rosen-Zvi, *The Mishnaic Sotah Ritual*, 89–95.

as part of her measure-for-measure punishment, it is an *obligation* for other women to view her as a warning to them not to behave in a similar way.[50] Perhaps the female slave and her male counterpart are not able to participate in this spectacle not only because the *sotah* has "no shame in front of them" but also because their sense of familiarity with their mistress means that the ritual will not have the desired impact *on them* as viewers; it will be wasted on them. For instance, since the female slave is accustomed to her mistress' nakedness, she will not feel embarrassed by it and hence she will not be taught to avoid lewdness. The female slave is not in the same category of women as the respectable Women Spinners. She is someone who is not generally granted the status of personhood. Consequently, the female slave is not the target of the lesson that the *sotah* ordeal is meant to convey, so she is not invited to participate in the public humiliation. As we have seen, of the three groups of incomplete testifiers, the charges of the female slave seem to have the most serious consequences for the *sotah*. Here the rabbis are recruiting the most trusted and potentially loyal workers in a person's home to turn against them. For a brief moment the slave is elevated to the status of full person, but only at the expense of the woman whom she has been serving.

THE ADULTERESS VS. THE ADULTERER

It is notable that in all these discussions of the *sotah's* putative transgressions, one key player is conspicuously absent. In the Rabbinic discussion regarding seclusion versus misconduct, we see how quickly the rabbis believed that a man and a woman alone in a room together would cross into the realm of the sexual. In the debate about whether it takes the time to walk around a palm tree or the amount of time to knot

---

[50] See *b. Sotah* 8b.

ISLAMIC AND JEWISH LEGAL REASONING

a piece of thread, it is noteworthy that the male who has besmirched the reputation of this married woman suddenly comes into view, if only for a brief moment. It is interesting to consider that in both the Jewish and Islamic texts the key figures are the accused woman and her accusers, but not the alleged male fornicator. These males are present, but mostly as background noise. Who are the people who are monitoring him? Are there no virginity checkers to establish his chastity? Are the Women Spinners less interested in the potential offenses of the men in their neighborhood? Or are these cultures less invested in cultivating informants to keep tabs on the bodies and whereabouts of males?

CONCLUSION

In both the Jewish and Islamic texts we see cultures that invest community members with the power not only to change the personal status of another person through their testimony (from married to divorced), but also to give forms of testimony which could result in bodily harm (lashes or other forms of corporal punishment) as well as a forever-tarnished reputation. Although women are generally not regarded as reliable witnesses on a par with men in either of these legal systems, when it comes to patrolling women's chastity and defining the social boundaries of these communities, women's eyes, ears, and hands (in the case of the virginity testers) are suddenly valuable because they have access to information and spaces otherwise denied to men. In this way, certain women—either respectable women or non-threatening ones—are lauded for their expertise and insider knowledge and persuaded to turn against other women. As witnesses, they become part of systems that otherwise regarded them as outsiders. In the cases of the virginity checkers, the Women Spinners, and the *sotah*'s female kin, their testimony will only go so far. It is efficacious enough to set certain consequences into motion (initiating divorce, clearing a woman's name), but because they are women they are not sufficiently trusted to bring the full effects of the legal system into force (to deprive a woman of her *ketubah* or to punish slanderous witnesses).

The social effects of recruiting women to do the work of patriarchy run deep. Although the *sotah* ritual is no longer practiced in Jewish communities, the fear of being labelled "immodest" is still strong. Hence the self-regulation among ultra-Orthodox women on public buses and turning a blind eye to other women who are harassed and assaulted for not conforming to the same standards. Both in the case of the *sotah* and in the public shaming on the bus, all women are invited to be part of the spectacle. Although disciplining perceived acts of immodesty may seem a far cry from punishing suspected acts of adultery, it is interesting to note that, according to Rosen-Zvi, the *sotah* ritual may not be about adultery at all:

> The [*sotah*] ritual serves a textual locus for analyzing and pub-licizing the threats inherent to womankind and for portraying an ideal, non-seductive woman...Marriage is not a major part of the ritual, and the husband and children of the *sotah* are not major players, since the ritual addresses all women...the problem it purports to solve is not adultery but seduction... We may read Mishnah Sotah as a ritual devised to instill in the hearts of its audience awareness of the dangers dormant in women by presenting a "well-managed woman," utterly neutral-ized and exposed.[51]

Much of the text, then, seems to be about encouraging women to toe the line, to keep them under control. That Naomi Ragen, like the *sotah*, should be regarded as guilty by her community for having overstepped the bounds of appropriate behavior is apparent from the

---

[51] See Rosen-Zvi, *The Mishnaic Sotah Ritual*, 225, 231, 236.

unusual postscript to her act of speaking out against the segregated buses. After helping to get the legitimacy of gender-segregated buses overturned by the Supreme Court of Israel, Ragen was accused of having plagiarized parts of the novel *Sotah* from the work of another Orthodox female author. Although Ragen eventually agreed to a settlement in this case, it does seem odd, as Ragen herself has noted, that this claim should suddenly be brought forward over twenty years after *Sotah* was first published.[52]

Ragen and Bahar Ebrahim understand all too well that there are consequences to stepping out of line in a close-knit community. The fear of her daughter's virginity being called into question, thereby bringing shame on the whole family, compelled Johra Kaleki to take matters into her own hands and physically assault her daughter, Bahar. That Bahar then turned around and forgave her mother, becoming the image of the pious woman that her mother longed for, confirms the hold that dusty legal texts—and the way that interpretive communities understand them—can have on contemporary lives. As we can see from the recruiting of the female slave, the Women Spinners, the virginity checkers, and even one's own family members, social coercion is not only about big explosive events like trying to kill someone for departing from the morality or modesty code, but also applies in small, banal moments of women's lives. When you are told by your texts that the women you might otherwise trust are watching you, you moderate your behavior so that it appears exemplary, even to the "bird" flying overhead.

---

[52] See Ben Hartman, "Court Rules Naomi Ragen Plagiarized in Best Seller," *Jerusalem Post*, December 13, 2011, http://www.jpost.com/National-News/Court-rules-Naomi-Ragen-plagiarized-in-best-seller. To be fair, this is not the first time that Ragen has been accused of plagiarism. Author Michal Tal also brought a case against her in 2007. However, the Tal case was overturned in 2012. See "Court Rules: Naomi Ragen Did Not Plagiarize," Ynet.co.il, May 1, 2012, http://www.ynet.co.il/articles/0,7340,L-4171752,00.html. Again, it is notable that both claims emerged in the aftermath of Ragen's activism pertaining to the segregated buses.

5

Sovereignty, Law, and the Pedagogy of Historical Fantasy

On the Halakha *on the Laws of War and the* Fiqh *on* Dhimmis

ARYE EDREI AND ANVER M. EMON

INTRODUCTION

The nineteenth and twentieth centuries were intellectually challenging and momentous periods for both Muslims and Jews. That historical period witnessed the development of a Zionist ideology of Jewish nationhood whose fulfillment came only in the wake of horrific violence against the Jewish people. It also witnessed the rise of colonialism in the Muslim world and then the formation of new Muslim-majority states. For both religious communities these historical developments posed significant challenges with respect to the way their religio-legal traditions should react and/or adapt to the shifting conditions of sovereignty. These changes were dramatic and complex in that they involved a fundamental change in the political realities that had become ingrained in the religious thought of each group—the idea of exile and diaspora on the part of the Jews and the idea of an at least nominally unified empire on the part of the Muslims. The realization of the need for change demanded (and still demands) innovative and creative thinking on both the ideological and legal levels. This has often engendered resistance among conservative adherents who refuse to acknowledge the legitimacy of the changing circumstances.

For instance, in the context of the Jewish diaspora the absence of a halakha relating to the laws of war was a sign that the Jews, as a minority population in a variety of host countries, viewed the military as an evil entity that often perpetrated persecution and violence in the name of a sovereign. Although the Hebrew Bible connects the fulfillment of Israel's historical destiny with the wielding of military force, there is considerable ambivalence toward military force in Rabbinic literature. The Talmudic sages imagined Torah study as the substitute for war, transferring the virtues often associated with the military hero to the Torah scholar.[1] Thus, for example, the biblical description of King David as "a brave fighter and a man of war" (I Samuel 16:18), is explained in the Talmud as follows: "brave fighter— that he knows what to respond; man of war—that he knows how to give and take in the war of Torah" (*BT Sanhedrin* 93b). The hero of the battlefield is transformed into the hero of the study hall—the sharp scholar. This reflects the Jews' diasporic self-perception as an ahistorical people who exist and function beyond the parameters of military and political power. The realization of the Zionist ideal with the founding of the State of Israel challenged this identity; Jewish thinkers and halakhic scholars who accepted this approach had to justify their position and to contend with a fundamental change in identity with broad halakhic implications. What does the absence of laws of war in Rabbinic law suggest about the extent to which the

---

[1] See Ehud Luz, *Wrestling with an Angel: Power, Morality, and Jewish Identity*, trans. Michael Swirsky (New Haven: Yale University Press, 2003), 21–23. See also Aviezer Ravitsky, *Messianism, Zionism and Jewish Religious Radicalism* (Chicago: University of Chicago Press, 1996).

Halakha can or should contribute to the Zionist imperative of a "return to history"? It is important to note in this context that the State of Israel defines itself as a secular state that has no formal commitment to Jewish law. The discussion has taken place largely as an intellectual debate among Religious Zionist rabbis seeking to minimize the gap between Jewish tradition and the Jewish state. Nevertheless, the halakhic deliberations on this topic had an important place in public discourse in general and in the military protocols developed by the Israel Defense Force in conjunction with the military rabbinate. At the same time, there is also a reluctance to involve religious law in state issues among some elements of the religious community. There remains a significant Jewish religious school of thought that refuses to legitimize the change in reality and rejects attempts to reconcile the Rabbinic tradition to that reality.

In contrast, the Islamic legal tradition was developed by jurists for whom Islamic law and governance were premised upon the complementary dynamics of conquest and a monist empire. Despite humble beginnings as an outcast community in Mecca, the Muslim imperium spread from the city-state of Medina to encompass much of the Arabian Peninsula by the time of the Prophet Muhammad's death in 632 C.E.. By the eighth century, that imperium extended west to the Iberian Peninsula and east into Afghanistan and South Asia. Muhammad's universal message was mechanized through conquest into imperial governance, which became the idealized means to implement God's will and extend the prophetic mission to all of humanity. As pre-modern Muslim jurists developed various strands of legal doctrine, in particular the rules governing non-Muslims living in Muslim lands (dhimmis), the logic of empire animated how they imagined the relations between Muslims, non-Muslims, and an Islamic governing enterprise, and how they clothed those imagined relations with the vestments of law.

The revolutionary political dynamics of the twentieth century drew the Jewish and Muslim communities in contrasting directions. While the Jews achieved sovereignty in the State of Israel, the Muslim world experienced the destruction of the last remaining Muslim empire (the Ottoman Empire), the colonization of Muslim lands, and ultimately the creation of new, territorially bounded states. Furthermore, the migration of Muslims to Europe and North America created Muslim minorities within non-Muslim states. The new states that were created, many of which were and continue to be majority Muslim, were separate, distinct political entities demanding equal sovereignty and respect, in contrast to the monist (or nominally monist) imperial model imagined under Muhammad and thereafter. In this sense, this collection of states represented a departure from the ideal of a monist empire that inspired the pre-modern jurists developing Islamic legal doctrine. Far from exercising an expansive imperium over Muslim lands, new Muslim-majority states exercised sovereignty over a limited geographic space in an international state system that is premised upon the equal and legitimate sovereignty of every state. None of this is to suggest that pre-modern Muslim empires (the Umayyad, Abbasid, or Fatimid, for instance) were united, cohesive, or without internal dissent. We merely wish to suggest that the move from empire to modern state has altered the underlying conditions of sovereignty that informed the logic of pre-modern doctrines, such as those on the dhimmi. If the dhimmi rules were informed by conditions of empire, it follows that departure from the empire-as-political-form to the state-as-political-form will occasion rethinking about these rules. Yet, despite this shift to the prevalence of the statist model, the dhimmi rules remain part of an ever-present discourse among many Muslims about how to engage the religious "other." With limited exception, they are not legally implemented in Muslim-majority states, but they nonetheless inform Islamist discourse, such as the 2007 Muslim Brotherhood platform of principles that precluded non-Muslims from serving as the president or prime minister of a

Muslim state,[2] and contribute content to pedagogic materials such as high-school textbooks and religious training manuals, as seen on pp. 206–12. Their ongoing influence reflects a presumption about the relevance of a past reality (a turn to a particular history) for the purposes of normative ordering today.

Juxtaposing Islamic and Jewish legal discourses makes possible a greater appreciation of the relationship between law, sovereignty, and history. In short, this chapter will demonstrate the impact that the ability or inability to properly perceive and accept changes in political reality has on both Jewish and Islamic law. In Jewish law, we will focus on the halakhic issues created by the renewal of Jewish sovereignty in the modern Zionist era vis-à-vis the lack of laws of war in the Rabbinic tradition. The absence of laws of war in the Halakha and the adoption of a somewhat anti-military outlook reflect a paradigmatic change that took place during the course of Jewish history in response to the loss of Jewish sovereignty in late antiquity. The exile of the Jews from their land and the complete failure of violent Jewish revolts against the Roman Empire led to a Rabbinic consensus regarding the need to adapt the halakhic vision to the new conditions. The return of Jewish sovereignty in the State of Israel has raised the question of whether contemporary Rabbinic scholars can make a counter paradigm shift and adapt the Halakha to new conditions that are somewhat similar to those that existed before the previous shift, but with modifications to accommodate modern political forces, such as the modern secular state and global standards of combat and international law. We will identify two main schools of thought regarding this. The conservative (*haredi* or ultra-Orthodox) world is not prepared to make changes in the accepted Rabbinic law and concordantly either rejects the legitimacy of Jewish sovereignty or marginally accommodates it. In contrast,

---

[2] Kristen Stilt, "'Islam Is the Solution': Constitutional Visions of the Egyptian Muslim Brotherhood," *Texas International Law Journal* 46:1 (2010), 101.

the Religious Zionist camp fully accepts and values the legitimacy of Jewish sovereignty, and its rabbis believe that the Halakha must be adapted to the renewal of Jewish military enterprise as well as to other issues of state. We will examine several approaches to this adaptation within the Religious Zionist camp.

In Islamic law, we will focus on the pre-modern dhimmi laws that regulated the approach to non-Muslims. Early Islamic doctrines on the dhimmi presumed certain features of governance, namely a conquest model that brought with it an expansive imperial outlook. As jurists of different persuasions considered the implication of religious diversity in an expansive empire, they differed on the scope of liberty that religious minorities could exercise in an Islamically governed empire. The question that arises today is whether the shift from the imperial mode to the modern state mode of governance also requires a paradigm shift in how contemporary Muslim scholars consider the religious "other." Contemporary scholars have not accomplished such a paradigm shift to deal with the loss of imperial Islamic governance. Some of the internal conflict within the Muslim world in recent decades, as well as contemporary relations between the Muslim world and the West, reflects this controversy. This raises the question of whether, how, and under what conditions pre-modern Islamic law is applicable in a post-colonial context where there is no Islamic empire but rather a collection of geopolitically demarcated sovereign states where Muslims are in majority, as well as Muslim minorities in regions such as Europe and North America. In other words, does the underlying shift in governance demand that Muslim jurists adopt paradigm shifts that will enable them to adapt pre-modern Islamic law to the modern reality?

The reader will immediately notice a curious inversion when reading this chapter. There is little focus on the early halakha regarding the laws of war, in large part because of its absence. Thus the Jewish legal debate on the laws of war is a contemporary one. In contrast, the Islamic legal analysis focuses on pre-modern debates, with limited focus on contemporary debates. It is not that there are no contemporary debates on the dhimmi rules or the status of the non-Muslim in Muslim-majority states. Rather, whatever the contemporary debates may be, they seem unable to escape the vast historical record of the dhimmi rules. This inversion is best appreciated by reflecting on the underlying political conditions that inform the law of both religious traditions. Moreover, this chapter reveals a stark irony that is perhaps only best appreciated by juxtaposing these two traditions. The irony is that both Religious Zionists and conservative Muslims invoke history as a way to reflect on the content and scope of religious law, whether Islamic law or Jewish law. For religious Zionists, internalizing the idea of the *return to history* promoted by the Zionist movement requires distancing contemporary Jewish thought and practice from a mythic and largely imaginary consciousness, and instead embedding it in the realities of mundane statecraft; history in this sense is about participating in and (re)making the world. For conservative Muslims, the *turn to a particular history*, whether to the life of the Prophet and his Companions or to the supposed heyday of the pre-modern legal tradition, reflects a desire to recreate an ahistoric, utopic vision of a glorious past that came to an end but which might promise glory once again if brought back into the present. Similarly, ultra-Orthodox Jews refuse to accept the idea of a return to history, preferring to remain in an ahistoric reality that maintains the utopic vision of an ultimate divinely imposed redemption.

In both communities the (re)turn to the law reflects both their normative vision of the world, and the individual believer's place within it. Consequently, as much as these rules have marginal effect in any secular governing regime, whether Israel or a Muslim-majority state, the articulation of a halakha on the laws of war and the persistence of the dhimmi discourse among conservative Muslims reveal how the law, whether the Halakha or the pre-modern *fiqh*, helps believers in these traditions situate themselves in an otherwise complex and ambiguous world. Moreover, the pedagogic effect of this (re)turn to history reveals how different means of relating a pre-modern legal system to a modern reality help define one's own place and standing in the world in relation to one's Others who inhabit it alongside one. On this understanding, the Jewish discourse regarding halakhic attitudes toward war and the Muslim discourse on the dhimmi rules reveal less about Jewish or Islamic law than they do about the worldview of those who would proffer certain interpretations for the diverse communities in each religious tradition.

EARLY RABBINIC AND ISLAMIC LEGAL TRAJECTORIES

Exile and the Laws of War: A Historical Backdrop to a Rabbinic Lacuna

The establishment of an army, and the use of arms and force, is one of the far-reaching changes in Jewish life resulting from the success of Zionism. The image of the degraded Jew who is incapable of defending himself was central to Jewish self-perception, as well as the reality, throughout the Middle Ages until the height of World War II. The new self-image of the Jew after the establishment of the State of Israel became the Jew who bears arms and is capable of defending himself or herself.

One who wishes to reconstruct Jewish laws of war will quickly discover that, as in other areas, this topic was not addressed by the Halakha during the period of exile. Thus, the "laws of war" almost completely disappeared from the corpus and were certainly not part of the active Jewish tradition. We have no relevant rules or traditions of what is permissible and forbidden in times of war, or the legitimate methods and limitations of the use of force.

Furthermore, the fact that for generations Jewish society never had the option of using force understandably made its mark on the ideological and psychological relationship of Jewish tradition to the use of force. Yeshayahu Leibowitz, one of the prominent religious intellectuals in Israel in the second half of the twentieth century, described the problem in the introduction to his famous article, "After Kibiyah," as follows:

> The great test to which we as a nation are put as a result of national liberation, political independence, and our military power—a society and culture that for many generations, derived certain spiritual benefits from conditions of exile, foreign rule, and political impotence. Our morality and conscience were conditioned by an unnatural, insulated existence in which we could cultivate values and a heritage that did not have to be tested in the crucible of reality. We viewed ourselves, and to a certain degree we were viewed by others, as a people who had controlled one of the most awful inclinations that ensnares the soul of man, and as those disgusted by the display of dreadful behavior found in every human society: the inclination to internecine murder.[3]

The reality of the lack of power not only led to a lack of norms but also created an ethos of opposition to the use of force, an idealization of the reality of powerlessness, a world of values in which the use of force was not an option in both a normative and an ethical sense. Thus, anyone wishing to establish Jewish laws governing the use of

---

[3] Yeshayahu Leibowitz, "Aharei Kibiyah," in *Yahadut Am Yehudi u-Medinat Yisrael* (Jerusalem: Schocken, 1976), 229–230 (author's translation). This article also appears in English translation as Y. Leibowitz, "After Kibiyeh," in *Judaism, Human Values and the Jewish State*, ed. Eliezer Goldman et al. (Boston: Harvard University Press, 1992). The article first appeared in 1954.

force would have to overcome both the psychological block against the use of force and the idealized perspective that was internalized in Jewish culture and tradition.[4]

An initial look at classical Jewish sources reflects a clear duality in the fundamental attitude to the use of force. This duality begins with the tension in the Bible regarding the use of force. On the one hand, force is viewed as a legitimate instrument. On the other hand, the use of force is restricted and there are clear warnings about the dangers inherent in its use. The Bible discusses desirable wars but in parallel expresses a prophetic vision that attacks belief in force and extols the ideal of world peace. Therefore, Joshua's conquest of the land of Canaan and King David's wars of conquest were viewed in a positive light (Joshua 4:12; 2 Samuel 6:18), yet King David was considered unsuitable to build the Temple because his hands were defiled with the blood of his enemies (1 Chronicles 22:8). Study of the layers of the Bible reveals an approach that legitimates the use of force in specific circumstances but warns against the danger of the use of force, especially a belief in reliance on force. A coherent formulation of the complex biblical position can allow the establishment of a political sovereignty that includes an army, while calling for a large degree of discretion in utilizing the military and requiring that it not occupy a primary position in the society.

In the Talmud, the classic site of Rabbinic literature, a different attitude is taken. The biblical tension disappears and the prophetic

---

[4] Discussion of the parameters and limitations of the use of force in the wake of the Zionist enterprise and the establishment of the State of Israel was obviously not limited to religious thinkers and rabbis. This issue generated a vibrant debate among Zionist leaders and occupied a central position in public deliberations for many years. There were two reasons for the centrality of the issue: the lack of Jewish sources relating to the use of force, as discussed here; and the confidence of the early Zionists that their program would be well received without a necessity to use force. See the address of Berl Katznelson to the 21st World Zionist Congress entitled "Yehi Nishkeha Tahor" [Your Weapons Shall Be Pure], in *Kol Kitvei Berl Katznelson* [The Complete Works of Berl Katznelson] (Tel Aviv: Workers Party of Eretz Israel, 1948), 9:65 (in Hebrew).

stance that demeans the use of force, or confidence in it, becomes the only viewpoint. While it is true that the Mishnah, the Talmud, and subsequently the law codes recognize the concepts of a permissible war (*milhemet reshut*) and an obligatory war (*milhemet mitzvah*), these concepts always refer to the wars that occurred during the times of the Kingdom of Israel and are not considered relevant to contemporary times. Essentially, the positive connotation of war in the Bible takes on a completely different, spiritualized, interpretation in Rabbinic literature. The biblical war is now treated allegorically, relating not to military battle but to the war of Torah (*milhamtah shel Torah*, i.e., the battle to study, preserve, and interpret the Torah). The legitimate and positive battle becomes the effort of scholars to convince each other of the correct interpretation of the Torah; power is the ability of scholars to distinguish, to refute, and to make legal determinations. The example of King David illustrates how the "brave fighter" was transformed from the hero on the battlefield to the hero of the study hall. Another image of the hero used by the sages is the person who controls his inclinations, who succeeds on the internal battlefield. "Who is strong?" the Mishnah asks rhetorically, and answers, "One who conquers his inclination, as it says:'He who is slow to anger is better than a strong man, and a master of his passions is better than the conqueror of a city'" (Mishnah *Avot* 4:1). Thus, Jews who conducted wars—e.g., Bar-Kocvah who led the revolt against the Romans in the second century, the *ribalieros* who rebelled against the Romans in the first century, and the Hasmonean kings—are almost ignored in Rabbinic literature, which was most influential in shaping Jewish thought in medieval and modern times. Although it is easy to understand why an anti-militaristic attitude developed among diaspora Jews, it does not change the fact that these are the texts that the traditionalists had before them when confronting the changing Zionist reality.

There is thus no doubt that Leibowitz's characterization is accurate. The archives of Jewish tradition are not empty: not only do they not contain sufficient norms for the conduct of war; they also include an anti-military ideology. It is important to point out that this approach was translated during the Middle Ages into a coherent doctrine of passivity vis-à-vis redemption. The dream of returning to Zion and the establishment of a Jewish society there remained a central part of public awareness, but took on a deterministic quality that precluded human initiatives and the use of force. Therefore, one who wishes to characterize the tradition as relevant to a period of Jewish sovereignty has a double challenge—to overcome the ideology and to create new laws relating to war. In a traditional legal culture that builds every stage of development upon the previous layer, this is a truly difficult challenge.

Islamic Empire and the Dhimmis: Historical Backdrop to the Dhimmi Rules

The Islamic legal treatment of non-Muslim permanent residents in Islamic lands has often been framed in terms of "tolerance." In other words, these legal rules, called the "dhimmi rules," are the site of ongoing debate about whether Islam and Muslims are tolerant of the non-Muslim "other," or not. To appreciate the significance of these rules, however, "tolerance" as an analytic term of art seems to miss the point. As many have already noted, tolerance talk covers up the underlying dynamics of governance and power that allow one group to "let" another group do something different, or, in other words, to "tolerate" them. To posit oneself as tolerating another by implication suggests that one could choose not to tolerate the other at all and instead demand conformity to some alternative, presumably majoritarian norm.

The dhimmi rules are better understood as reflecting a particular Muslim juristic imagination, namely the imagination of a universal empire as the normative mode of governance for which Islamic legal doctrines (*fiqh*) must be developed. The Islamic tradition has no shortage of materials professing that the Qur'an and prophetic message were not just for the Arabs of Medina but rather for all of humanity. Qur'anic verses can be read as characterizing the Qur'an and the prophetic mission of Muhammad as having universal appeal and aspirations. One verse that addresses Muhammad's mission characterizes it in aspirational terms: "Say...This Qur'an has been revealed to me so that by it I can warn you and all it may reach [*wa man balagha*]."[5] Later exegetes interpreted this verse to give an expansive import to Muhammad's prophecy and the aspiration of the Qur'anic message. For instance, al-Tabari (d. 310/923) held that the warning the Prophet was to issue concerned God's punishment of all those who disbelieve. That warning extended beyond the confines of the Arabian Peninsula, where Muhammad met opposition; it applied to all people without limitation (*sa'ir al-nas*), since there is no end to effectuating the Qur'anic aspirations (*in lam yantahin ila al-'amal bi ma fihi*).[6] Moreover, the later exegete al-Qurtubi (d. 671/1273) explained the implications of the universal aspiration of the Qur'anic message for the purposes of governance. To have the Qur'an and the Prophet's tradition reach others was to make a normative claim upon their obedience and allegiance. According to al-Qurtubi, once the Qur'an and the Prophet's tradition (Sunna) has reached people, it follows that those people are commanded by God to accede to the values and requirements elaborated therein (*tabligh al-Qur'an wa al-sunna ma'mur bihima*).[7]

The universalist ethos of Islam offered jurists and rulers a normative vision or telos to be manifested in the world through an imperial model of formal governance. Khalid Blankinship, writing about early

---

[5] Qur'an 6:19.
[6] Muhammad b. Jarir al-Tabari, *Tafsir al-Tabari*, ed. Bashshar 'Awad Ma'ruf and 'Isam Faris al-Harastani (Beirut: Mu'assasat al-Risala, 1994), 3:231.
[7] Muhammad b. Ahmad al-Qurtubi, *al-Jami' li Ahkam al-Qur'an* (Beirut: Dar al-Kutub al-'Ilmiyya, 1993), 6:257.

Islamic expansion under the Umayyad Dynasty, argues that the this dynasty (41–132/661–750) based its legitimacy in large part on its effort to manifest a universalist Islamic faith through conquest and expansion, or through what he calls the "Jihad State." From a purely pragmatic perspective, conquest provided the Umayyads sufficient spoils of war with which to pay their soldiers and feed the imperial coffers. As Muslims conquered more land and taxed non-Muslims, the revenues provided financial support to uphold and expand the empire.[8] By linking conquest to the universalist Islamic ethos using the jihad ethic, the Umayyads converted what might have been viewed as an opportunist use of force into an imperial mission legitimated by reference to Islam and the fulfillment of God's will on earth.

The non-Muslim living under the authority of a Muslim polity presented to Muslim jurists the fact of diversity to which the law had to respond. The importance of cultivating lands for the empire's economic well-being forced jurists to contend with the implications for Islamic universalism of permitting non-Muslims to reside in Muslim lands and retain their faith commitments. As Muslim forces continued to expand the Islamic empire, they soon found themselves to be a minority ruling over regions populated by non-Muslims. Conversion to Islam may certainly have reduced the disparity, but, as Richard Bulliet and others have suggested, conversion to Islam seems to have occurred gradually over generations.[9] In other words, imperial expansion had

---

[8] Although the *jizya* offered an important source of tax revenue for the Muslim polity, it was not always applied in fact. Khalid Yahya Blankinship, *The End of the Jihad State: The Reign of Hisham Ibn 'Abd al-Malik and the Collapse of the Umayyads* (Albany: State University of New York Press, 1994), 23, 27.

[9] Richard Bulliet, *Conversion to Islam in the Medieval Period: An Essay in Quantitative History* (Cambridge, Massachusetts: Harvard University Press, 1979); Michael G. Morony, "The Age of Conversions: A Reassessment," in *Conversion and Continuity: Indigenous Christian Communities in Islamic Lands, Eighth to Eighteenth Centuries,* ed. Michael Gervers and Ramzi J. Bikhazi (Toronto: Pontifical Institute of Medieval Studies, 1990), 135–150. For demographic accounts of the experience of non-Muslims under Islamic rule, see Courbage and Fargues, *Christians and Jews under Islam.*

to be envisioned and framed in light of both the fact of diversity and an Islamic universalist ethos.

The result was a pluralist approach to governance of which the dhimmi rules were a by-product. Indeed, helping to negotiate the tension between empire and universalism was one of the fundamental tasks the dhimmi rules fulfilled.[10] Dhimmis were, on the one hand, excluded from the *Muslim community* because of their difference in faith. On the other hand, dhimmis were included in the *Muslim-ruled polity* because of their physical residence and payment of a poll tax, called the *jizya*, for the benefit of the governing enterprise. Legal doctrines regarding the dhimmi reflected this insider–outsider duality. For instance, the dhimmis' *jizya* liability provided a significant tax base to support the Muslims who fought the jihad to expand the empire. At the same time, the *jizya* presented an opportunity to hierarchize society along confessional lines to uphold the superiority of the Islamic message and its adherents over and against all "others." Historians have noted that under the Umayyad regime dhimmis began to convert to Islam. With their conversion, Islamic law rendered them immune from any *jizya* tax burden, thereby diminishing the empire's tax revenue. However, historical records indicate that the Umayyads nonetheless continued to impose the *jizya* on newly converted Muslims, a position that aroused considerable controversy given its departure from the prevailing legal requirements about the cessation of *jizya* liability upon conversion.[11] Before their conversion, these new Muslims were mere residents in the Muslim polity. After their conversion, they became more than residents; they were insiders of the Muslim community. The dhimmi as insider was entitled to the same protections as Muslims, but the dhimmi as outsider was a reminder of the ongoing universalizing mission of the Islamic faith. Conversion was the mark of the mission's

---

[10]   Blankinship, *The End of the Jihad State*, 3–13.
[11]   Ibid., 87–9, 114.

success. To continue taxing newly converted Muslims with the *jizya*, therefore, prioritized empire over universalism—a prioritization that jurists criticized.

The tension between the universal ethos and the fact of diversity brought on by an imperial agenda was jurisprudentially negotiated by jurists using the contract of protection, called in Arabic the *'aqd al-dhimma*. They used the contract of protection to move from the fact of diversity to a commitment to a pluralistic ethic of imperial governance. The dhimmi, as a non-Muslim permanent resident, paid the *jizya* and thereby entered the contract of protection. This contract governed the relations between the Muslim polity and the dhimmis. This is not to suggest, as a historical matter, that each and every dhimmi signed or otherwise consented to the terms of a specific contract. Rather the contract provided a paradigm by which jurists developed legal expectations in the form of regulations for the dhimmis, Muslims, and officials who oversaw the enterprise of governance. The dhimmis' rights and entitlements in the Muslim polity did not inhere in the dhimmi as an individual but rather derived from a contract whose terms and content were the subject of considerable legal debate over the centuries. The contract of protection, in Islamic legal theory, served both political and legal functions. It was political in that it was the conceptual device jurists used to reconcile an Islamic universalist ethos with the fact of diversity arising from a commitment to empire. It represented the political agreement between the Muslim sovereign and the non-Muslim community in the interest of the latter's relative freedom and the sovereign's efficient management of the empire. Legally, the contract was the site of debates about the scope of the dhimmis' freedom in the empire. In other words, the contract represented a juridified political site for legal debates about the content of what we are calling the dhimmi rules.

For example, the general rule prohibiting alcohol consumption did not apply to a dhimmi who consumed alcohol; instead, an exception was created for the dhimmi, given a contractarian theory that paid respect to the dhimmi's tradition. Yet the very rule that prohibited consumption of alcohol and that was suspended in the case of the dhimmi nonetheless operated at a different level—the level of public policy or public weal—to inform a conception of the public good that thereby justified a different legal rule that prohibited any public drunkenness by the dhimmi. In this sense, the general legal prohibition helped to constitute the ethos of the Islamic polity and gave "Islamic" content to the enterprise of governance. Although the jurists themselves focused on general rules and exceptions, their debates operated at multiple levels, both as an articulation of the dhimmis' scope of legal liability and as a mechanism for constituting political society, political order, and the guiding principles of an empire that contained diverse peoples.

Three legal issues exemplify the way in which the dhimmi rules were framed in terms of a presumption of empire. The first concerns whether and to what extent a dhimmi can endow a charitable trust. The second involves whether dhimmis can build or repair their houses of worship (churches and synagogues). The third and final example has to do with whether and under what conditions dhimmis could perform their religious rituals in public.

Dhimmis and Charitable Endowments

To endow property in a trust was a right that accrued to a property owner as a private individual. To use one's property to create charitable endowments, however, was often intended to influence the public weal, whether in small or large part. Thus, at the intersection of private rights of ownership and charitable bequest were concerns about regulating philanthropic giving that could contravene the public good. In other words, although private property rights might be protected, the scope of protection was limited in light of competing interests of a more general, public nature. Consequently, the juristic debate about whether and to what extent a dhimmi could endow a charitable trust had to account for the need to respect both the dhimmi's private property interests and the imperative to protect an Islamic public order. Examining how jurists defined the public good and thereby resolved this balance will reveal the presumptions of conquest, empire, and governance that gave the legal doctrines and debates their meaningfulness.

Two ways to create a charitable endowment were (1) a bequest that would take effect upon the testator's death (*wasiyya*), and (2) an *inter vivos* transfer of property directly into a trust (*waqf*). Shafi'i and Hanbali jurists generally agreed that dhimmis could create trusts and issue bequests for the benefit of any specified individual (*shakhs mu'ayyan*), regardless of the beneficiary's religious background, although some jurists limited the beneficiaries to one's kin group.[12] This permissive attitude was based on the legal respect for private ownership (*tamlik*) and the rights the property owner had to dispose of his property as he saw fit.[13] Shafi'i and Hanbali jurists held that the dhimmi's private property interest was sufficiently important to warrant the right to bequest property to other individuals.

However, if the dhimmi's bequest was to establish something that might adversely affect the public interest, as framed in terms of Islamic

---

[12] Abu Hamid l-Ghazali, *al-Wasit fi al-Madhhab*, ed. Abu'Amru al-Husayni (Beirut: Dar al-Kutub al-'Ilmiyya, 2001), 2:397–398. Abu al-Hasan al-Mawardi, *al-Hawi al-Kabir*, ed.'Ali Muhammad Mu'awwad and'Adil Ahmad'Abd al-Mawjud (Beirut: Dar al-Kutub al-'Ilmiyya, 1994), 8:328–330, wrote that there is dispute about whether a non-Muslim can make a bequest to anyone other than a free Muslim of legal majority; al-Nawawi, *Rawdat al-Talibin wa 'Umdat al-Muftin*, 3rd edn. (Beirut: al-Maktab al-Islami, 1991), 5:317, held that a *waqf* could be for the benefit of a dhimmi but not for an enemy of the state (*harbi*) or apostate; Abu Ishaq al-Shirazi, *al-Muhadhdhab fi Fiqh al-Imam al-Shafi'i*, ed. Zakariyya'Amirat (Beirut: Dar al-Kutub al-'Ilmiyya, 1995), 2:323–324, allowed *waqf* for specified dhimmis but noted the debate about *waqf* for the benefit of apostates or enemies of the state.
[13] Al-Ghazali, *al-Wasit*, 2:397–398; Abu 'Abd Allah b. Muflih, *al-Furu'*, ed. Abu al-Zahra' Hazim al-Qadi (Beirut: Dar al-Kutub al-'Ilmiyya, 1997), 4:513; Ibn Qudama, *al-Mughni* (Beirut: Dar Ihya' al-Turath al-'Arabi, n.d.), 5:646.

universalism, then the bequest was a sin against God and could not be valid under sharia.[14] To hold otherwise would be to use the legal institutions of an Islamic enterprise of governance to legitimate practices that contravene an Islamically defined public good. Specifically, if a dhimmi created a charitable trust to support building a church or a school for Torah or Bible studies, Shafi'i jurists would invalidate the *waqf* because it constituted a sin (*ma'siya*) and thereby fell outside the scope of activity the law could uphold and protect.[15] The Shafi'i jurist al-Shirazi provided a logically precise argument justifying this position. First, he held that a charitable *waqf*, in its essence, is a pious endowment that brings one close to God (*qurba*). Second, anyone who creates a charitable endowment through a bequest or *wasiyya* will create an institution that bestows bounties (*hasanat*) on others. Lastly, he concluded, any charitable endowment that facilitates sin (*i'ana 'ala ma'siya*) is not lawful.[16] Al-Shirazi held that charitable endowments that support a church or Torah-reading school perpetuated disbelief in the land of Islam and thereby were tantamount to sin. Consequently, because the bounties from such charitable endowments were sinful, any such endowment was void (*batila*) as a matter of law.[17] Al-Shirazi went so far as to liken such bequests to a bequest that armed the

---

[14] Al-Ghazali, *al-Wasit*, 3:41–2; al-Nawawi, *Rawda*, 6:107, allowed a *wasiyya* to be for the benefit of dhimmis, harbis, and apostates; Ibn Qudama, *al-Mughni*, 6:103, analogized a *wasiyya* to a gift and said that both could be given to dhimmis and harbis in the *dar al-harb*; Abu 'Abd Allah b. Muflih, *al-Furu'*, 4:513l; al-Bahuti, *Kashshaf al-Qina' 'an Matn al-Iqna'* (Beirut: Dar al-Kutub al-'Ilmiyya, 1997), 4:442; al-Muhaqqiq al-Hilli, *Shara'i' al-Islam fi Masa'il al-Halal wa al-Haram*, ed. Sadiq al-Shirazi, 10th edn. (Beirut: Markaz al-Rasul al-A'zam, 1998), 1:482.

[15] Al-Ghazali, *al-Wasit*, 2:397; Shihab al-Din al-Ramli, *Nihayat al-Muhtaj ila Sharh al-Minhaj*, 3rd edn. (Beirut: Dar Ihya' al-Turath al-'Arabi, 1992), 5:366. The Ja'fari al-Muhaqqiq al-Hilli held that a Muslim could not create a *waqf* to support a church, synagogue, or school for studying the Torah or Bible. However, he allowed a non-Muslim to do so, thus introducing yet another complicated idea into the debate. Al-Muhaqqiq al-Hilli, *Shara'i' al-Islam*, 1:459.

[16] Al-Shirazi, *al-Muhadhdhab*, 2:323–324.

[17] Ibid., 2:341–342.

Muslim polity's enemies, thereby equating the two in terms of their potential to inflict harm on the Muslim polity.[18] In other words, for al-Shirazi, a charitable endowment that supported the perpetuation of value systems that were contrary to the Islamic universalist ethos was not simply sinful and thereby legally invalid; it was a security threat that had to be contained for the benefit and perpetuation of the Islamic governing regime.

Contrary to this approach, Hanafi jurists addressed the power to bequeath using a hypothetical case about a dhimmi who bequeathed his home to be a church, as opposed to leaving it to a specific named person. Abu Hanifa held this bequest lawful on the ground that this act constituted a pious, devotional act for the dhimmi (qurba) and must be respected just as Muslims respect the dhimmi's faith in other regards. In other words, whereas both al-Shirazi and Abu Hanifa viewed charitable endowments as bringing one closer to God, Abu Hanifa appreciated that bringing someone closer to God cannot be defined only in Islamic terms; closeness to God takes different forms depending on the tradition to which one belongs. Abu Hanifa's students Muhammad al-Shaybani and Abu Yusuf, however, disagreed with their teacher. They invalidated such a bequest because they (like al-Shirazi) deemed its subject matter sinful (ma'siyya haqiqa) despite the dhimmi's belief that it was a pious act.[19]

This dispute within the Hanafi school raised a fundamental question for jurists operating at the intersection of law and governance:

---

[18] The Hanbali Ibn Qudama argued that a bequest could not be made to support schools for teaching the Torah or the Bible because these scriptures had been abrogated by the Qur'an and contain corruptions. Ibn Qudama, al-Mughni, 6:105. See also al-Bahuti, Kashshaf al-Qina', 4:442.

[19] Badr al-Din al-'Ayni, al-Binaya Sharh al-Hidaya, ed. Ayman Salih Sha'ban (Beirut: Dar al-Kutub al-'Ilmiyya, 2000), 13:495; Ibn Nujaym, al-Bahr al-Ra'iq (Beirut: Dar al-Kutub al-'Ilmiyya, 1997), 9:302; al-Kasani, Bada'i' al-Sana'i' fi Tartib al-Shara'i', ed. 'Ali Muhammad Mu'awwad and 'Adil Ahmad 'Abd al-Mawjud (Beirut: Dar al-Kutub al-'Ilmiyya, 1997), 10:500–501.

by what terms of reference should one determine and evaluate the dhimmi's act of charity?[20] To resolve this question, the Hanafi al-'Ayni offered four possible outcomes:

+ If a bequest involved a pious act in the dhimmi's tradition but not in the Islamic tradition, many Hanafis held that it should be allowed, although other schools (as well as other Hanafis) disagreed.
+ If the dhimmi made a bequest that would be a pious act for Muslims, like donating to support the Muslim pilgrimage to Mecca (*hajj*) or for building a mosque, the bequest was invalid; it was contrary to the dhimmi's faith. However, if the bequest benefited specific named individuals (for the purpose of going on *hajj*, for instance), it was valid, since the dhimmi's private interest as property owner was to be respected under the law.
+ If the bequest concerned a subject matter that was lawful under the dhimmi's beliefs and Islamic beliefs, it was valid.
+ If the bequest involved a subject matter that was unlawful in both the dhimmi's faith and the Muslim faith, it was invalid. The underlying subject matter would be a sin for both Muslims and dhimmis to allow.[21]

By offering these alternatives, al-'Ayni illustrated the underlying issues at stake, namely the dhimmis' private property interests, the limits on dhimmis in light of their tradition's requirements, and lastly a jurid-ically defined public good that limited the dhimmis' scope to make charitable bequests. In the interest of upholding the dhimmis' private

---

[20] This was the dilemma in the jurisprudence noted by al-'Ayni. Al-'Ayni, *al-Binaya*, 13:495.

[21] Al-'Ayni, *al-Binaya*, 13:496; Ibn Nujaym, *al-Bahr al-Ra'iq*, 9:302; al-Kasani, *Bada'i' al-Sana'i'*, 10:500–501.

property interests, al-'Ayni granted them the authority to create pious endowments that did not violate any precept in the dhimmis' traditions or the Islamic one. In other words, if the charitable endowment was lawful under both the dhimmis' and the Islamic tradition, there was no real conflict; to allow such bequests would uphold the Islamic values underlying the enterprise of governance and respect the dhimmis' tradition pursuant to the contract of protection. In such a case, the claim space of sharia would not countenance something that would run contrary to sharia-based doctrines, the public good, or the Islamic enterprise of governance.

Interestingly, the dhimmi could not bequest a charitable endowment for something that was lawful under Islam but unlawful or of no legal significance under the dhimmis' tradition, such as the *hajj*. Respect for the dhimmis' tradition, as required under the contract of protection, arguably animated this legal outcome. However, one cannot ignore the fact that the dhimmis' private rights of property disposition are limited by their own tradition, regardless of how a particular dhimmi-grantor might subjectively feel about the matter.

The most difficult issue had to do with whether dhimmis could create a charitable endowment that was valid in their own tradition but was contrary to Islamic values. This is the case on which jurists disagreed, as noted above. For some, to give legal effect to such endowments would be tantamount to giving legal cover and protection to sin. Some jurists went so far as to consider such endowments security threats to the well-being of the polity. Others, such as some Hanafi jurists, allowed such endowments. They recognized that the dhimmis' traditions considered such endowments valuable, and Muslim rulers were required to respect the dhimmis' traditions under the contract of protection.

To further complicate matters, the Malikis had their own approach, which carved out a middle ground between the two positions noted

above. Importantly for the purpose of this essay, the Maliki position also reveals the extent to which this legal issue was embedded
within a larger vision of empire, governance, and regulation. Malikis
addressed the issue of charitable endowments by reference to the
religious association of the testator, the framework of Islamic inheritance law, and the prevailing tax regime. Under Islamic inheritance
law, two-thirds of a decedent's property was distributed pursuant to
a rule of inheritance that designated percentage shares for specifically
identified heirs. The decedent could bequest the remaining one-third
to non-heirs.[22] Malikis asked, though, whether a Christian dhimmi
with no heirs could bequest all of his property to the head of the
Church. Generally, the Christian could give one-third of his estate
to the Patriarch, while the remaining two-thirds escheated to the
Muslim polity, which was considered his lawful heir in this case.[23]
Even if the testator left a testamentary instrument that transferred
his whole estate to the Patriarchate, the above arrangement was to
be carried out.[24]

However, the application of this general rule depended on whether
the dhimmi decedent was personally liable to the governing regime for
the *jizya* or whether the dhimmi's community was collectively liable
for the tax payment. If the dhimmi was personally liable for paying
the *jizya* directly to the government, the above ruling on escheat to
the government applied. The rationale for this rule was as follows:

---

[22] On the rules of inheritance in the Qur'an and Islamic law, see Qur'an 4: 11–12;
David Powers, *Studies in Qur'an and Hadith: The Formation of the Islamic Law of
Inheritance* (Berkeley: University of California Press, 1986).

[23] Ibn Rushd al-Jadd, *al-Bayan wa al-Tahsil* (Beirut: Dar al-Gharb al-Islami, 1988),
13:326–327.

[24] Ibn Rushd al-Jadd, *al-Bayan*, 13:326–327. See also al-Hattab, *Mawahib al-
Jalil*, ed. Zakariya 'Amirat (Beirut: Dar al-Kutub al-'Ilmiyya, 1995), 8:515, which
relates this view and critiques another that upholds the validity of any *wasiyya*
by a kafir; al-Qarafi, *al-Dhakhira*, ed. Sa'id A'rab (Beirut: Dar al-Gharb al-Islami,
1994), 7:12.

with the death of the dhimmi, the ruling regime lost its annual *jizya* revenue from him. Consequently, the escheat of his estate was designed to account for the regime's lost revenue.[25]

But suppose the leaders of the dhimmi's community's collected the *jizya* from the community's members and delivered the payment to the ruling regime on behalf of the community. Furthermore, suppose the *jizya* tax liability was fixed, such that the total sum did not decrease with the deaths of community members. Under such circumstances many Malikis allowed individual dhimmis (presumably without heirs) to bequeath their entire estate to whomever they wished.[26] This particular ruling worked to the financial benefit of the ruling regime. The ruler still received the same *jizya* revenues. Any financial loss was distributed to the dhimmi's community, since its tax liability did not diminish with the death of its community members. To offset that financial loss, the Malikis permitted dhimmis to bequeath their entire estate to the community when they lacked any heirs.

In conclusion, when a dhimmi sought to donate money to endow a religious institution, Muslim jurists were concerned about giving such charitable institutions legal recognition. To use sharia-based legal categories and institutions to uphold non-Muslim religious institutions would seem awkward and ironic at best, and illegitimate at worst, given a public good defined in terms of a universalizing Islamic ethos. The legal debate about the scope of the dhimmi's power to bequeath property for religious purposes shows how Muslim jurists grappled with the effects of diversity on the aspirations and efficiency of an Islamically defined governing enterprise. The disagreements and alternative outcomes can be appreciated as juridical attempts to

---

[25] Ibn Rushd al-Jadd, *al-Bayan*, 13:326–327. See also al-Qarafi, *al-Dhakhira*, 7:35.
[26] Ibn Rushd al-Jadd, *al-Bayan*, 13:326–327. However, Ibn Rushd did note others who disagreed with him and held that the estate escheats to the state when there is no heir. Al-Qarafi, *al-Dhakhira*, 7:12, held the same view as Ibn Rushd al-Jadd but also noted the disagreement on this issue.

account for and respect the dhimmi's conception of piety and property interests, preserve the public good, and enhance the efficiency and efficacy of the ruling regime. Regardless of the analytic route any particular jurist adopted, the legal debate in the aggregate illustrates that the intelligibility of the legal doctrines depended on circumstances such as source texts and legal doctrine, as well as institutions (e.g., adjudication and taxation) of the enterprise of governance legitimated by the Islamic public ethos.

Building Religious Sites in an Islamic Public

If the contract of protection was designed in part to allow the dhimmi to retain his or her faith, did that also permit the dhimmi to ensure the continuity of his or her faith by passing it on to future generations? If so, the previous discussion on charitable endowments should raise some concerns. If charitable endowments to support Torah and Bible schools were restricted, if not void, under the law, how could dhimmis build or maintain their communities and faith practices? It is one thing to retain one's faith; it is another to pass it on to future generations. If the preservation of a religious tradition other than Islam through a charitable endowment was considered a sin among some jurists, could sharia-based legal doctrines and institutions countenance dhimmis' effort to preserve their religious spaces, such as churches or synagogues, while living in a Muslim polity? This is the fundamental question that is hidden from view in Keller's quasi-translation as discussed below. By his translation omission he avoids engaging the historical backdrop that gave these rules intelligibility as law for purposes of governance.

Hunwick writes that whether non-Muslims could build new religious places of worship depended in large part on whether the town was purely dhimmi, newly conquered, or a brand new Muslim-built town.[27] This discussion will show that the ability of dhimmis to build and repair places of worship depended on the type of land they occupied, their land tax liability, and whether the Islamic ruling regime had taken control of the land by conquest or treaty. Implicitly invoking the pragmatics of empire, an Islamic universalizing ethos, and the contract paradigm, Muslim jurists used demographic, historical, and financial arguments to determine the degree to which the dhimmis could develop and enjoy places of worship for their respective communities.

In regions where the land was cultivated by Muslims (e.g., *amsar al-islam*), such as Basra and Kufa, dhimmis were not allowed to build new places of worship. These were lands that Muslims occupied and claimed suzerainty over, as if the land were *terra nullius*, despite dhimmis having lived there and erected places of worship. In such cases, places of worship that existed before the Muslim arrival could remain intact, according to some jurists, although others counseled their destruction.[28]

If the land came under Muslim suzerainty by military conquest against the dhimmis, the dhimmis could not erect new religious buildings, and jurists debated whether old ones could remain or be refurbished.[29] Malik, al-Shafiʿi, and Ahmad b. Hanbal required old religious buildings that remained after conquest to be destroyed.[30]

---

[27] John O. Hunwick, "The Rights of the Dhimmis to Maintain a Place of Worship: A 15th Century Fatwa from Tlemcen," *Al-Qantara* 12.1 (1991), 133–156, 140, 145.
[28] Al-Ghazali, *al-Wasit*, 4:207; al-Mawardi, *al-Hawi*, 14:320–321; al-Muzani, *Mukhtasar al-Muzani*, in al-Shafiʿi, *Kitab al-Umm* (Beirut: Dar al-Fikr, 1990), 5:385; al-Nawawi, *Rawda*, 10:323; al-ʿAyni, *al-Binaya*, 7:255–256; Ibn Nujaym, *al-Bahr al-Raʾiq*, 5:190; al-Qarafi, *al-Dhakhira*, 3:458; Ibn Qudama, *al-Mughni*, 8:526–527; al-Bahuti, *Kashshaf al-Qinaʿ*, 3:151; al-Muhaqqiq al-Hilli, *Sharaʾiʿ al-Islam*, 1:262.
[29] Ibn Nujaym, *al-Bahr al-Raʾiq*, 5:190. See also al-Mawardi, *al-Hawi*, 14:320–321; Ibn Nujaym, *al-Bahr al-Raʾiq*, 5:191, held that existing buildings can be repaired but not expanded or transferred; Ibn Qudama, *al-Mughni*, 8:527–528.
[30] For example, see the Maliki al-Qarafi, *al-Dhakhira*, 3:458; Ibn Qudama, *al-Mughni*, 8:526–527; al-Nawawi, *Rawda*, 10:323. See also the discussion by the Maliki al-Hattab, who surveyed the juristic disagreement about whether to allow old religious buildings to remain intact in areas conquered by Muslim forces. Al-Hattab, *Mawahib al-Jalil*, 4:599.

A dominant Hanafi position was to require the dhimmis to convert such buildings into residences rather than destroy them.[31] The Hanafi al-'Ayni argued differently, suggesting that in such cases, if the dhimmis' religious buildings became dilapidated, they could refurbish them and retain them as religious buildings. Dilapidated religious buildings, however, could not be abandoned to erect others in their place at different sites, since that would be akin to building anew. Furthermore, such religious buildings could not be rebuilt or renovated to be bigger than they were before.[32]

If the land at issue fell under Muslim rule by means of a treaty between the dhimmis and the Muslim forces, authority over the land (*mulk*) and land tax liability (*kharaj*) became decisive factors in determining whether dhimmis could build or repair religious buildings. There were three possible outcomes that jurists contemplated:

+ If the Islamic ruling regime assumed both authority over the land (*mulk al-dar lana dunahum*)[33] and responsibility for land tax liability (*kharaj*), the dhimmis could keep religious buildings already present but could not build new ones.[34]

+ If the Muslim enterprise of governance assumed authority over the land but the dhimmis were collectively liable for the land tax, the existing religious buildings could remain. Whether dhimmis could build new religious buildings

---

[31] Al-'Ayni, *al-Binaya*, 7:255–256.
[32] Ibid., 7:256.
[33] This particular Arabic phrase is used by al-Mawardi, *al-Hawi*, 14:322.
[34] Al-Mawardi, *al-Hawi*, 14:320–322; al-'Ayni, *al-Binaya*, 7:255–256. The Hanbali Ibn Qudama held that in cases where Muslims retain sovereignty of the land and the dhimmis only pay the *jizya*, one must look to the terms of the treaty to determine whether the dhimmis have the liberty to erect new religious buildings. Ibn Qudama, *al-Mughni*, 8:526–527. On this Hanbali opinion, see also al-Bahuti, *Kashshaf al-Qina'*, 3:151.

depended on the terms of the contract of protection that
they negotiated with the Muslim conquerors.[35]
+ If the dhimmis retained authority over the land (*mulk al-dar
lahum dunana*)[36] and were also responsible for the land tax
(*kharaj*), they had the right both to keep the old religious
buildings and to build new ones.[37]

In these examples, the determining factors were authority over the
land and tax liability. If the dhimmis enjoyed the benefits that accrued
from holding authority over the land and bore the burden of tax liability, they were permitted to enjoy certain privileges. If the Muslim
authorities held the land and bore the tax burden, they could deny
those privileges to the dhimmis. Where the Muslims enjoyed the
benefit of authority, but the dhimmis bore the burden of tax liability,
the jurists allowed some negotiation given the distribution of benefits
and burdens. Notably absent was a conceivable fourth option, where
the dhimmis enjoyed authority over the land, but Muslims bore the
tax burden payable to the Muslim enterprise of governance. The
absence of this fourth option may have to do with the ambiguity of
the Arabic term translated as "authority," namely *mulk*. The term can
imply possession and authority but may also reflect an imperial division

---

[35] Al-Nawawi, *Rawda*, 10:323; Ibn Nujaym, *al-Bahr al-Ra'iq*, 5:190. The Maliki
al-Qarafi held that if the dhimmis are responsible for the land tax then they can
keep their churches. But if they include in the treaty a condition allowing them to
build new religious buildings the condition is void except on land where no Muslims
reside. However, in such regions dhimmis can erect new religious buildings without
having to specify their right to do so in any treaty. Al-Qarafi, *al-Dhakhira*, 3:458.
[36] For this Arabic phrasing, see al-Mawardi, *al-Hawi*, 14:322.
[37] Ibid., 14:320–322; al-Ghazali, *al-Wasit*, 4:207; al-Nawawi, *Rawda*, 10:323; Ibn
Qudama, *al-Mughni*, 8:526–527; al-Bahuti, *Kashshaf al-Qina'*, 3:151. Fred Donner,
The Early Islamic Conquests (Princeton, New Jersey: Princeton University Press,
1981), 240, indicates that early Muslim conquests did not aim to dispossess the
indigenous peoples of their lands. Rather the focus was upon seizing political control
over lands and drawing off tax revenues to support the Islamic governing regime.

of power, decentralized authority being a common characteristic of imperial regimes. If this were the case, then it would explain the absence of a fourth option. The Muslims were always sovereigns of the land; the only real question was the degree to which they directly ruled the region or delegated authority to other communities. Indeed, given the imperial assumptions that made the dhimmi rules intelligible, such a fourth option would be *unintelligible*. It is therefore not surprising that no such fourth option was mentioned by the jurists.

The Hanafi jurist al-'Ayni approached the issue differently. He relied on demographic analysis to arrive at an appropriate accommodation. He held that dhimmis could not build new religious buildings in the towns that Muslims had built and cultivated (*amsar*). However, his general ban did not apply to the villages in which non-Muslims predominantly resided.[38] The Hanafi Ibn Nujaym qualified al-'Ayni's exception by upholding the ban in both Muslim towns and dhimmi villages that were *in the Arabian Peninsula*, since the Prophet indicated that there could not be two faiths in the Arabian Peninsula.[39] Al-'Ayni considered this prophetic tradition to be weak in its authenticity, yet he recognized that it conveyed a general attitude against erecting religious buildings in the region and so might be read as providing

---

[38] Al-'Ayni, *al-Binaya*, 7:257. See also al-Marghinani, *al-Hidaya*, 1:455. See also the Maliki al-Hattab, *Mawahib al-Jalil*, 4:600.

[39] Ibn Nujaym, *al-Bahr al-Ra'iq*, 5:190. See also al-Marghinani, *al-Hidaya*, 1:455. The conquest of the Arabian Peninsula saw an expulsion of non-Muslims from the region. Relying on a tradition in which the Prophet rejects the possibility that there could be two faiths in the Arabian Peninsula, the second caliph 'Umar b. al-Khattab (r. 13–23/634–644) instituted a policy of expulsion, causing the Banu Najran tribe of Arab Christians to leave the region. Hugh Goddard, "Christian–Muslim Relations: A Look Backwards and a Look Forwards," *Islam and Christian–Muslim Relations* 11:2 (2000), 196. This tradition was read by jurists as one of the bases for prohibiting dhimmis from constructing religious buildings in Arab lands. Hamidullah, however, argues that this prophetic tradition was not premised on an agenda of minority religious persecution or intolerance. Rather it reflects the Prophet's political aim to secure a region of safety, security, and homogeneity for Muslims. Muhammad Hamidullah, "Status of Non-Muslims in Islam," *Majallat al-Azhar* 45.8 (1973), 10.

an exception to his exception.[40] Other Hanafis rejected al-'Ayni's initial demographically based exception to the general ban. Instead, they banned non-Muslims from erecting new religious buildings in both Muslim towns and dhimmi villages. They argued that Muslims resided in both areas. Their argument implicitly made it possible for the universalizing Islamic ethos of the public good to prevail, despite the limited Muslim population in predominantly dhimmi villages.[41]

For many jurists, the rationale for limiting the extent to which dhimmis could build new religious buildings or preserve old ones had to do with ensuring the Islamic character of lands falling under the imperium of the Islamic ruling regime. For instance, the Shafi'i al-Mawardi held that churches and synagogues could not be erected in lands under Muslim rule (amsar al-Islam), since they would undermine the dominance of Islam. He argued that allowing such construction would be a sin (ma'siyya), since non-Muslims congregated in these buildings to preserve disbelief (kufr). In Islamic lands, he said, no faith other than Islam should be prominent (zahir).[42] Even al-'Ayni, who permitted exceptions to the general ban, knew that to allow Jews and Christians to construct religious buildings would impede the universalist imperative of Islam.[43] He wrote that such religious buildings in the land of Islam (dar al-Islam) enfeebled the presence and strength of Islam in the land (turithu al-da'f fi al-Islam).[44] The question for him and others concerned the extent to which the Islamic empire could sustain its character while accommodating the religious "other."

The justifications for these building restrictions and their exceptions show how Muslim jurists believed that dhimmis counted as

---

[40] Al-'Ayni, al-Binaya, 7:255.
[41] Al-Marghinani, al-Hidaya, 1:455.
[42] Al-Mawardi, al-Hawi, 14:321.
[43] Al-'Ayni, al-Binaya, 7:255.
[44] Ibid.

members of society and yet should be regulated so that the public presence of their contrary religious values would not compromise the integrity of an enterprise of governance premised upon a universalist Islamic ethos. No single approach dominated the legal tradition; nonetheless the differences among jurists reveal the mutually constitutive relationship between the law and the enterprise of governance. The presumptions about the enterprise of governance contributed to legal decisions about the scope to which the dhimmis' claims and interests could be accommodated. Although jurists sought to accommodate dhimmi interests, the scope of that accommodation could not be so large as to threaten the well-being of an Islamic ruling regime imagined in the light of a universalizing Islamic ethos made manifest through both empire and legal doctrine.

Dhimmi Rituals in an Islamic Public

A second issue, related to the one above, concerned the extent to which dhimmis were allowed to engage in public displays of religious practice. Jurists of both Sunni and Shi'a schools generally agreed that, although dhimmis could practice their faith in Muslim lands, they could not proselytize, recite publicly from the Torah or Bible, or engage in public rituals of religious significance, such as carrying a cross or ringing church bells (naqus).[45] If they did so, jurists would not necessarily consider the contract of protection breached, but they would allow the ruling authority to subject the dhimmi to discretionary punishment (ta'zir).[46] If, through proselytization, dhimmis directly or indirectly

---

[45] 'Abd al-Karim Zaydan, Ahkam al-Dhimmiyyin wa al-Musta'minin fi Dar al-Islam (Beirut: Mu'assasat al-Risala, 1988), 84. For Shafi'i authors, see al-Mawardi, al-Hawi, 14:316; al-Muzani, Mukhtasar al-Muzani, in al-Shafi'i, al-Umm, 5:385; al-Shirazi, al-Muhadhdhab, 3:314. See also the Shi'a Muhaqqiq al-Hilli, Shara'i' al-Islam, 1:260–261.
[46] It was a matter of debate whether breach of such conditions voided the contract

ISLAMIC AND JEWISH LEGAL REASONING

caused dissension in the faith of Muslims, Shafi'i jurists would consider the contract void, thereby revoking the dhimmis' protected status under the Islamic imperium and transforming them into an "enemy of the state." The legal effect of such revocation and redesignation was that if the dhimmis were killed while residing in the Muslim empire their killers would face no legal consequences, akin to what Giorgio Agamben calls the *homo sacer*.[47] These examples illustrate how the dhimmi's otherness constituted not just an alternative set of values, but was viewed as a potential threat. Recalling al-Shirazi's concerns about charitable endowments, dhimmis who engaged in public displays of religious ritual, and indeed went so far as to challenge Muslims in their faith commitments, at the very least had to be punished and at worst were security threats to the polity.

Importantly, for some jurists, the threat was not in the fact that the dhimmis performed their religious rituals, but arose when they performed them *in public view*. For example, the Hanafi al-Kasani did not permit dhimmis to display the cross in public because the cross was a sign of disbelief; but he did permit dhimmis to display the cross and ring their bells privately in their churches. In other words, dhimmis could practice their faith freely among themselves. Allowing them to practice their faith in public was an entirely different matter. It might be construed as granting their faith tradition equal or equivalent standing with the Islamic values and traditions that gave content to the public good of the Muslim polity, and which the Islamic enterprise of governance upheld and protected.

Whether such a threat was serious or not depended on the public

---

or preserved the contract while allowing discretionary punishment. See al-Nawawi, *Rawda*, 10:328–9, 333; al-'Ayni, *al-Binaya*, 7:260.

[47] Al-Mawardi, *al-Hawi*, 14:316; al-Muzani, *Mukhtasar al-Muzani*, 5:385. For a similar conception of the "enemy of the state," see Giorgio Agamben, *Homo Sacer: Sovereign Power and Bare Life*, trans. Daniel Heller-Roazen (Palo Alto, California: Stanford University Press, 1998).

sphere in question. In some cases the public sphere comprised both Muslims and dhimmis. In other cases the public sphere was composed predominantly, if not entirely, of dhimmis. Given these demographic differences, the Hanafi jurist al-Kasani made exceptions to the general prohibition if the dhimmis were the predominant, majority population in the village, even if some Muslims lived there.[48] However, the Hanafi al-Marghinani rejected this exception, noting that those who transmitted the teachings of the Hanafi school's leading jurist, Abu Hanifa, generally lived in villages where dhimmis were the majority. He argued that Abu Hanifa's students would have been sufficiently familiar with such demographic contexts and would have provided such exceptions if they were warranted. Since his students did not make such exceptions, al-Marghinani held that even where dhimmis were the predominant group in a region they should still be restricted from public displays of religious ritual.[49]

Hanbali jurists analyzed the legality of dhimmi public displays of religious ritual by reference to the kind of land at issue. For instance, Ibn Qudama would not permit dhimmis to engage in public religious displays—e.g., ringing church bells—in towns that Muslims had built, such as Basra or Kufa.[50] In these cases the land was regarded as *terra nullius*, thereby granting the Islamic enterprise of governance an uncontested imperium. Likewise, if dhimmis lived in townships that had come under the Islamic ruling regime through conquest, the Hanbali Abu 'Abd Allah b. Muflih prohibited the dhimmis from public displays of their faith tradition, presumably because of the imperium that accrued to the regime as a consequence of conquest. But if dhimmis lived in lands subjected to a negotiated treaty the dhimmis' legal capacity to publicly express their faith depended on the

---

[48] Al-Kasani, *Bada'i' al-Sana'i'*, 9:449; see also the Maliki al-Qarafi, *al-Dhakhira*, 3:458–459.
[49] Al-Marghinani, *al-Hidaya*, 1:455.
[50] Ibn Qudama, *al-Mughni*, 8:526–527.

negotiated terms of the contract of protection agreed upon between them and the ruling regime.[51] In this case Hanbali jurists used the contract paradigm to introduce a negotiative, accommodative spirit.

Muslim jurists did not *universally* prohibit dhimmis from practicing or exhibiting their faith publicly, or developing institutions to transmit their religious values to future generations. They did, however, limit the scope of the religious other's public presence in order to preserve the dominance of the Islamic character of the public sphere. Muslim jurists relied on an Islamic universalist ethos and an imagined imperial reality to determine whether, as a matter of law, dhimmis could establish charitable endowments, publicly perform religious rituals, build new places of worship, and maintain older ones. Their legal arguments had an intelligibility that drew upon different types of arguments that reflect the connection between law and governance. Such arguments may refer to tax liability, demographics, conquest, and treaty relationships. The different arguments across the legal schools reveal the extent to which the content of the law and an imagined reality of empire and governance were tightly interwoven.

INVERTING THE POLITICAL FORM

Religious Zionism and the State of Israel: Competing Interpretations of the Rabbinic Lacuna on the Laws of War

This section will describe the Rabbinic deliberations with regard to whether it is necessary and even possible to establish halakhic laws governing the use of force in contemporary times. The specific content of the laws of war will not be elaborated except when important for clarifying our discussion of the primary question, "Do we need to fill

---

[51] Abu 'Abd Allah b. Muflih, *al-Furu'*, 6:250.

this void in Jewish law, and, if so, how can this be done?"

Jewish identity was understood throughout the Middle Ages as revolving around two foci—observance of the Halakha and connectedness to the Jewish collective. Observance of the Halakha, i.e., the fulfillment of the normative Jewish legal system in both the individual and communal realms, was a central element defining the identity of the individual Jew and the Jewish community. This view of Jewish identity was shared by the surrounding society, including the supposition that Jewish law purports to encompass all areas of life. Classical Jewish tradition does not include the well-known Christian perspective of "grant unto God that which is God's and grant unto Caesar that which is Caesar's." The modern Jewish nationalist movement, the Zionist movement, questioned the balance between these two foci and aspired to strengthen the communal element at the expense of the legal component. The rise of Jewish nationalism was a process that took place over the course of a century within the European Jewish community, a period that included the elimination of the ghetto walls that divided the Jewish community from the surrounding non-Jewish society and the process of secularization that created a full range of Jews with varying degrees of reduced commitment to Jewish law. The idea of establishing a Jewish state essentially paralleled the aspiration to strengthen the communal element of traditional Jewish identity, which was certainly compatible with the secular outlook of a majority of its proponents. The fact that Jewish law was not equipped to deal with issues related to sovereignty was not problematic for them. It did, however, trouble the segment of the Zionist movement that considered itself committed to both Jewish law and the Zionist idea—the Religious Zionists.

There are a number of ways that one may deal with this lacuna in the Rabbinic tradition.

1. One approach, which as we will see was adopted by some of the legal authorities, is to see the lack of norms on the topic

as an explicit legal position, i.e., to claim that the absence of these norms is ideological in nature. In other words, Jewish law did not develop a normative system dealing with the use of force because it is opposed to the use of force.

2. On the other hand, we also find an opposite position that views this lacuna not as an ideological–legal position but rather as a pragmatic consequence of the Jewish condition in the diaspora. From this perspective, the Halakha should and can develop laws of war that respond to a new and very different Jewish reality. This approach is based on a worldview that sees the Zionist enterprise as a very positive development from a traditional Jewish perspective, and on the argument that the Halakha was always able to adapt to new situations. Based on these perspectives, many Rabbinic leaders of Religious Zionism viewed it as the obligation of contemporary rabbis to try to fill in this gap and create a Jewish legal corpus relating to war in order to reconcile the Halakha to sovereignty-related issues that were irrelevant during the exile. The laws of war constitute only one notable example of the need perceived by the Religious Zionist rabbis and thinkers to extend the Halakha beyond the private domain to deal with issues relating to the public realm in the reborn Jewish state.

Within this camp, two basic approaches developed as to how such a corpus should be created—i.e., what sources could be utilized, and what methods of interpretation could be employed to establish a normative system relating to war and the use of force. One approach was to turn to halakhic sources relating to the saving of life and the right of self-defense (*pikuah nefesh*). These laws recognize the right to harm a person who is pursuing another with the intent to kill them, and delineate the parameters for such actions. The implication of turning to these sources is that it involves turning to criminal law in order to establish a normative system for the laws of war. It reflects an assumption that war does not constitute an independent normative category. This line of thinking does not require one to develop a different category of laws that we might call "state laws," but rather continues an ongoing halakhic discussion that dealt with such questions throughout the period of exile. This approach was adopted by a significant number of Rabbinic authorities because it is a less radical and innovative methodology that seems more compatible with a traditional legal system such as the Halakha.

Many religious Zionist rabbis and thinkers, however, pre- ferred to build a separate normative system relating to war. In the discussion below, we will see that several approaches have been suggested to identify a foundation for such a nor- mative system. We will examine this approach by looking at the writings of two important and influential personalities, Yeshayahu Leibowitz and Rabbi Shlomo Goren. Leibowitz, one of the most prominent thinkers of the period, and Rabbi Goren, a prominent rabbi and the founder of the Israeli military rabbinate, both contended that it was obligatory to fill in the gap. Rabbi Goren, as an expert legal authority and a military man, took the initiative and tried to build a corpus based on the normative halakhic system. From his military perspective, he objected vociferously to basing the laws of war on the principles of criminal law and sought to build a unique corpus of laws on the subject. To that end, he utilized innovative methods of interpretation. He sought to shape a corpus that would be relevant to modern times by connecting the biblical attitude to power with the more pacifist Rabbinic attitude.

3. A third approach is to obviate the need for the Halakha to
   address the issue. This approach too includes two possible
   positions. One position is to accept the gap and to argue
   that the law is indifferent to this issue. According to this
   approach, the laws of war are beyond the scope of Jewish
   law. Proponents of this view believe it is not the place of
   Rabbinic authorities or religious thinkers to deal with
   political and state issues that are not addressed by the
   Halakha. One prominent advocate of this position was
   Rabbi Joseph B. Soloveitchik, the Rabbinic leader of the
   Religious Zionist Mizrachi movement in North America.
   The second possibility is to turn "outward," i.e., to incorporate an external legal standard into the Halakha. This
   approach was adopted by Rabbi Shaul Yisraeli, one of the
   prominent Religious Zionist rabbis in Israel, who advocated
   adopting accepted international norms as the halakhic
   guidelines for conducting war. A well-known precedent
   of this method is the halakhic principle "the law of the
   land is the law" (*dina demalkhuta dina*), which has been
   part of the Jewish legal system since the third century.
   Here we are not dealing with the complete detachment
   of Jewish law from the topic, but rather with a lack of
   pretension by the Halakha to create its own normative
   system.

As we discuss these different approaches, we will also see that the distinctions between them reflect a very significant difference of opinion
regarding the essence of the Zionist enterprise and the significance of
the State of Israel in religious terms. In these distinctions we confront
the connection between ideology and interpretation.

The Lacuna as Normative: The Conservative (Haredi) Critique of Innovation

As a prelude to the discussion, it is important to note the larger Rabbinic context within which these approaches took shape. Perhaps most notable is that a significant portion of the Orthodox rabbinate fundamentally opposed the Zionist idea from its inception, and so rejected the very idea of a religious Zionism that would inform the development of Rabbinic law. From their religious perspective, it was forbidden to engage in any initiative that has pretensions to advance the redemption; rather one should leave it to a deterministic intervention. This opposition began at a point when nobody even considered the possibility that the realization of the Zionist program would require the use of force. The subsequent necessity for military action created an additional anchor for Orthodox Rabbinic opposition to Zionism. Some of the rabbis saw the necessity for the use of force as a categorical proof that the Zionist idea was fundamentally illegitimate from the perspective of Jewish tradition.

From this critique of Zionism, it necessarily followed that, since Jewish law addresses all relevant areas of life for the Jews, the lack of laws of war in Jewish law is a convincing proof that military action is not to be undertaken. According to this view, Jewish law does not deal with laws of state and of war because it opposes the establishment of an independent Jewish state and the use of force for the purpose of gathering the exiled Jews before the advent of the messiah. The position of Jewish tradition on these matters is the opposition to the use of force that flows from the Talmud. It is therefore inappropriate for Jewish legal authorities to render decisions or participate in deliberations on these issues, since to do so lends support to a process that is entirely in opposition to the central ethos of the Halakha.

Rabbi Yoel Teitelbaum (1888–1979), the Satmar Hasidic Rebbe, the leader and spokesman of radical Haredi Orthodoxy after the Holocaust, wrote as follows in his anti-Zionist manifesto, *Va-Yoel Moshe*:

> Their hands are also stained with bloodshed, and they are the reason for the great tragedy in which six million Jews were killed. From then until now, tens of thousands of Jews have been killed because of this impure idea of establishing a state by means of the sword and strength... Anyone who brings about a war that endangers life against the opinion of the Torah is a murderer.[52]

Thus, a Jew who goes out to war in our times is a murderer. The argument against war came to expression conspicuously and eloquently in the speeches and writings of Rabbi Menachem Shach (*ca.* 1898–2001), the leader of Lithuanian Haredi Orthodoxy for several decades. He does not deal with the question of how to conduct oneself in war, for in his opinion the very establishment of an army and the conducting of war are a negative situation and unnatural for Jews. Since the messiah has not yet come, the Jews are still in a state of exile. Jews, according to this view, must be passive and survive in the world until the redemption in the messianic days. They must take their Torah with them everywhere and be sustained by it. Rabbi Shach believed that the ongoing cycle must be broken, i.e., the intoxicated faith in power that leads to war, the war that leads to acts of bloodshed and subsequently causes the spiritual and moral destruction and impurity of humankind. From this perspective, Jewish law does have pretensions to regulate all aspects of life, including use of force, but the current reality cannot be considered a "Jewish reality" and thus cannot be regulated according to Jewish law.

---

[52] Yoel Teitelbaum, *Va-Yoel Moshe*, 212.

Toward a New Halakha I: Yeshayahu Leibowitz and the Religious Duty to Fill Rabbinic Lacunae

Yeshayahu Leibowitz (1903–94), a prominent and influential Jewish thinker of the twentieth century, dedicated his early writings, from the 1930s until the middle 1950s, to a vociferous demand that the Religious Zionist rabbis deal directly and seriously, on the normative level, with the challenges posed to Jewish law by Jewish sovereignty and all of its implications. In his opinion, Jewish law was capable of responding to the realities of sovereignty, and it was imperative for the rabbis to do so through drastic legislative intervention. Leibowitz raised this argument aggressively for decades until he gave up and admitted his failure in bringing it into reality.

In his original approach the religious significance of the establishment of the State of Israel was the revival of the Halakha, the fact that it was necessary to derive answers and operative procedures from Jewish law in many areas of public life which had not previously been addressed during the period of exile.

> Our definition as Zionists teaches us that the fault lies not in the Torah, but rather in our historical situation that prevented us from implementing the noble power hidden in the Torah. Under these circumstances, it is our duty to strive to redeem the Torah.[53]

The blossoming of a normative Jewish system that would bring to realization the great potential buried within it had, in his mind, a deep religious significance and therefore placed responsibility upon the shoulders of the Rabbinic leadership of that generation. Leibowitz

---

[53] As cited Aryei Fishman, *Judaism and Modernization on the Religious Kibbutz* (Cambridge: Cambridge University Press, 1992), 75.

saw in the rabbis' lack of responsiveness to this challenge a proof that they had not internalized the new reality and were still functioning as if they were in exile. In a speech delivered in 1943 regarding modern religious education, Leibowitz claimed that "the Jewish people were torn away from independent political, social, national, and economic life" and that as a result of that "not only...the complete application of the Torah was halted, but also the struggle to apply it within a societal context." He saw the perpetuation of this reality in the context of the State of Israel as an "educational crisis."[54] We can say that Leibowitz tried to cast the Zionist enterprise in a context that related not only to the Jewish people "breaking into" the process of history, but to a "breaking out" of Judaism into all of the normative areas that it was careful not to address during the years of exile.

One of the last articles Leibowitz wrote before changing his focus to other topics was his famous piece "After Kibiyah," which dealt with the ethics of war. This article was published in the aftermath of the controversial military action by the Israeli army in October 1953 in the village of Kibiyah, located in territory that was then in the control of the Kingdom of Jordan. The action came as a response to terrorist attacks staged from Jordanian territory, apparently from Kibiyah, which resulted in the death of an Israeli women and her two children. The Israel military response caused the loss of life of innocent civilians and ignited both a public outcry in Israel and, for the first time, piercing international criticism of Israel. In the public debate at that time, many arguments arose that are familiar to us today in the discussion of the war on terror. What are the limits of the right of self-defense? Does the fact that terrorists kill innocent civilians and afterwards hide within supportive civilian populations permit one to attack those civilians? Is it possible to fight terror without harming innocent people? Leibowitz posited

---

[54] Yeshayahu Leibowitz, *Torah u-Mitsvot ba-Zeman ha-Zeh* (Tel Aviv, 1954), 58–62.

that the issue is not the justification of war itself—which may be seen as a necessary evil[55]—but the manner in which war is to be conducted (*jus in bello*):

> This moral problem did not arise in connection with the war we conducted for our liberation and national restoration...Only one prepared to justify historically, religiously, or morally the continuation of the exilic existence could refuse to take upon himself the moral responsibility for using the sword to restore freedom. Therefore, in our religious–moral stocktaking, we neither justify the bloodshed of the war (in which our blood was spilled more than that of our enemies) nor do we apologize for it. The problematic issues concern the manner of conducting that war, which goes on to this very day.[56]

Leibowitz attempted to internalize the changes, to relate to contemporary reality, and to deal with the real and difficult challenges of military ethics. To that end, he turned to Jewish sources and his religious worldview. There is no doubt that his discussion of the issues is incomplete, and even perhaps does not reflect a consistent approach, but it is certainly interesting because of its pioneering quality and its creativity.

As we have seen, Leibowitz did not reject the legitimacy of waging war, but he did vociferously negate the international criticism leveled against Israel. He argued that in order to end World War II the

---

[55] He also denigrates the Haredi position mentioned above: "Attachment to the *Galut* (exile) and the opposition of many of the best representatives of Judaism to political redemption within historic reality was, in no small measures, a form of escapism reflecting the unconscious fear of such a test—fear of the loss of religious–moral superiority, which is easy to maintain in the absence of temptation and easy to lose in other circumstances" (Leibowitz, "Aharei Kibiyah," 230).

[56] Yeshayahu Leibowitz, "Aharei Kibiyah," 231 (author's translation).

United States killed with a nuclear bomb 100,000 people, most of them innocent women and children. How much more so were the Israelis justified in their actions, engaged as they were in a daily struggle "that has turned into a continuous nightmare of dread of violence and murder."[57] Nevertheless, he strongly rejected the idea of merely adopting the values that other nations apply in their wars. Thus, although the Kibiyah operation may have been justified according to international standards of military practice, that fact is not enough to grant it halakhic justification:

> It is therefore possible to justify this action, but let us not try to do so. Let us rather recognize its distressing nature. There is an instructive precedent for Kibiyeh: the story of Shekhem and Dinah (Genesis, 34). The sons of Jacob did not act as they did out of pure wickedness and malice. They had a decisive justification: "Should one deal with our sister as with a harlot?!" (Genesis 34:31)...Nevertheless, because of this action, their father Jacob cursed the two tribes for generations.[58]

Jewish tradition, according to Leibowitz, must go beyond accepted international standards and provide rules for such situations based on its unique worldview. He thus considered it an obligation to undertake moral deliberation and establish halakhic rules on questions of war.

The biblical story of Shimon and Levi—killing the men of Shekhem out of vengeance for the rape of their sister—and their father Jacob's reaction to it constitutes a biblical precedent for the claim that even a justified act may be accursed and unethical, especially in war. Leibowitz

---

[57] Ibid., 232.
[58] Ibid.

claimed, based on Maimonides, that Shimon and Levi were justified in what they did. Yet, in spite of this justification, Jacob cursed them with a harsh curse for generations.[59] From this Leibowitz derived the principle that in war the fact that an action is formally justifiable by law is not the complete picture. The act must be examined on an additional level, that of the ethics of war. Leibowitz concluded his article with the dramatic declaration, "Let us not establish our third commonwealth on the foundation of the curse of our father Jacob!" A number of weeks later, he expanded his article and added to this basic idea that there are ethical values that go beyond the rules of warfare, the imperative to eradicate any religious significance from war. These two principles, according to Leibowitz, are Jewish principles that are embedded in Jewish tradition.

The point of departure for Leibowitz's fundamental position was his religious ideology. It is therefore understandable that his target audience was primarily the rabbis and halakhic authorities whom he wished to activate to realize his vision of creating a serious legal corpus relating to the laws of war. Leibowitz's position, as it found expression in many of his writings, was not limited to the laws of war. He advocated the same process for all issues relating to sovereignty that arose from the establishment of a Jewish state, including many areas that had escaped the attention of the Halakha because of the historical circumstances of the diaspora. It is very plausible that the

---

[59] See Genesis 49:5–7. Apparently, Leibowitz adopts Maimonides' interpretation of the incident. See Maimonides (Rambam), *Mishneh Torah* (The Code), Book of Judges, Laws of Kings and Wars (*Hilchot Melahim*) 9:14. Maimonides established that the brothers acted in accordance with the law—that the men of Shechem were guilty enough to die because they had not prosecuted the perpetrator in accordance with the Noahide law requiring the establishment of a court system. Nevertheless, Maimonides does not state anywhere that the act was immoral. Nachmanides directly refuted the position of Maimonides. In his opinion, Jacob called the act "violence" and cursed his sons because there was no justification for the act that thy perpetrated. See Nachmanides (Ramban), *Commentary on the Torah*, Genesis 34:13, 49:5.

reason Leibowitz's voice was unheeded and did not impact on the Rabbinic leadership is related to the fact that he called for radical steps, involving far-reaching legislation. Leibowitz was unwilling to accept the traditional halakhic methods characterized by the reinterpretation of classical sources.

Toward a New Halakha II: Rabbi Shlomo Goren—Finding Modern Relevance in Ancient Sources

One of the prominent and interesting personalities who accepted the fundamental position of Leibowitz regarding the obligation to update the Halakha in order to address issues relating to sovereignty was Rabbi Shlomo Goren (1917–94). Yet, Rabbi Goren, who addressed this issue in the early days of the State of Israel, was only prepared to act within the context of the accepted parameters of halakhic discourse. Rabbi Goren founded the rabbinate of the Israel Defense Forces immediately after the establishment of the state and served as its head for approximately two decades. Subsequently, he served as the chief rabbi of Tel Aviv and then as the chief rabbi of the State of Israel. The scope of his literary work is broad, and many of his publications deal with military issues and the laws of war. He dealt with the many sides of military law, from the operation of a military camp to rules of engagement. The role of the military rabbis in modern European armies was to help Jewish soldiers maintain a Jewish lifestyle under military conditions. Even in Israel, many of the military rabbis perceived their role similarly. Rabbi Goren, however, sought to infuse the fabric of the evolving Jewish army with the spirit of Jewish law and ethics. He believed that the era of Jewish sovereignty demands that military rabbis relate to the army rather than to the individual soldier. He therefore aspired to write a codex of the laws of war that would fill in one of the gaps in existing codes of Jewish law such as the *Shulhan*

Arukh.[60] In the introduction to his book *Meshiv Milhamah,* which deals with military law, Rabbi Goren declares his objective clearly: "This book is intended to be a *Shulhan Arukh* for the military."[61] In essence, Rabbi Goren responded to the challenge voiced by Yeshayahu Leibowitz decades before, and expressed by many Religious Zionist leaders—the need for laws of state. The source of his pretension to create new laws was his religious Zionist belief that the significance of the Jewish state relates directly to the degree to which it reflects the Halakha. In a public debate in 1966 that dealt with spiritual perspectives on the Jewish people and the State of Israel, Rabbi Goren stated, "Jewish education is education for practice, for Judaism is manifested in the fulfillment of commandments. There is no Judaism that is just embedded in the heart."[62]

This is true not only on the individual level but also on the national level. Unlike other nations, Jewish nationalism is defined by its law rather than by territory or other sociological categories. Jewish law and its commandments are the essence of the Jewish experience. Thus the State of Israel has ethical and practical significance as a Jewish state only inasmuch as it functions according to the Torah. Goren based his argument on the famous statement of Rav Saadia Gaon (882–942), "Our Nation cannot be called a nation, but by its law." For this reason, Rabbi Goren was drawn to create a corpus of laws relating to the army and issues of security. He saw this as a mission and destiny that was timely at this turning point in the history of his people. Yet, how can a corpus be written in an area that has never before been addressed?

---

[60] *Shulhan Arukh,* written by Rabbi Josef Caro in the sixteenth century, is considered to be the authoritative code of Jewish law.

[61] Shlomo Goren, *Meshiv Milhamah* (Jerusalem: ha-Idra rabah, 1982/83), 1:10–12.

[62] Shlomo Goren, "Jewry and Judaism in the Modern World—the Jewish People, the Jewish State, the Jewish Law…and their Inter-relationship," paper presented at the Forum for Jewish Thought, Tel Aviv, September 5, 1966. The speakers were former prime minister David Ben Gurion, Dr. Nahum Goldman (the head of the World Zionist Congress), and Rabbi Shlomo Goren.

In the introduction to his main book on the subject, Rabbi Goren informs us of the heart of the problem:

This book of rulings is different...than all other books of responsa. On the topics of this book, we do not have an on-going tradition of rulings from generation to generation. There is nothing parallel in the *Shulhan Arukh*, or in other codes of law.[63]

Rabbi Goren contends that, although the Jewish law is a traditional spiral system in which each layer is built upon the previous one, it has the ability to deal with situations that have no precedent and require a high degree of creativity. Jewish law includes mechanisms that allow flexibility and the ability to respond to unprecedented situations:

In the laws of the Torah it states: "And you shall live by them." The Torah was given for life. There is room to delve into the sources in order to reveal creative ideas and derive innovative interpretations. I believe and am convinced that it is possible to solve the problems of our generation according to the Torah. For our Torah is not frozen in its context. The Written Torah and the Oral Torah are eternal, and have the strength to stand up to the difficulties of the generations...There is a saying in the Jerusalem *Talmud* (*Sanhedrin* 4:2): "If the Torah had been given in a clear and explicit fashion, we could not live by it. Why was it not? So that it could be interpreted either as the forty-nine aspects of impurity or the forty-nine aspects of purity." In other words, if the Torah had been given as a set code—this you can do and this you can't do—we would not

---

[63] Goren, *Meshiv Milhamah*, 1:10.

be able to live by it. But it was given in a flexible fashion...In this generation, we need the great scholars of Torah and Jewish law to take a "state approach" to issues and to relate positively to the historical turning point for the Jewish people represented by the establishment of the state.[64]

This would appear to be an accepted and self-evident line of thinking in the Talmud and the halakhic tradition. Clearly, the Talmud interpreted sacred texts in a very creative manner. Nevertheless, the crisis that modernity posed to the traditional community in the nineteenth century caused a conservative reaction within the Orthodox community that opposed any change. Rabbi Goren's approach was in its time bold and revolutionary. The individual capable of dealing with the creative rulings and interpretations required to meet this challenge would be a person who identified ideologically with Zionism and recognized the need to reformulate Jewish law to be compatible with the new reality of sovereignty, a person with a positive perspective on this historical turning point. A rabbi of this nature could rehabilitate Jewish laws in areas in which it is lacking, and formulate a corpus—a *Shulḥan Arukh*, in Rabbi Goren's words—on the subject of war and the use of force.

Rabbi Goren not only wanted to create a normative system; he also felt the need to define the ideological relationship to the use of force, i.e., to redefine the ideology and Jewish values relating to the use of force, to the military, and to war. Rabbi Goren wanted to revise the exegesis reflected in the Talmudic allegorical interpretations of the biblical approach to war. A significant number of his articles attempt to redefine the relationship between power and spirit in Jewish thought. He contended that Jewish tradition should not be viewed negatively because it praised the spirit at the expense of physical power, nor

---

[64] Goren, "Jewry and Judaism in the Modern World," 23.

should it be understood as taking a stance in opposition to the use of force. On the contrary, in his opinion, power is a necessary element of life, but it must be a means and not an end—it must be controlled and restrained by the spirit. The spirit that was used as an excuse to attack Jewish tradition as irrelevant at the time of the renewal of Jewish sovereignty and Jewish power became in Rabbi Goren's hands a source of glory for the tradition that sought to deeply implant an ethic of restraint to guide the use of force.

In Jewish law, as we have already mentioned, biblical law is applied in the manner that it was interpreted by the sages, and Rabbi Goren was certainly aware that the legitimacy of the use of force disappeared in Rabbinic literature. Nevertheless, he claimed that this happened because of the historical conditions imposed by the exile. In applying Rabbinic sources to modern circumstances, it is therefore necessary to take into account the historical circumstances in which Rabbinic literature took shape. Rabbi Goren therefore granted himself the liberty to return to the basic biblical texts and their simple meaning and to ignore some of the allegorical exegesis through which biblical wars were reinterpreted in Rabbinic literature. Rabbi Goren turned as well to post-biblical literature from the Second Temple period which was never considered in halakhic rulings, such as the Books of the Maccabees, works that traditionally were not utilized as normative sources and are not part of the Jewish canon. In practice, he embarked on a process that redefined the parameters of the canon. He implied that the canon of the rabbis was a canon from the period of the exile, and suggested the need, in the period of Jewish sovereignty, to broaden the canon and return to earlier sources from historical periods in which Jews had exercised political power. This process enabled Goren to return to the biblical wars and the Maccabean wars and to view them as legitimate sources for the creation of a new Jewish legal and ethical code for the contemporary wars of Israel. In this way, he sought to revive the relevance of the traditions, negating both the Haredi anti-Zionist arguments on the right and the arguments of those on the left who opposed the integration of Jewish values into issues of state. This process enabled him to say the following words that reflect his view on the reinterpretation of traditional sources:

[We see in the Talmudic sources:] "Who is the mightiest of the mighty?—One who controls his inclination, as it says: 'Forbearance is better than might.'" We learn that this definition does not come to negate physical heroism, but to define the mightiest of the mighty. From here, we learn that there are two levels of heroism. The lower level is physical heroism, and the higher level is spiritual heroism.[65]

As we have seen, Leibowitz viewed the biblical story of the rape of Dinah as a potential cornerstone upon which to build ethical principles of war. It is, therefore, of interest to examine Rabbi Goren's interpretation of the same story. There is a sharp debate among medieval commentators as to how the story should be understood. Maimonides (1135–1204) held that Shimon and Levi acted in accordance with the law when they killed the men of Shechem. In his opinion the men of the city were culpable because they did not prevent the rape *a priori* and did not prosecute the perpetrator after the fact. Nachmanides (1194–1270), in contrast, harshly criticized their action. In his opinion, Jacob cursed his sons who perpetrated the massacre because there was no justification for what they had done. The act of the brothers was considered "violence" and was cursed by Jacob because they killed innocent people. Not only were they innocent, but they were righteous in that they had circumcised themselves and taken on the laws of God

---

[65] Shlomo Goren, "ha-Gvura be-Mishnat ha-Yahadut" [Might in Jewish Thought], *Mahanayim* 7:9 (1979), 120 (in Hebrew).

that were in force at the time.[66] Rabbi Goren proposed an alternative interpretation of the story which sought to harmonize the approaches of Maimonides and Nachmanides. In his opinion, Maimonides is speaking about law and Nachmanides is speaking about ethics on an extralegal level. Indeed, Rabbi Goren concludes, it is impossible to conduct a war based solely on law. War must be conducted on the ethical level as well. In other words, although it may not be possible to prosecute Shimon and Levi for what they did, it was prohibited for them to do it. Rabbi Goren wanted this ideology to guide the Israel Defense Force. The harmony that Rabbi Goren created in the interpretations of Maimonides and Nachmanides reflects the greater harmony that he sought to create between the biblical and Rabbinic perspectives on the use of force, a harmony between the legitimacy of the use of force and the spirit that must guide it.

The analyses of Leibowitz and Goren of this biblical story are similar, yet there is an important difference between them. With regard to the question "What produced this generation of youth?" Leibowitz answered in the later version of his article that it was the result of attributing the concept of holiness to war. In contrast, Goren responded that it happened because they did not apply Jewish concepts of holiness to war.

Dhimmis in Translation in the Post-Imperial Post-Colony

Though very much part of pre-modern legal debates, the dhimmi is also a point of contemporary debate. For some, the dhimmi is an

---

[66] In Jewish tradition, there are other interpretations of this story, such as that of Judah Loew ben Bezalel (the Maharal of Prague 1525–1609), who claims that during a time of war it is impossible to differentiate between the guilty and the innocent. Maimonides justifies the action of Shimon and Levi by assigning guilt to the men of the city.

outmoded category that ought to be discarded with the advent of the state and citizenship as the principle marker of political community. For others, it remains a category that is politically relevant for Muslim-majority states that embrace an Islamist political stance while governing a religiously diverse polity. Outside the realm of formal state governance, the dhimmi also operates as a trope by which to articulate the boundaries of community and belonging.

In this last sense, the dhimmi curiously features in a passage of an Arabic book translated into English by the American convert to Islam, and Sufi shaykh, Nuh H. M. Keller. The book, entitled *Reliance of the Traveller*, is an English "translation" of a fourteenth-century Shafi'i *fiqh* source entitled '*Umdat al-Salik* by Ahmad b. al-Naqib al-Misri.[67] Originally published in 1991 and then revised in 1994, Keller's text provides both the original Arabic text and a facing English "translation," with commentary and appendices. Keller's text is worth examining because of the specific pedagogic protocols it applies to translation. Keller's "translation" of '*Umdat al-Salik* is not a full or complete translation of the pre-modern text. Keller states in his introduction that "[n]ot a single omission has been made from [the Arabic text], though rulings about matters now rare or nonexistent have been left untranslated unless interesting for some other reason. Parts untranslated are enclosed in brackets [in the Arabic]."[68] Although Keller encloses the untranslated *Arabic passages* in brackets, he does not indicate in the English text when and where he omits these passages. He refuses to include ellipses in the English section, since the omitted section is provided fully in Arabic and in brackets, which he says "was felt to suffice."[69] *Reliance*

---

[67] Ahmad b. al-Naqib al-Misri, *Reliance of the Traveller: A Classic Manual of Islamic Sacred Law*, trans. Nuh H. M. Keller, rev. edn. (Evanston, Illinois: Sunna Books, 1994).

[68] Al-Misri, *Reliance*, ix.

[69] Ibid., xi.

of the Traveller is a modern (re)presentation of a pre-modern text. Consequently, its intelligibility and significance cannot be measured in terms of the historical context in which the original text was written. Nor can the words on the page, in particular the English words, be read uncritically, as if their meaning is transparent.[70] Of course, there is a wide range of plausible examples to focus upon regarding contemporary debates on the dhimmi. But, given space limitations as well as the representative power underlying Keller's translation protocol, focusing on his treatment of the dhimmi will suffice as we bring this chapter to a close.

The relevant passage on the dhimmi is reproduced below. It concerns the terms of the contract of protection that non-Muslims are presumed to enter in order to live within the Islamic imperium. The quotation on the next page reproduces the English translation that Keller provides. Notably, in Keller's text, each page is divided into two columns, the English translation on the left-hand side and the Arabic on the right-hand side. The Arabic text that corresponds with the English translation of the quote contains passages that are not translated at all into English.[71] In the Arabic column, Keller designates those untranslated sections by enclosing them in brackets ([...]). In the reproduction of Keller's translation, the untranslated Arabic phrases appear in italics in order to distinguish them from what Keller actually chose to translate:

---

[70] Some who adopt the myth of persecution read the English text in Keller's *Reliance* as if it were transparently meaningful. They do not problematize the text or consider the ideological aim of the translator as equally significant, if not more so, as the design and structure of the text. See, for instance, Spencer, *Islam Unveiled*, 143–150. As suggested above, such a reading of *Reliance* ignores the way the text does more than simply convey the past tradition to a modern audience. It reshapes it and repackages it in light of conceptions of identity and community that are not explicitly acknowledged in the text.

[71] Others have criticized his work for excluding entirely the discussion on slavery in the original pre-modern text. See Kecia Ali, *Sexual Ethics in Islam: Feminist Reflections on Qur'an, Hadith and Jurisprudence* (Oxford: Oneworld, 2006).

Such non-Muslim subjects are obliged to comply with Islamic rules that pertain to the safety and indemnity of life, reputation, and property. In addition, they:

(1) are penalized for committing adultery or theft, though not for drunkenness;

(2) are distinguished from Muslims in dress, wearing a wide cloth belt (zunnar), *and wear around their necks a bell when in the public bath and not ride horses, but instead a mule or donkey in public;*

(3) are not greeted with "as-salamu ʿalaykum;"

(4) must keep to the side of the street;

(5) may not build higher than or as high as the Muslims' buildings, though if they acquire a tall house, it is not razed;

(6) are forbidden to openly display wine or pork, (A: to ring church bells or display crosses,)[72] recite the Torah or Evangels aloud, or make public display of their funerals and feastdays

(7) and are forbidden to build new churches. *If they enter a peace treaty concerning their territory for payment of the poll-tax, they are not prevented from that.*[73]

The difference between what the Arabic text provides and how the English is "translated" begs various questions about how Keller is using

---

[72] In the Arabic, he puts the phrase *wa naqus* in brackets but provides this translation of what that phrase is meant to convey.

[73] Al-Misri, *Reliance*, 608.

the dhimmi rules to educate a transnational, post-colonial Muslim readership.

Without an express explanation from Keller, any assessment of why certain portions are translated and others are not translated is tentative. But a comparison of Keller's choices with the historical analysis of the rules addressed below may reveal how *Reliance* is very much a modern project of edification in a context of fantasy. The pre-modern doctrines concerning what dhimmis could wear, what sorts of animals they could ride, and where they can walk in the street were legal modes of humiliation and subordination through demarcation. Why Keller refused to translate one set of provisions but translated another, given that they all evince what we moderns would call discrimination, is perplexing. Perhaps public baths are not as common today as they once were in the pre-modern period. Likewise, as the principal mode of transportation is motorized, the reference to horses, mules, and asses may seem outdated and irrelevant for a modern audience concerned with how to live in today's world. But walking in the street, greeting people, and living in community with people (e.g., in neighborhoods) are all things that remain part of contemporary experience.

To omit the license for dhimmis to build or repair their places of worship is also significant. Pre-modern Muslim jurists debated whether dhimmis could erect new religious buildings or renovate dilapidated ones. Whether dhimmis could do so depended on the type of land they occupied, their land tax liability, and whether the Islamic enterprise of government took control of the land by conquest or treaty. But in the modern context none of these factors would seem relevant given the absence of an Islamic imperial enterprise of governance. There is no Islamic empire that is conquering new lands where non-Muslims reside. Even the Islamic State in Iraq, though it may claim to be an expansive caliphal power, remains tied to a geopolitical territory as it performs its state functions. In the absence of such an enterprise of governance, the exception to the general ban is hardly relevant to the modern Muslim. However, and most tellingly, the same could be said about the general ban itself. In the absence of an imperial enterprise of governance, why the need to preserve the general ban on the construction of churches?

Arguably, the general ban is translated without the exception to proffer a romantic image (a fantasy) of a Muslim world repossessed of its former glory, which through the expression of law was an imperial splendor. The translation of the ban without the exception gives Muslims a telos of redemption, a romantic image of hope, at a time when Muslims live in a post-imperial and post-colonial world where the former glory of Muslim empire has ended and Muslims are increasingly the subject of suspicion, surveillance, and subordination. It acts like a balm to the modern pain of subservience that Muslims and Muslim-majority states suffer in their post-imperial *and* post-colonial condition.[74] This is an important point of contrast to the efforts of religious Zionist authorities to develop halakhic rules of war to fill the gap that came about during the long period in which the Jewish people lacked sovereignty. In the context of a very real Israeli sovereign the laws of war speak to a lived reality that, according to these rabbis, the Halakha ought to be made to address. But in the case of Keller and the dhimmi rules, the preservation of these rules (as opposed to their outright dismissal as legal relics) bolsters the bruised self-image of a people whose imperium has been penetrated, undercut, and dispersed.

---

[74] Scholars and Muslim reformists have deeply criticized the effect of the West and modernity on the nature and organic integrity of Islam for Muslims today. These criticisms are perhaps so ingrained in and accepted by the likes of Keller and the authors of the Saudi textbooks as to animate a framework of analysis that requires no justification. Much has been written on Islam and modernity. For some useful references, see Bassam Tibi, *The Crisis of Modern Islam: A Preindustrial Culture in the Scientific-Technological Age*, trans. Judith von Sivers (Salt Lake City: University of Utah Press, 1988); Fazlur Rahmn, *Islam and Modernity: Transformation of an Intellectual Tradition* (Chicago: University of Chicago Press, 1982).

CONCLUSION

The underlying thesis of this chapter is framed in ironic terms. All too often the relationship between Jews and Muslims is viewed through the lens of the Israel–Palestine conflict. That geopolitical conflict over land that is sacred to Jews, Christians, and Muslims becomes a lens through which to posit a more fundamental conflict between Muslims and Jews. On this reading of the political conflict, it is as if the two religious communities are in an interminable religious conflict and the Israel–Palestine conflict is merely a contingent, political manifestation of something deeper, abiding, and transcendent. This chapter, on the other hand, seeks to illuminate the striking similarity between Religious Zionists and conservative (e.g., Salafi) Muslims who invoke history to legitimate their political aims in the present. In both cases the resort to history does important political work, though not the political work that these groups might hope.

To (re)turn to history, or return to a particular history, is prospectively programmatic. For Religious Zionists the return to history is a call to action. For conservative Muslims the return to a particular history draws upon the past to frame the path to the future, and ultimately redemption. Given the politics implicit in their (re)turn to the past, it is perhaps more appropriate to suggest that, rather than returning to history, they are invoking "memory." As Michael Rothberg states, "memory is the past made present."[75] Memory, he writes, has two corollaries. First, "memory is a contemporary phenomenon, something that, while concerned with the past, happens in the present."[76] Second, "memory is a form of work, working through,

---

[75] Michael Rothberg, *Multidirection Memory: Remembering the Holocaust in the Age of Decolonization* (Stanford, California: Stanford University Press, 2009), 3.
[76] Ibid., 4

labor, or action."[77] In other words, memory is not simply a recounting; it is a contemporary activity with deeply political implications for the present and the future. It is, in short, a political project in which the past does political work in the present to chart the trajectory of the future.

Another way of analyzing these returns to history might be in the psychoanalytic terms of fantasy which Joan W. Scott brings to her historical scholarship. Writing about history and identity, she notes that our presumptions about certain identities (e.g., women, Muslims, Jews) as given, natural, or self-evident actually have a history to them as well. They do not "preexist their strategic political invocations" and are "invented as part of some effort of political mobilization."[78] For Scott the mechanics of this invention can be captured by reference to the phrase "fantasy echo." She writes, "Depending on whether the words are both taken as nouns or as an adjective and a noun, the term signifies the repetition of something imagined or an imagined repetition. In either case, the repetition is not exact, since an echo is an imperfect return of sound. Fantasy, as noun or adjective, refers to plays of the mind that are creative and not always rational."[79] The Religious Zionist's return to history and conservative Muslims' turns to a particular moment in history are both "retrospective identifications" that imagine repetitions, or in our case the repetition of a past tradition made present. But it is in the "making" present that the political work of memory or the fantasy lies.

In the case of Religious Zionists committed to the State of Israel and a Rabbinic way of life, creating a Rabbinic law of war makes the past (the Rabbinic tradition) present in a way that also defies the past of diaspora and the absence of sovereignty that the State of Israel has

---

[77] Ibid., 4.
[78] Joan W. Scott, *The Fantasy of Feminist History* (Durham, North Carolina: Duke University Press, 2011), 46, 47.
[79] Ibid., 48.

changed. The return to history, then, is not history in any positivist sense—there was no Rabbinic tradition on the law of war for reasons that are no less part of Jewish history than is the modern State of Israel.[80] Rather, the return is a call for struggle, action, and activity in the making of history. For Muslims who invoke the dhimmi rules, the invocation of the past in the present is also a memory or fantasy of a past made present. Their ability to do so without attending to the political context in which these rules were developed reflects the imperfection of memory as it echoes across time while reverberating in a present for very different purposes. In the case of modern Muslims invoking the dhimmi rules, the invocation of past legal doctrines does the very active work of soothing the pains of a present that is a constant reminder of the lost power, authority, and glory of an Islamic imperial past. In both cases the (re)turn to history is both an invocation and a subversion of the past in the present in order to make, if not remake, the present.

Certainly there is a bit of fantasy in thinking that a Rabbinic law of war might become the governing doctrine of the State of Israel.[81] The State of Israel does not seem likely to implement any new halakha of the law of war. Likewise, Muslim groups such as the erstwhile Muslim Brotherhood of Egypt sought to frame citizenship and leadership by reference (at least implicitly) to the dhimmi rules. Their platform was not so much an attempt to provide a pluralist approach to political belonging (state citizenship, religious identity,

---

[80] The law of war is merely one example of a lacuna in early Rabbinic legal history. The contemporary legal debates about it are part of a larger phenomenon of reviving the Rabbinic legal tradition in various areas of law that did not exist historically.

[81] Fantasy is particularly relevant to understanding the salience of Rabbinic Judaism, where the study of the law is about transmitting memory or the fantasy of a lost world that, for Religious Zionists, may be on the verge of returning, if it has not already. Other examples of Rabbinic law as fantasy include the intensive study of agriculture doctrines in the period of exile, given that such doctrines are only valid in the land of Israel.

ethnic identity, etc.) as it was an attempt to subvert the status quo model of state citizenship[82] with their memory of an Islamic ideal of political belonging. The current regime of citizenship is part of a political reality that invocations of dhimmi rules either ignore or seek to subvert in whole or part. That subversive potential is made very real in the case of ISIS (Islamic State of Iraq and Syria), which has already invoked the dhimmi rules in Syria as a mechanism of governance. The exceptional case of ISIS reveals the power that inheres in the fantasy, the memory, of (re)turning to history.

As much as the prospects of governance in accordance with a halakha of the law of war or an Islamic law of the dhimmi may be a fantasy, the echoing discourse of such memories has a pedagogic reality that reveals the power of law in constituting identities in opposition to one's proclaimed "other." For the halakhic law of war, what matters is how one treats one's enemy in war. But the very idea of a law of war presupposes that one has enemies, thus delineating a distinction between an "us" and a "them" to which the law—here Rabbinic law—ought to give content. Likewise, when Keller provides a quasi-translation of the dhimmi rules in a pre-modern Islamic law treatise, he is instructing his reader how to view himself or herself in relation (and in contrast) to the "other," cast here as the dhimmi. In other words, as much as some may see these (re)turns to history as fantastical, delusional, or even in breach of political realities, they

---

[82] Admittedly, even this form of citizenship seems to be under attack as governments increasingly treat citizenship as a state-managed asset to be granted or denied under circumstances (or prices) they deem appropriate. On citizenship for sale, see Youcef Gamal El-Din, "Buying Citizenship: Which Nations Are Affordable?" CNBC, November 14, 2013, http://www.cnbc.com/id/101198433. On Canada's legislative attempt to revoke the citizenship of those found guilty of major crimes, such as terrorism, see Michael Adams, Audrey Macklin, and Ratna Omidvar, "Citizenship Act Will Create Two Classes of Canadians," Globe and Mail, May 21, 2014, http://www.theglobeandmail.com/globe-debate/citizenship-act-will-create-two-classes-of-canadians/article18778296/

nonetheless exert political power through the formation of the religious self in part by defining the "other." These memories or fantasy echoes of a new halakha or an old dhimmi rule may never find their way into state governance, as their adherents and advocates may want, but they nonetheless do their political work pedagogically, in the formation of both the "self" and its "other."

PART II

6

Cross-Textual Reflections on Tradition, Reason, and Authority

ADAM B. SELIGMAN

To stand within a tradition does not limit the freedom of knowledge, but makes it possible.[1]

INTRODUCTION: TRADITION AND REASON

In their introduction to this volume, Anver M. Emon and Robert Gibbs discussed issues of authority, reason, and, critically, tradition. They pointed out that not only did the interlocutors of our chapters stand in different traditions but they carried within them different "internal libraries" that are, in essence, the struts and frames of each tradition. Traditions bridge reason and authority. Reason is in its nature universal, shared by all and an aspect of every tradition. Authority is somewhat different. Authority can never be fully identified with reason, and reason in itself is not authoritative. It is always mediated by a particular, idiosyncratic, and unique voice. In Hans Gadamer's terms, "Reason exists for us only in concrete historical terms, i.e., it is not its own master, but it

---

[1] Hans-Georg Gadamer, *Truth and Method* (New York: Crossroads Press, 1988), 324.

remains constantly dependent on the given circumstances in which it operates."[2] Reason may be as universal as a logical syllogism; authority—which is reason's enactment—always speaks a specific language. What gives a certain ruling, or social role, authority (and not just the power embodied, say, in the state's monopoly on the means of violence, to paraphrase Max Weber) is its connection to a particular set of cultural referents or meanings, to a sense of a shared past or the feelings of a shared community of fate among the different individuals, both those endowed with authority and those subject to it. Authority always contains an element of legitimacy that pure reason lacks, precisely because the makings of legitimacy always have some particular cultural and social locus, a shared sense of the sacred around which a moral community can cohere.[3] Reason does not know, from such an idea of moral community or from the particular character of its social ties, the obligations such ties engender and the commitments they entail. Reason, in its abstract universality, can make little sense of those human communities within which moral credit is granted and which we may consider to be communities of belonging. Such communities of course have their own beliefs, codes, and myths, indeed their own traditions. For such reasons, communities of belonging can never be universal. They are always bounded (just as families are bounded) and so set off from other communities. They have their own histories and their own trajectories, their own languages and jokes, their own obligations, their taken-for-granted worlds, their own flavors and smells—their own understandings of home. They may be more or less open, more or less ascribed, and their boundaries may be more or less permeable; but they do have boundaries and always define some "us" as against some "other." In this sense they always stand in some tension with

---

[2] Ibid., 245.
[3] Emile Durkheim, *The Elementary Forms of Religious Life* (London: George Allen & Unwin, 1915).

reason whose very universality challenges the particularist cast of each and every authority.

Traditions are those sites within which reason and authority come together. This is their strength, their defining cast, and their ambiguity as well. A tradition that claimed solely the universality of reason could evoke no authority—just as Esperanto has given birth to no Shakespeare, Goethe, Racine, or Rumi. On the other hand, a tradition that totally abjured reason and reasoned arguments could not last and maintain itself in the face of the world's challenges over generations. Religious and other movements that have rejected the reasonableness of daily life (millennial movements for example) have been short-lived.

In the simplest of terms, a "tradition" means simply a *traditum*, something that is passed down from the past to the present.[4] The objects and beliefs handed down can be, and are, infinite in variety and encompass the whole range of human production—material and spiritual. As the sociologist Edward Shils has taught us, we "live in the present of things from the past. Much of what [we] do and think and aspire to, leaving aside idiosyncratic variations, is an approximate reiteration of what has been done and thought for a long time, long before anyone still alive was born."[5] Traditions, then, are not to be identified with the type of static society that early social scientists imagined, a society "bound by the cultural horizons set by tradition, while modern society was seen as culturally dynamic oriented to change and innovation."[6] Rather we have come to recognize (as the quote from Shils above indicates) that in modern societies too our answers to some of the most fundamental problems of human existence— defining the major dimensions of social and individual meaning; the

---

[4] Edward Shils, *Tradition* (Chicago: University of Chicago Press, 1988), 12.

[5] Ibid., 34.

[6] S. N. Eisenstadt and S. R. Graubard, eds., *Intellectuals and Tradition* (New York: Humanities Press, 1973), 2.

relations between the cosmic, cultural, social, and political orders; the importance of such for the formation of collective identity; and the distribution (and redistribution) of resources—are informed by the "presence of things past." As Hans Gadamer explained, "That which has been sanctioned by tradition and custom has an authority that is nameless, and our finite historical being is marked by the fact that always the authority of what has been transmitted—and not only what is clearly grounded—has power over our attitudes and behaviors."[7]

TRADITION AND DIALOGUE

Crucially, we have come to recognize that every tradition addresses the above challenges by posing certain questions about the basic problems facing both societies and individuals as well as by providing a range of possible answers. The renouncer in Indian civilization is not identical with the monk in the Eastern Christian Church, nor is the Buddhist scholar/monk identical with the Jewish ideal of the *talmid chacham* (meaning both student of the wise and wise himself). The Islamic umma is not the people of Israel, nor—at the end of the day—is the Islamic legal decisor the same as his Jewish counterpart. Again, the universalism of reason, including of legal reasoning, is highly mediated within any given tradition by its particular languages, resonances, moral commitments, and revelations. It is these that provide the "ground of their validity" to what we see as our own moral choices and autonomous decisions.[8]

For this reason intellectual work (including the works in this volume) is always produced within an existing intellectual tradition. "An intellectual tradition is a set or pattern of beliefs, conceptions of

---

[7] Gadamer, *Truth and Method*, 249.
[8] Ibid., 249.

form, sets of verbal (and other symbolic) usages, rules of procedure, recurrently and unilaterally linked with each other through time. The linkage is the identity between two or more temporally sequential works. An intellectual tradition exists in a stock of works which those who participate in the tradition 'possess', that is, assimilate into their own intellectual culture and to which they also refer."[9] This "stock of works" is precisely that internal library referred to in the introduction.

It is here that we can begin to assess the boldness, uniqueness, and daring of this book's collaborative venture. For although there are many voices today, especially in the humanities and cultural studies— extolling the virtues of hybridity, multicultural, and cross-cultural production, decrying the discriminatory effects of essentialism and modernist or national culture, calling instead for the decentering of culture and its de-essentialization—very few of these voices take tradition seriously.[10] Very few of them bother to understand just how traditional and imitative are their own clarion calls. Their calls echo the voices of those modernist sociological thinkers that Eisenstadt and Shils were arguing against close to fifty years ago. Moreover, the "hybridity" they call for today can be found in traditional texts half a millennium old (to which we shall turn shortly).

What is so unique and important in this work is precisely that it seeks, not a new hybrid (which make sense for automobiles or Mexican television shows, but not for traditions going back millennia) but a dialogue across traditions. Dialogue is a vanishing art, as is listening and forbearing and bearing the *other* in a manner close perhaps to Rimbaud's dictum: *Je est un autre.* (Literally, "I is someone

---

[9] Ibid., 23.

[10] There is a vast literature on hybridity, much connected to post-colonial studies. One of the major texts in this genre is Homi Bhabha, *The Location of Culture* (London: Routledge, 2004). See also Anjali Praju, *Hybridity: Limits, Transformations, Prospects* (Albany: State University of New York Press, 2007); Marwan Kraidy, *Hybridity or the Cultural Logic of Globalization* (Philadelphia: Temple University Press, 2005).

ISLAMIC AND JEWISH LEGAL REASONING

else," meaning that, in reflecting on the self, one recognizes one's own strange, foreign, uncanniness.) This is precisely what is essayed here and, although some of the chapters are more explicitly dialogical than others, the give and take between traditions—a rhythm as each respectively appears and gives way to its "other," only to reappear again and so on—is evident in each. It may therefore be wise to remind ourselves of some pre-modern precedents (again, a *traditum*) of such writing.

The centrality of dialogue between traditions, and hence also by implication the self-restraint of bearing one's own silence which makes dialogue possible at all, is evident in all traditions. Thus, the injunction of the Apostle James, "let everyman be quick to hear but slow to speak," is quoted in the preface to Peter Abelard's *A Dialogue of a Philosopher with a Jew and a Christian* (1136). This quote, following a similar thought brought from the biblical book of Proverbs is, I believe, a reference to that silent speech between traditions upon which the understanding of each must rest. The point of Abelard's *Dialogue* was less to uphold traditional Christian assumptions as to highlight the thread of common reason in all positions: the Law of the Jews, the natural law of the philosophers, and the supreme Good of the Christian God. As noted by Peter Mews, Abelard in his dialogue "was primarily concerned not with proving Jews wrong, but with understanding the supreme good and how that supreme good should be reached. In terms of existing dialogue literature this was a novel perspective. By drawing attention to the common ground that was the goal of the philosopher, the Jew and the Christian, Abelard avoided the customary arguments generated by the uniqueness of the Christian claim."[11] Abelard was writing within a distinct genre of medieval dialogue which included such works as Gilbert Crispin's *Disputatio Judei et Christiani* (1092) and *Disputatio cum gentili* (1093)

---

[11] John Laursen and Cary Neederman, eds., *Beyond the Persecuting Society: Religious Toleration Before the Enlightenment* (Philadelphia: University of Pennsylvania Press, 1999), 39.

and Ramon Llull's *Liber de gentili et tribus sapientibus* (1275). Mews and Neederman both make the interesting claim that Abelard's dialogues go a step further than most in transforming such a genre from a demonstration of Christian superiority to an exercise in mutual edification.

Over four hundred years after Abelard, Jean Bodin wrote his famous *Colloquium heptaplomeres de rerum sublimium aracnis abditis* (*Colloquium of the Seven about the Secrets of the Sublime*), which is a dialogue between a Catholic, a Lutheran, a Calvinist, a Jew, a Muslim, an advocate of natural religion, and a skeptic. As argued by Gary Remer and Marion Kuntz, Bodin's dialogue departs from the accepted humanist script by refusing to reconcile all differences of religion in one single and unitary truth claim.[12] Though it was judged by many to be a "failure" for precisely this reason (failing that is of the accepted humanist resolution), Remer and Kuntz show how the dialogue itself points the way to a vision of "a unity based on multiplicity."[13] Unintentionally resonant with certain Sufi views of religious truth, Bodin's argument saw "religious truth as composed of distinct elements whose differences cannot be ignored."[14] A vision of the harmony of diverse perspectives (*concordia discours*) is presented as an essential element of religious truth. This harmony of beliefs is set off by the physical venue of the meeting, in Venice, which in the sixteenth century was the most international of cities, where the "commensality" of different faiths and religious creeds was more evident than anywhere in Europe.

Not published until the nineteenth century (although Leibniz had prepared a copy for publication in the seventeenth), Bodin's

---

[12] Gary Remer, *Humanism and the Rhetoric of Toleration* (University Park: Pennsylvania State University Press, 1996); Marion Kuntz, "Dialogue," in *Colloquium of the Seven about the Secrets of the Sublime*, ed. J. Bodin (Princeton, New Jersey: Princeton University Press, 1975).

[13] M. Kuntz quoted in Remer, *Humanism and the Rhetoric of Toleration*, 219, note 37.

[14] Remer, *Humanism and the Rhetoric of Toleration*, 219.

work was circulated in manuscript form for centuries.[15] Beyond the argument from conscience, Bodin's *Colloquium* makes a subtle and, for our purposes, a critical point. This is the valuation of dialogue for dialogue's sake. The art of discourse valued not for the sake of achieving a single and unitary truth, but, as it were, for itself (something perhaps analogous to the Jewish notion of *torah l'shma*—the pursuit of the Torah for its own sake rather than for any reward). The exchange of diverse views is of itself valuable. Not the negation of difference but its very upholding is the point of dialogue. This is not a Millesian use of dialogue to urge on reason in the pursuit of a knowable (though yet unknown) truth. It is rather a use of dialogue to school the interlocutors in the act of living in a *concordia discours*. None of the participants decides to change their position on the basis of the discussion. None converts. None is bested in the sense of having lost their argument. Nor do they agree that their differences are only in matters inconsequential, marginal, or inessential. Nor, yet again, do they espouse a lack of faith, or adopt arguments of relativism or skepticism toward religious truths (which would be the modern version of such a dialogue). All keep their faith or their belief in both the existence of truth and their own version of the truth. Yet, they tolerate difference and argument, even revel in it. (What comes to mind as analogy is the metaphor that Bodin puts in the mouth of one of his protagonists when discussing the meaning of harmony: "the flavor of fresh oil and vinegar is very pleasing but it cannot be mingled by any force.")[16]

To moderns, schooled on the absoluteness of the principle of contradiction, such an approach verges on the incomprehensible. Yet it

---

[15] Its call to religious tolerance preceded many later arguments, including those of John Locke, since it ends with the argument that "no one can be forced to believe against his will." (This was of course the central feature of John Locke's argument for religious toleration in his 1689 *Letter Concerning Religious Toleration*).
[16] Bodin, *Colloquium of the Seven about the Secrets of the Sublime*, 145.

is precisely here that we can see how much the current collaboration shares with such ancients in their ideas of dialogue, of restraint, and of that art of translation which is predicative of tolerance and living with the other. We may be schooled in a humility that is not skeptical, a modesty that is not relativist, just as we may learn a belief that is not absolutist. This is really the essence of dialogue, at least of Jean Bodin's *Colloquium* as well as in the work before us. What the participants of Bodin's *Colloquium* (as well as our own authors) endure (*tolerer*) are not others' beliefs but an aspect of their own act of believing and affirming. It is here that we can find the crux of both the dialogical act and its inherent restraint.

We may wish at this point to remind ourselves of Martin Buber's characterization of the three faces of dialogue, which I quote at some length, since it well illustrates both the dialogue of mutual restraint and its opposite—the absoluteness of the self, capable of only a mirrored monologue.

> There is genuine dialogue—no matter whether spoken or silent—where each of the participants really has in mind the other or others in their present and particular being and turns to them with the intention of establishing a living mutual relation between himself and them. There is technical dialogue, which is prompted solely by the need of objective understanding. And there is monologue disguised as dialogue, in which two or more men, meeting in space, speak each with himself in strangely tortuous and circuitous ways and yet imagine they have escaped the torment of being thrown back on their own resources. The first...has become rare; where it rises, in no matter how "unspiritual" a form, witness is borne on behalf of the continuance of the organic substance of the human spirit. The second belongs to the inalienable sterling quality of "modern existence."...And the third...a conversation characterized by the need neither to

communicate something, nor to learn something, nor to influence someone, nor to come into connection with someone, but solely by the desire to have one's own self-reliance confirmed by marking the impression that is made...an underworld of faceless specters of dialogue![17]

What our authors have achieved here is what Buber calls "genuine dialogue," which is the real meeting of an I and a Thou and through which—and only through which—are the creative potentialities of human cultural production possible. It is not coincidental that this "genuine dialogue" has taken place around what is perhaps the most traditional of all concerns—that is the twin axes of law and religion. Both have been handed down over millennia of human cultural production and in both we truly live in "the present of things from the past."[18] This is true even in our seemingly more secular cultural pursuits—as we see from debates on the preamble to the European Constitution; on issues surrounding religious education the world over; and on legal pluralism, multicultural jurisprudence, and the current rethinking of the famous secularization theses of the mid twentieth century.[19] All point to just how much our present is continually being made and made anew by our past. Religious traditions are still very much alive and playing a defining role in the lives of the majority of human societies. It is thus only to be hoped that the type of deep respect, restraint, and dialogue that makes itself felt in these chapters be explored in this realm.

---

[17] M. Buber, *Between Man and Man* (Boston: Beacon Press, 1954), 19–20.

[18] Shils, *Tradition*, 34.

[19] On education, see Adam Seligman, ed., *Religious Education and the Challenge of Pluralism* (New York: Oxford University Press, 2014). On multicultural jurisprudence, see Marie-Claire Foblets and Alison Dundes Renteln, eds., *Multicultural Jurisprudence: Comparative Perspectives on the Cultural Defence* (Oxford: Hart, 2009). On the secularization thesis, see David Martin, *On Secularizaton: Towards a Revised General Theory* (Oxford: Ashgate, 2005).

CROSS-TEXTUAL REFLECTIONS

In Islam too we can find a similar concept of restraint and forbearance before the other, which provides a similar repertoire. The
concept of *hilm* combines qualities of "moderation, forbearance and
leniency with self-mastery and dignity." In some ways it is surprisingly
akin to the idea of civility among the eighteenth-century Scottish
Moralists.[20] According to the great Islamic scholar Ignaz Goldzhier,
hilm combines moral integrity with mildness of manners and is
juxtaposed to al-Jahiliyya, that pre-Islamic period of Arab tribal
warfare when emotions governed actions and when "haughtiness,
arrogance and insolence" ruled, rather than the humble submission
of Islam.[21] Toshihiko Izutsu's study of *jahiliyya* and of *hilm* provides
a good sense of how central these terms are to appreciating the
inner phenomenology of Islam: how the "haughtiness" of the *jahiliyya* is contrasted with the forbearance of the *hilm* in defining the
idea of Islamic behavior.[22] In the Prophet's transvaluation of values
wrought on Arab society the practice of forgiveness and leniency
was considered *hilm*—an attribute of the patriarch Abraham and
ultimately of Allah. In this move the Prophet replaced the values
of tribal vengeance with those of forgiveness. Existential modesty
and humility, no less than epistemic doubt, exist in religious traditions as paths to the other, as ways of knowing, and as constitutive
of the space we can share with the other—again Buber's dialogue
of mutual relation. In sum, and as Gadamer has taught, tradition
is the genuine partner of communication "within which we have

---

[20] Adam Seligman, *The Idea of Civil Society* (New York: Free Press, 1992); idem,
"Animadversions on Civil Society and Civil Virtue in the Last Decade of the Twentieth
Century," in *Civil Society: Theory, History, Comparison*, ed. J. Hall (London: Polity
Press, 1995), 200–223.
[21] Ignaz Goldzhier, *Muslim Studies*, vol. 1 (London: George Allen, 1967), 201–208.
[22] Toshiko Izutsu, *Ethico-religious Concepts in the Qur'ran* (Montreal: McGill
University Press, 1966); idem, *God and Man in the Koran: Semantics of the Koranic
Weltanschuung* (Tokyo: Takeio Institute of Cultural and Linguistic Studies, 1964),
198–229.

fellowship, as does the I with a Thou."[23] As Gadamer makes clear again and again, the Thou, though always a specific one, is never an object, but always "in relation with us"—which is precisely what has been sought (and to no small measure achieved) in the essays that make up this volume.

AUTHORITY AND RELIGION

It is no mere coincidence that in this volume the dialogical production of individuals from within their respective traditions progresses on the plane of matters pertaining to authority and religion. For what can be truly countenanced from a religious position is a grounding of the individual not in a socially determinant and yet accidental community of his or her birth but in a set of "ultimate concerns," to use Paul Tillich's phrase.[24] This has provided an argument for human dignity and worth in all the monotheistic traditions. It is rooted in the very breakthrough to transcendence that characterized the Axial Age.[25] In the Western tradition and its modes of institutionalizing the Axial chasm, the individual came to exist primarily as an individual-in-relation-to-God, which, as Jaspers notes, is precisely what provided the "resoluteness" of "personal selfhood...experiencing the highest freedom in the limits of freedom in nothingness." Each individual became a unique entity "immediately responsible to God for the welfare of his soul and the wellbeing of his brother."[26] The valorization of the indi-

---

[23] Gadamer, *Truth and Method*, 321.

[24] Paul Tillich, *Systematic Theology* (Chicago: University of Chicago Press, 1971).

[25] Karl Jaspers, *The Origin and Goal of History* (London: Routledge & Kegan Paul, 1952); S. N. Eisenstadt, ed., *The Origins and Diversity of Axial Age Civilizations* (Albany: State University of New York Press, 1986); Benjamin Swartz, ed., *Wisdom Revelation and Doubt: Perspectives on the First Millennium B.C.* (Cambridge, Massachusetts: American Academy of Arts and Sciences, 1975).

[26] Jaspers, *The Origin and Goal of History*, 63.

vidual is through his or her "consecration to God." It is, in Troeltsch's words, "only fellowship with God which gives value to the individual."[27]

Thus, the transcendent, the first fully generalizable other, becomes the basis for a non-negotiable sacred, one seen to exist beyond all possible social constructions, beyond all negotiation. It provides the definitive description of reality, especially of normative reality or rather the normative aspects of our material reality. Transcendence, together with the authority inherent to it, reorganizes the relations within the mundane realm. The authority of the transcendent sets it off from what we may term the merely material or physical power of magic. Magic relates to the supernatural realm as simply another form (or extension) of the natural world. Consequently, magic has its own set of tools to mediate the impact of the supernatural on the world of humanity. (Just as one must engage in the chopping down of trees to make a house, magic does something similar in the realm of the supernatural.) Thus one may, in particular circumstances, need to sacrifice one's daughter in order to get the wind up to continue the course of the fleet to Ilium.[28] A comparison of the sacrifice of Iphigenia with that of Isaac highlights this difference between a magical manipulation of the cosmos and the bending of the will to the dictates of a transcendent deity. For transcendence is not concerned with building houses or keeping the wind in one's sails, but with reorganizing the mundane world in accordance with principles now deemed transcendent in nature—which are precisely the themes addressed by all our authors as together they illuminate, through a dialogue, the nature of the sacred law in Jewish and Islamic traditions.

In this reorganization the individual emerges as a moral evaluator (as for example in the prophet Nathan's admonishment of King

---

[27] Ernst Troeltsch, *The Social Teachings of the Christian Churches*, vol. 1 (New York: Harper & Row, 1960), 55.
[28] See Adam Seligman, *Modernity's Wager: Authority, The Self and Transcendence* (Princeton, New Jersey: Princeton University Press, 2000).

David). The idea of transcendence provides a locus of moral authority and selfhood, albeit one foreign to modern sensibilities. It does so, moreover, without falling back on ascriptively defined and primordial categories of selfhood. However paradoxical it may seem to us, its very authority calls the self into being as moral evaluator, as agentic in a sense other than power. The chapters devoted here to issues of gender roles, virginity checkers, and the rights of fathers over daughters illustrate just how far this moral evaluation—rooted in tradition—can question and upturn authority's received assumptions.

Problematizing existence, transcendence drives the self to encounter Being. In this encounter, agency can become an existential and moral endeavor rather than simply the exercise of power. A heteronomously constituted self is constructed in tension with transcendent dictates—even in issues extending beyond human social relations and encompassing, as Beth Berkowitz and Marion Katz show us, our relations with animals.

It is this truth that, for philosophers like Hermann Cohen, provided the basis for the possibility of an ethical stance and hence the "recognition of the particular and personal being" that Buber notes above. Thus Cohen explains:

> The correlation of man and God is in the first place that of man, as fellowman to God. And religion proves its own significance first of all in this correlation of the fellowman to God, in which, indeed, man as fellowman becomes a problem and is engendered through this problem. The share of religion in reason is the share of religion in morality, and no problem of morality takes precedence over this problem of the fellowman. The possibility of ethics is tied to this problem.[29]

---

[29] Hermann Cohen, *The Religion of Reason out of the Sources of Judaism* (Atlanta: Scholars Press, 1995), 114.

CROSS-TEXTUAL REFLECTIONS

Again, as we have seen in this book, this ethical stance can be directed in many different directions, both within the social world and reaching out to our relations with others of God's creatures. The unique dialogical nature of each chapter here, the bringing into dialogue of two traditions, achieves but a heightening of this ethical stance in the mutual recognition of more than one tradition and set of texts.

This takes us immediately to issues of authority. For it is in the roles and figures of authority that traditions connect the organization of the social and political world to the terms of individual and social meaning and solutions posited to the overarching dilemmas of human existence, especially as these come to define matters of collective identity and the distribution of resources (symbolic and material) in society—in the differences say between a Christian *ecclesia*, Muslim umma, and *am Yisroel*, or the existence of priests, prophets, or, for that matter, business elites within different social formations. Or think of the debates over usury in all the monotheistic traditions and their implications for economic development, social stratification, and elite development.[30] Authority is thus the subject of the chapter by Cohen and Ahmed, whose concern is the link between the institutional structures of Rabbinic or 'ulamic authority and the transcendent terms legitimizing that authority (the legitimation challenged in some of the other chapters in this book). The chain of authority and its links are thus matters of grave concern in both traditions, where at the end of the day, in Gadamer's words, "authority has nothing to do with obedience, but rather with knowledge."[31]

---

[30] See Max Weber, *The Protestant Ethic and the Spirit of Capitalism* (New York: Scribner, 1958); R. H. Tawney, *Religion and the Rise of Capitalism* (Piscataway, New Jersey: Transaction Press, 1998); S. N. Eisenstadt, ed., *The Protestant Ethic and Modernization: A Comparative Perspective* (New York: Basic Books, 1968); Benjamin Nelson, *The Idea of Usury, From Tribal Brotherhood to Universal Otherhood* (Chicago: University of Chicago Press, 1969).

[31] Gadamer, *Truth and Method*, 248.

The ultimate challenge of any tradition is how it negotiates its boundaries with other traditions, with other sources of authority, in terms of meaning-giving order and definitions of collective belonging—in short, with other frameworks and sources of knowledge. No tradition exists in splendid isolation from the world. Although the rabbis of the Talmud engaged in such a conceit, it was always clear just how much foreign and gentile realities influenced the construction of the Jewish legal codex. This was especially true in the Middle Ages, as Haym Solevitchik has shown in his study of regulations concerning gentile wine.[32] We know that in late eighteenth-century France a copy of the *Shulchan Aruch*—the definitive code of Jewish law, used to this day to regulate the daily life of observant Jews—was placed in every parliamentary court in France on order of the king. Presumably this was done because Jews made much use of gentile courts, even though they clearly were forbidden to do so by Jewish law.[33] In some decisions on issues of tort law, Jewish decisors in eighteenth-century France explicitly followed non-Jewish rulings, again in clear violation of what the authority and "tradition" of Jewish legal doctrine.

Traditions, then, are not closed systems, not absolutes, and not directed solely inward. They cannot be, since the societies they regulate are always in contact with an "other," a gentile, or unbeliever, someone inhabiting other frames of meaning, knowledge, and authority—other "communities of belonging," to use our earlier locution. This is the theme addressed in the chapter by Emon and Edrei: the Jewish "return to history," that is, to concrete, iterated, institutional

---

[32] Haym Soloveitchik, *Wine in Ashkenaz in the Middle Ages* (Jerusalem: Zalman Shazar Center for Jewish History, 1988) (in Hebrew); Haym Soloveitchik, *Principles and Pressures: Jewish Trade in Gentile Wine in the Middle Ages* (Tel Aviv: Am Oved, 2003) (in Hebrew).

[33] See Jay Berkowitz, *Protocols of Justice: The Pinkas of the Metz Rabbinic Court 1771–1789*, vol. 1 (Leiden: Brill, 2014).

relations with gentiles, from—and this is crucial—a position of power and control. How can a tradition, developed under conditions of powerlessness and (relative) isolation, reinterpret itself to fit the reality of the power that comes with a state, and with it the forces of violence that a state controls. The Muslim tradition, on the other hand, through its dhimmi rules has a long history of governing and regulating the other and, though it be no longer in force, of providing a template through which observant Muslims can orient themselves to an always existing, if no longer subservient, other. Contemporary developments in the Israel Defense Force's rabbinate show that this orienting-through-tradition is happening, in perhaps a very unfortunate manner, in Israel as well.[34]

In many countries of the Middle East and South and Central Asia, and in Europe as well, all traditions are facing more and more the challenge of an encounter with external bases of knowledge, authority, meaning, and identity. How this encounter will be negotiated will to no small extent define the world we leave to our children. This slim volume is a small attempt to present—*lege artis*—a model predicated on dialogue, forbearance, and mutual engagement. It draws inspiration from Karl Jaspers' insights into the nature of truth, its plurality, and the means given to access it:

> The plurality of truths…becomes even more untrue when they become mutually indifferent and simply rest alongside one another…There is a sophistry of easy tolerance which wishes to be valid, but not to be really touched. On the other hand, there is the truth of tolerance which listens and gives and enters into

---

[34] See, for example, Gerald Blidstein, "The Treatment of Hostile Civilian Populations: The Contemporary Halachic discussion in Israel," *Israel Studies* 1.2 (1996), 27–45; Stuart Cohen, "Safra v'Saifa vma Shebenehem, Itzuv Halachat Tzava v'Milchama B'Yisrael" [Halakhic Discourse of War in Israel, 1948–2004], *Iyyunim b'tekumat Yisrael* 15 (2005), 239–274.

the unpredictable process of communication by which force is restrained in such a process, man reaches from his roots to the heights possible for him.[35]

Only thus, our authors seem to indicate, do traditions provide, as Gadamer claimed in our opening quote, the possibility of knowledge.

---

[35] Karl Jaspers, *Reason and Existenz* (New York: Noneday Press, 1954).

7

The Social Life of Reason

ROBERT GIBBS

F or many readers, especially philosophers, the texture of the
chapters in this book display too little of what they would consider philosophy. What seems to predominate is the scholar's
interest in legal matters, rulings, cases, classic texts, jurists' disagreements; and upon those matters are woven complex reflections about
the role of law in society and the task of reading law. This recourse
to legal matters animated our project from the start, and indeed we
chose to address the questions that concerned us by reading legal matters—rather than by abstract argument or by navigating conceptual
analysis. Although we dared to claim to engage the minds of jurists
and scholars of earlier ages, what we have witnessed most readily is
the thinking of each other—thinking formed in school (both the
university and religious circles). This engagement with each other
has produced a different sort of book, and quite a different sort of
philosophy, if we can claim that name. Adam Seligman reflects in
Chapter 6 on the sociological implications of this project; my task
is to take a philosophical view—which is easier than it might seem,
for this book emerged, through ongoing conversations with Anver
Emon and several others, from a project that was designed to explore
a philosophical point of view.

I will locate the work we have done and the writings before you as both "philosophy of law" and as "jurisprudence," but I begin with two sets of confusions. There are distinct pairs of meanings for both "philosophy of law" and "jurisprudence." First, philosophy of law. (a) Philosophy as a second-order reflection on a field of knowledge and practice (the law). We could speak of philosophy of science, or philosophy of language—and in each case we would assume that the field (e.g., law, science, language) is both given and distinct *before* we start to philosophize. (b) The "of" means that law, rather than being a given field of knowledge, is rather a kind of judgment and so is central to philosophy. Philosophy, in this case, concerns universal judgments, which are called, generally, "laws," and so philosophy is primarily about reasoning with laws. In this sense there is no philosophy without law. If the first instance suggests that philosophy's task follows or even depends on legal matters, the second will say that a specific general view of logic and law governs both philosophy and any body of concrete laws, e.g., political, social, physical, linguistic.

"Jurisprudence" is also capable of being two quite different sciences. (a) The study of the reasoning used by jurists, again explored for the sake of insight into their reasoning. (b) A philosophical exploration in political philosophy of root concepts of justice and authority, or lawfulness and order. Both pairs of concepts are quite intriguing. The first terms of each set seem, if not empirical, at least concrete and filled with particular stuff; the second terms of each set are the site of conceptual and abstract work that many regard as the core of philosophy. My own work has been led by a desire to see what happens if we argue from the first term in each pair to the second. Taking legal matters and legal reasoning in their concrete forms, we would first philosophically attend to the legal matters. We might from that study discern a philosophical vision of logic and law in general, which itself might discern not only the root concepts of justice but also the originary shape of philosophical judgment and reason.

Such a view of philosophy raises the stakes for the essays in this volume a bit high: in my reading they become a guide to reason in general and philosophy expanding beyond the study of laws. My argument proceeds from casuistry and specific legal texts. What we may see there are models of reasoning or even abductive cases, from which the legal matter can be clarified. The root concepts will be authority, history, boundaries of the law, invention, personhood, and witness. These are features of many traditions of laws—features in play and also made explicit by reflection. I am not saying that any reflection on the limits of invention from a tradition is philosophy. Rather, I am suggesting that exploring how juridical invention is limited in a tradition may allow us to achieve philosophical insight about those limits. But, and this is the key point for this project, such reflection is heightened greatly by contrast with a second tradition. If one tradition depends extensively on the assessment of the reliability of historical lines of transmission and another one has no interest in this assessing exercise, then how do we understand the role of such assessment in law? Do we say these and those are both the words of law? Are we obliged to find a common ground? Do we leave the conversation with a deeper sense of the correctness of one tradition—or perhaps the justification for and explanation of making (or omitting) such assessments are more salient ?

At the heart of this project is a way of thinking that brings philosophical reflection to matters of law and brings important insights from these discussions to philosophy. I will first offer a philosophical framework for the work in the project. Then in the second part I will draw on several chapters to indicate what philosophical questions have become visible for me through the writings of my colleagues. All of this will happen pretty quickly, in order to give a sense of why a philosopher would want to turn to this activity and what he or she can learn from these readers and readings.

A PHILOSOPHICAL FRAMEWORK

Although I would hesitate simply to subscribe to the system of
Hermann Cohen, I will follow his strong claims for jurisprudence as
an organon for ethics.[36] That is, the way to study ethics is to study
the laws and the human science of interpreting laws. Cohen's philosophy takes as its "given" not experience or tradition but the sciences.
Mathematics serves as the organon for philosophical interpretation
of the theoretical sciences. Hence philosophical logic has mathematics
as its organon for constituting knowledge. The parallel argument will
be that in the human sciences (*die Geisteswissenschaften*) the science of
law or jurisprudence is an organon for philosophy forming ethics. This
is a bold claim. Ethics must arise from the human sciences, and not
from some sort of moral experience or, even more troubling for Cohen,
from some inner personal struggle. And it points to the intimacy of
law and ethics. In another essay, I would explore how this challenges
the division of law and ethics in Kant and trace the division back to a
Protestant tradition that diminishes the role of law in ethics. What is
required for this essay is simply the recognition that the ethical self and
its relations to others are actually formed in law, allowing both a moral
and normative space in legal matters, and a constructive role for laws,
including coercive law, in ethics. Thus we do not have a sequestered
private court (the isolated soul) for ethics, any more than there is a
private mind for knowing. But a thorough connection of legal reasoning
and ethics is what leads ethics to consider these specific legal matters.

To give two short examples from Cohen of what this might mean:
ethics concerns actions (*Handlungen*). Usually one tries to get access to
what an action is through an account of psychology and one often has
recourse to a will that is internal and becomes externalized. Or action
is interpreted as a bodily motion of a person, particularly some kind

---

[36] Hermann Cohen, *Ethik des reinen Willens* (Berlin: Zweiter Teil, 1904).

of voluntary motion. For Cohen, action is first of all something that could be brought forward in court, playing on the Latin *actio*. Thus the actions that are ethical and are subject to ethical judgments will be those that are claimable in court, that are subject to adjudication. Jurisprudence will help us clarify which sorts of bodily motions or utterances, etc., are attributable to a person from the shape of the jurisprudence of imputation. The boundaries of my actions will be sorted by legal cases and reasoning.

Alternatively, and this is a key insight in Cohen, my agency itself is created in the legal fiction called a contract. Cohen was one of the inventors (discoverers?) of the I/you relation, and one form of that occurs in contract. The specific responsibility and rights of the *I* arise in relation to another (a *you*) and do not precede it. Property, status, and contract all arise from this I/you relation, in which self-consciousness arises through a relation with another, a legal relation, and which engenders my self as beholden to the other in reciprocal relation. No *I* without *you* means, specifically, that the ethical capacity of asserting my own rights emerges from a contract where I bind myself to a *you*. The jurisprudence of contracts will then allow us to see the limits of this emerging self-consciousness. This means that property derives from a relation to another person, indeed a duty to the other, and so economics in law will follow from ethical relations.

The second part of the framework is the claim that revelation is the creation of reason, also from Cohen.[37] Cohen recognizes that the ancient Greeks also framed a concept of reason, but he is interested in linking reason and revelation tightly together. Here, too, is a contrast to a predominantly Christian tradition (with exceptions), that sees revelation and reason as contrary, or at least as fundamentally independent. If they are opposed or at least separate, then philosophy must

---

[37] Hermann Cohen, *Religion der Vernunft aus den Quellen des Judentums* (Wiesbaden: Fournier Verlag, 1988).

adhere to reason and be suspicious and reluctant to take revelation seriously at all. In such a perspective, religious law will be of almost no intrinsic import for philosophy of law (but may matter to anthropology or sociology or history of law). For Cohen, the revelation to the Jews is the source for their learning to reason, and this occurs especially in the legal texts and their ongoing tradition of interpretation. Reason arises, in this tradition, when a revealed text is doubled up with a second or even a third version of the same. Such repetition requests reasoning, and often legal reasoning. For example, the Hebrew Bible has long been recognized to have two narratives of creation (Genesis 1:1–2:4 and 2:5–3:24). Twice the human being is created. The first is grand and cosmic—according to Cohen, mythic. The second is a narrative of commands, knowledge, and the fall—an ethical narrative for Cohen. In it man becomes an ethical agent through the dialogues.

But even more compelling is the repetition that occurs as the fifth book of the Bible (Deuteronomy), which is called "The Repetition of the Law" in Jewish tradition. Here not only narratives are repeated, but also laws, and there is subtle variation—even in the Ten Commandments. These repetitions of Deuteronomy are the birth of legal reasoning in the Jewish tradition. They have served as a well-spring for generations of scholars and allow the Jewish tradition to progress in scrubbing off the mythic in search of a rational jurisprudence and thus ethics. Perhaps this is most disruptive to the familiar account of revelation as it is supposed to partake of divinity and be utterly constant, with no variation. These repetitions, however, are characteristic of most scriptural traditions, and certainly of Judaism, Islam, and Christianity. Thus revealed texts incite one to reason and to interpret—precisely through their repetitions and variations. But before I move to the comparative aspect of our project, I wish to underscore again that revelation need not be opposed to reason, and that reason itself is linked to our creatureliness—to a relation to God. We can misuse reason, and we do sin, and we can also misconstrue revelation, but the claim here is that what calls for reason itself is revelation, and that ethics does not stand against religion.

This philosophical framework then doubles these two claims: a need to study jurisprudence to frame an ethics, and that religious law itself is a source of reason. Either of these claims might have disqualified what is happening in the essays that comprise Part I of this book as a resource for philosophical ethics, but in the combination we have the guiding principles that we outlined in the introduction: reason and authority. The historical reinterpretations of jurists negotiate ways to constitute the agency and complex set of responsibilities of each person. Religious law need not be seen as totally distinct from and opposed to the philosophical way to approach ethics; rather, in its ongoing negotiation with authorities, religious jurisprudence yields unique insights into the basic principles of ethics and philosophy of law.

The third part of the philosophical framework moves beyond the historical stretch of interpreters in any one tradition to seek a philosophical gain by contrasting two traditions. In religious discourse there is often a claim that the "other" should convert to my religion, because only one religion can be true, and so often is true to the exclusion of all others. In philosophical discourse, there is often a parallel claim that one perspective or system or even thinker is right and that reason would compel everyone to adhere to that philosophy. Again, there is an exclusive claim about truth, and a compulsion that embraces everyone. Ironically, the philosophers regard the religious believers as dogmatic and unjustified in insisting on conversion, while some theologians regard the compulsion of reasonable argument, with its compulsion toward compromise, as failing to provide the warrant of faith. Beyond these exclusive perspectives are two further options for comparison. The first is to find a common ground between the two traditions. Ironically, the search for common ground all too often reiterates the logic of exclusive universality: everyone should confess or adhere to this ecumenical truth, which will comprise only the essential part from either tradition. The second is relativism, that each tradition is true for its adherents and those raised with it, but false for others. For these latter two options conversion is not possible.

The logic of plural truth and traditions offers a different frame of philosophy. It is not easily discerned within these monotheist religious legal traditions. They tend to regard legal pluralism as a fact of political happenstance, and each understands its own ongoing tradition as not bound to the changes and jurisprudence of the other traditions. In the university context, however, this logic may arise from a historical or a philosophical viewpoint. That is, one may see that the jurisprudence of Islamic and Jewish law intersects and also diverges in historical events and discern this by a careful historical study. Alternatively, one could see those patterns by looking at the patterns of the jurisprudence and nurture openness to pluralism not so much from a historical vantage point as from rejection of a logic of exclusive truth. We can undertake to compare two traditions not so much from outside them as from interpreting jurisprudence within them, and at the same time, hold open the plural models of legal reasoning and theological reflection.

One key philosophical premise here is that each tradition does aspire to a universal truth on the basis of its singular perspective. Each can discern in its ongoing debates and reinterpretations that there is a desire to claim that this law is true, and true for everyone. But the pairing of traditions allows us to see paired aspirations and to see that the limits are not a simple rebuttal of that aspiration. Pluralism can help guide us to see how multiple traditions can contribute to truth and can permeate any specific tradition.

The fourth piece of the philosophical framework, however, is that the work of study is conducted by particular people, who can benefit by studying together. In the Scriptural Reasoning practice we mentioned in the introduction, there is ongoing discussion of how trust in each other produces a distinctive sort of fellowship through reading scriptural texts together. In our legal textual practice, that trust became real by engaging the expertise and knowledge that each person brings is vital to exploring the contrasts between the two traditions. In our intro- duction we wrote of the internal library. In any conversation, one brings one's own experience and mind into the dialogue, but when scholars read together, when they study complex texts, the discipline and the wealth of knowledge they bring are put in the service of interpreting and exploring the text. My own philosophical task tends to idealize the texts in relation to the philosophical task of ethics. Idealization is not necessarily a bad interpretative choice, especially to discern philo- sophic method and access to the highest kinds of truth, but the scholars assembled were not so rosy in their assessment of their own traditions. Our project created asymmetrical dialogues, but as such they created imaginative and reflective space. In each episode, we would stage a meeting between those for whom their own library included or would easily include the texts and the jurisprudence about the matter (the texts of their own scholarly tradition), and other readers whose library was parallel but separate from the texts. Thus we created a teacher– student dyad, but in a master class context where the student had an affiliated expertise. So the scholars were permitted to be ignorant and to learn from those from whose tradition the text came. This permis- sion for a scholar to be a novice is a hugely liberating experience. The process of learning in this context is rapid and exciting: the otherness of the text and the parallel expertise accelerate the excitement of engage- ment. And for the "teaching" partners, this need to explain a text or a specific principle of legal reasoning to a ready student is also liberating. Our familiar principles and texts, concepts and contexts are rendered new and disclose facets that go unnoticed in the scholarly enterprise conducted with scholars who already share one's own internal library.

If one tended to be critical of one's own tradition's texts, in this context we were usually able to extend much credit to the jurisprudence of the other tradition. Again, to acknowledge ignorance allows one to learn from a text and from the other tradition's scholars. Nonetheless, scholars take a stand near a tradition—and, in the cases where they have been adherents to the legal tradition, somehow within that tradition—but as scholars in the academy our participants challenged and criticized their own traditions. None was complacent, and what they discerned was that the jurists of old also were challenged and critical, allies but hardly passive to the tradition they received.

Our project reiterated this experience of learning with effects of delight and of humor, since none of us had power over the others in the way either of academic-field struggles or of competing religious authorities. But in such an environment insights are won and developed in safety and with the aid of great knowledge and skill. The chance to learn, to be engaged in pedagogy, was singular because we were not seeking a convergence of the two legal traditions; rather the paired asymmetrical learning embodied a specific epistemology. The absence of conversion and of consensus does not mean that insight is not garnered. What most of us know is that the discomfort in our own tradition is much sharper than that between traditions—because in part we know we don't know. The dialogue is constituted by the Socratic moment of learning that we don't know. There is here a complex mediation: the text is a medium between the scholars, and the scholars also mediate to each other the legal reasoning. In this complex interaction new insights emerge, and voices balance each other.

PHILOSOPHICAL QUESTIONS

The chapter in this volume emerged from this context of reading across traditions around a table. In several cases we had an opportunity to meet over the drafts and, indeed, to argue about them in a way quite different from the pedagogic dialogue about the legal texts themselves. The stakes became higher as we stepped onto the page in our own names and voices. This, too, accentuated the safety of our workshop practice, but also revealed the gap between the in-person experience and the representations of the dialogue. Nonetheless, against the background of this four-part framework, a brief tour of the chapter will offer us some important philosophical insights. These insights arise as questions that hold the two legal traditions apart but also allow them to intersect.

Question One:
How Does Law Define the Limits of Being a Person?

In close proximity to Cohen's claim that ethical action is based on legal proceedings and imputation of agency, the chapter by Katz and Berkowitz explores how reflection on animal suffering and duties to aid animals can plunge into reflections about human agency. The animals of their chapter (loaded beasts of burden, a calf for slaughter, cats and dogs, and weasels) are all regarded within the human environment. Although there are general human obligations to them that arise in large measure from their being alive and prone to suffering, there are also intersecting interests that intersect with legal requirements and prohibitions. Sometimes it seems as though the question of standing in court is held to trump all other qualities, but more important in Katz and Berkowitz's dialogic reading is the discovery that both legal traditions have a wider horizon for their reflection. Whereas today we would separate ethics from law, the scholars they review find them tightly bound in interaction and at times in tension. Katz cites a text that our project had explored, that understood normativity in a richer spectrum than merely obligation and prohibition. As the scholars analyse the complexity of legal distinctions, issues for ethics are brought to light. For in parallel with the animals who lack legal standing are human beings who similarly lack that standing: slaves, wives, children, and, of course, men from other religions. Jurisprudence revels in ranges and intersecting kinds of distinction because truth is found in these shades and limited parallels.

Moreover, this chapter, like others we will consider, discovers the tensions between strata of legal reasoning. As Berkowitz shows, Rava both initiates (in departure from his predecessors) a new attention to animal suffering, which almost succumbs to later interpreters' dissolution of the innovation. Early texts and general principles sometimes fight back against later jurisprudential assaults. The cast of characters in these texts, moreover, "personify" the animals, in a rhetorical move that the scholars note. Even if the animals are not ethical agents, they become more than mere objects. But the chapter alerts us to the way that texts interpret and reinterpret each other. The chapter, as a performance of dialogue itself, embodies the reasoning that allows us to discern the range and intensity of our ethical agency.

Question Two:
How Does Legal Reasoning Generate Moral Norms?

The challenging chapter by Chaudhry and Golberg explores how attitudes from legal process can become normalized in a society independent of current jurisdiction for those court processes. The topic of the legal reasoning in this essay is how to prove accusations against women by trial. Women cannot normally serve as witnesses in these legal traditions. If we construe agency exclusively through the power to bring an action in court, there is little range of action. But what the two sets of texts here explore is how the court should determine whether a bride is a virgin and whether a wife is not an adulteress. In the Jewish context the ritual required in the Bible and explored extensively by the rabbis—when the process no longer was possible—stands as a sign of a suspicion and the vulnerability of a wife to her husband's accusations. In the Islamic context, there is a complicated matter of the physical condition of virginity—which is not regarded as the integrity of the hymen. What emerges from the study of both accounts of juridical process is the power bestowed by the court on women, specifically some women's power over other women. Surveillance, gossip, physical examination, domestic intimacy—this chapter marks out spaces where greater proximity places women under threat and control by other women. As witness against another woman, a woman can be given more capacity for determining truth than if she were called to witness in relation to a man. The asymmetry of agency or legal personality, however, is really the frame for a more challenging reflection on law and ethics.

The intricate and extensive reflections on these matters in the legal texts have uncanny resonance in contemporary culture. The chapter looks to fiction and to news stories to see how the control of women, the subordination of them to men through the witnessing agency of other women, the humiliation of them before other women are still resonant in some places today. The norms of surveillance, of shaming and threatening other women are embedded in attitudes, practices, even the vocabulary of parts of religious communities. This showcases how law can become normalized as the habits and practices of society and in that way float as a stable practice of violence beyond the context of the court. The practices and values explored in legal matters can become normal and produce adherence independent of the court's action. Or worse, in this case, the oppression of women becomes normal, to the point that women controlling women, for the sake of men and the patriarchal system, now draws on the symbolic legal order.

The implications are quite harsh: when law is not merely external restraint, then its capacity to become normal and govern attitudes and practices of morality holds a danger that it will not be a merely external sanction of oppression but will lead to everyone adopting oppression as the moral course of action. The most intimate spaces and most proximate others are now enrolled as watchers and witnesses. Whether legal reasoning can provide an antidote to legally sanctioned oppression is a difficult matter, and we will return to that question, but one should not underestimate the symbolic normality that legal reasoning can bestow on abhorrent practices. More detail, as in the Rabbinic amplification of the trial of the suspected adulteress, seems not to mitigate against the violence, but rather to create an even stronger adherence to the values of suspicion and surveillance.

Such an exploration of legal amplification (beyond the courtroom) places us in a position where the questioning of law's place in ethics is much more fraught. It is easy enough to grasp the ethical and legal injunction against adultery or fornication—and it is also readily apparent that such injunctions in an oppressive culture will be used to oppress women. What is more complex is how the extensive legal reflection on what may constitute proof, and the creation of specific roles for women disciplining women, seems not only to follow from the plain sense of the prohibitions, but to weave a fabric of attitudes and practices that is more substantial and more stable than the simple prohibitions. The interesting question then arises: what happens when scholars of the two traditions explore these parallel texts together? Is the moment of critique enhanced by the parallel? Is this, despite the differences, a moment when the scholars gain insight into the shape of each other's tradition, or their own tradition? Or, perhaps the danger of oppression and normalizing this disciplining role for women in the different lines of jurisprudence poses the principal philosophical issue: to caution us to better scrutinize the social impulses at work in creating and in studying legal matters.

Question Three:
How Does Legal Imagination Bind and Unbind History?

Edrei and Emon have written a chapter that focuses on how changing political contexts create transformations in Islamic and Jewish law.

The mirroring of loss of imperial sovereignty and gaining of modern state sovereignty creates significant challenges for the legal order, a challenge to the image of these legal systems, and the image of the work the legal traditions do in their societies. At a first-level reflection, both writers attend to the change in legal figuring of relations to others (resident others in Islam, military enemies in Judaism). Whereas we see contemporary Islamic writers simplify the jurisprudence, in part in response to the change of sovereignty when they collapse a wider range of complexity into a blunter ideology, we see Jewish jurists spread out from an explicit refusal into a range of views on whether there can or should be Jewish laws of war in a modern state. There is in this chapter an interplay between facing reality, interpreting traditional texts, and imagining history.

One of the abiding contrasts in the workshop was the role of sovereignty in the framing of legal debates. Because the Rabbinic tradition coped with the absence of state authority, as well as the absence of a temple and priestly authority, its ongoing fantasies and exploration of matters relating to the king and the Temple pervade also the limited account of the courts. Often the historical reality becomes elevated to a retro-fit ideality: it is better not to use force, not to have an army, not to have authority over other communities. On the other hand, Islamic legal tradition arose in a period of expanding and imperial rule, and the rule over other communities became a source of special reflection on the place of Islam in the life of the lands with multiple communities. Our modern concepts of the role of coercion in law were interrogated, and the complexity of legal reasoning itself expanded the various tasks and kinds of law.

Such a contrast, which opens up a questioning of the modern assumption of law as a coercive and uniform rule, also inspired us to look more deeply into the value of imagining new views of the past and reimagining the present reality. If we start from the recent past, the Jewish tradition was almost bereft of laws for warfare, and the

Islamic tradition was more complex and subtle than some perceptions that dominate current political polemics. The Islamic campaigns for reasserting sharia often obliterate the complexity of the contexts and the jurisprudence of the past. The challenge of an Israeli army leads to a diverse series of positions about the desire or even necessity for laws of warfare: what was simple in the past now produces a range of tightly held positions. Thus the dynamic of changes in conditions prompts this elasticity of jurisprudence, from a narrower to a wider range. In the classical period of the two traditions, whatever the actions of the sovereign, the jurists pursued a limited but diverse range of legal positions. The upshot from this essay, however, is that such a wider range is not directly linked to sovereignty. It also remains to be seen how difficult it is to coordinate that multivocal jurisprudence with many forms of the modern state—which craves a uniform legal code and a unified ordering state.

More interesting still is the benefit from studying the two traditions together. Both faced new challenges in the twentieth century, but the empty space in Rabbinic jurisprudence is almost a full complement to the complex and multivocal in Islamic jurisprudence during the medieval period. In the two periods with diverse options, we can see that imagination generates complexity of legal views and that diverse ethical principles come into conflict and challenge each other. But what the essay also shows is that Islam struggles without its premise of imperial sovereignty and that Judaism abandoned the jurisprudence needed to address issues of war and state violence in order to survive without a state. There is no simple principle that connects changes in reality with the imagining of a complex jurisprudence or a constrained and limited one. Context is therefore relevant, but in some important way not determining—since one can have expansive jurisprudence in different contexts and also limited constraint with the change in power. Moreover, in the contemporary context religious authorities negotiate with the laws and legal images from the past and then are led to reimagine the conflicts and the shape of law from the present. However, it is the legal scholars that are most likely to notice this doubling of imagination: *in* the past and *of* the past. And, if I may so add, it is through the dialogue performed in our workshops that a third imagining comes most into focus: the relation of those two kinds of imagining.

Question Four: Can New Readers Renew Old Laws?

But the question of historical change can also be taken in another way: when readers gain access to texts of which they were never intended to be readers. When Adler and Chaudry explore the laws concerning the marriage of girls, they face a series of exclusions and in this context undertake a bold recasting of law from within. As dramatic as the project of revitalizing the law is (and I will say more about that shortly), even more challenging is the claim to the authority to interpret traditional laws. We saw above that women were excluded from most court roles and that their surveillance role was instituted in order to serve patriarchy. Women were not trained to be jurists, were not permitted to offer legal opinions, were not expected to read and master the legal texts that constitute the very project we have undertaken. Is it possible, is it permitted, is it required or possibly recommended for a tradition to renew itself by admitting new tradents?

There is a discovery of play-space in these legal traditions, once one studies the details of legal matters. The general legal schema may be warped, but disagreements generate at least a limited range of positions. Some rulings are much worse than others; some modes of reason deny a voice to women in the matter of marriage, whereas others defend the right to consent or refuse. The play-space depends on reading the details and also requires a stance that ascribes intentions to the different named authorities. This is not biographical or psychological intention, but in the conflicts studied in the legal texts one reads as though one authority is pushing the law in one direction and others are reasoning in opposed directions. The stakes are high. How will girls and women be treated? What sort of control can they exercise over their own bodies and their own destiny? Worse, as we saw with the persistence of symbolic norms, these practices survive and the norms of how to think about women's place in society persist.

Thus we can find in this chapter a discovery of a limited but real range of legal options. Again, plurality is welcome. But the fundamental norms and images for these espousals are oppressive. Adler, near the end, refers to her own bold and radical work to recast the fundamental image of marriage from acquisition to contract. What occurs throughout the essay is a give and take about both basic matters and fine-grained detail as the authors exchange their expertise and climb into the darkness of each other's texts. We leave the chapter with bright lines of questioning, not so much about the laws as about studying laws and about how to stand in a tradition. Perhaps one of the most challenging issues is whether one should not simply abandon studying the legal matters, shuck the norms, ignore the laws, and adopt a different community, where marriage may be utterly different. Or if one is too much a scholar to abandon studying the legal matters, then study them from a position of criticism and hostility, saying, "These are the very details that oppressed women for generations and are still operating today!"

In this chapter there is no attempt to apologize and justify these legal distinctions, but the task here was complex. I would suggest that ethics itself partakes of this complexity: that if one takes a position within a community, one is often at least partially confined to darkness. Even secular, rational ethics have been a tool of oppression, of colonization, of patriarchy, of exclusion. The explicit and complex negotiations of bad laws offer us insight into how we can cope with our own past and the norms of our present. The task for study is careful and highly critical, but it is not a slate wiped clean or an ethics from nowhere. Revising laws requires the jurisprudence that gives the laws their specific shape. Here is a model of ethics that is embedded and still critical.

But the situation here admits of one more dramatic question: if we can read against the text to allow all women to become ethical agents, can we also affirm the authority of women to become jurists, to revise and to interpret the laws of the tradition that excluded them from such roles? The opening of the chapter offers a model of talking one's way into a tradition. At some level, nobody feels comfortable with the new readers: the new readers wonder if they should just leave; the old readers feel that the new ones don't belong. But the real dialogue begins as each side learns how to think like the other. And, as should now be clear, such a dialogue is repeated in another degree by studying texts with the other tradition and its experts. Thus two women battling side by side with texts that are complex but unrelenting in their oppression learn not so much to share discomfort but to compare and to understand it better. Although the inclusion of new readers seems to cohere with Habermas' principle that all who are affected should take part in the conversation, it is truly a more significant negotiation even to join the discussion. One cannot simply eradicate the traditional constitution, but one also should not reinscribe it. This doubling up of traditions helps model the engaged expansion of the discussion, without presuming a consensus to be the goal.

Question Five: Is Jurisprudence Itself an Ethics?

The interplay of Cohen and Ahmed in Chapter 1 is a testimony to the creativity of the workshops and the project. The topic is the authority of judges; the seemingly paradoxical result is that religious authority, though explained as arising from God, seems to rest more and more in people, and the authority of the judge depends on sustaining the world (or, as we may translate it, repairing the world). The scholars interpret texts from both traditions, and in complex interactions a narrative emerges that divine authority is bound to the sustaining of the world more than to divine fiat or even divine knowledge of truth. This story is woven by exploring sequences of texts and specific matters of jurisprudence as the loss of a certified divinely appointed authority provokes both a sense of crisis and a need to reground judicial authority. Or perhaps we should say *un*ground judicial authority. The need to stop people from stealing and beating each other is fundamental, but matters of private right do not seem to depend on God's will. They are consistent with that will, but seem hardly theological and appear removed from what we would normally label religion. The story, at one glance, seems like a secularizing of legal authority. Well and good.

Except...it is not clear that the good old days were any more theological. In the times of the Sultanate or when the Temple stood, were the judicial matters of private right more dependent on divine will, or absolute truth? Were they seen as grounded in vast theological claims, or were they even then bound with the task of social justice and flourishing? Thus the deeper claim of the chapter is that a modern, Protestant-inflected view of religion separates religion all too much from the world, from secular concerns. These two scholars seem to converge on a space where law is concerned with sustaining our social relations, and is devoted to what I could term ethics. In this sense, religion should be regarded as concerning these socially regulated matters. As Ahmed observes, obedience is not the central quality of lawfulness.

There is, however, the mythic and theological story that operates in these texts, or rather in the background of them. Divine revelation, inspired judges, high priests, legitimate kings and sultans—these are evoked as part of a juridical order that is not currently in force. What the jurists seem most interested to do is get on with creating enough authority to settle disputes and provide a frame that sustains the world. Thus the authors in this volume note that their own chapter is more explicit about theology than the texts under consideration. One can imagine that, in much same way as Edrei confronted the absence of laws of war in Rabbinic jurisprudence, the space for Rabbinic law depends on crossing out the image of an explicit "normal" political order. But what strikes me is that what was normal was described as divinely governed, almost directly so. Viewed from the angle of jurisprudence, divine governance now appears to be fundamentally lost—it needs to be remembered or perhaps fantasized in order to be cancelled and thus leave the sustenance of the world as a task for the human scholars and jurists.

I wish to raise one final reflection on this particular story, complete with a cancelled divine governance—the question that Cohen raises at the end of the chapter about the value of study itself. Is philosophy a practice or a mode of thinking? And what about practical philosophy, either philosophy as ethics or as the philosophy of law? There is a deep question that we can pose here but not resolve. If the "normal" political situation is either not possible or no longer possible, or is invoked only as a fantasy, then what is the goal of jurisprudence? Guiding jurists or discerning what is just in the specific situation? We know that the rabbis elevated the scholar over the king and the soldier, even over the priest and the prophet—but although Ahmed is drawn to articulate a new Islamic diasporic conception of law, with no authority commanding obedience, in affinity with Rabbinic Judaism, it is not clear whether the goal is *not* to determine law. Of course, we sat in the room as a group of scholars, and here is the twist that is even more complex: the work in this group and in this book is not applicable or juridical. And a further issue: when we read in the context with others, and when we write for readers from diverse traditions, we are not agents in the legal order. We are scholars, engaged with texts that themselves straddle a line between reflection on law and the guidance of judges who must decide.

If I reiterate that jurisprudence is the organon for ethics, then we also need to see that ethics is not legislative or often even imperative. Ethics is practical philosophy, the study of how we reason about our responsibilities. It clearly has impact, and can help guide a person or a community, but it still hovers on that line between reflection and intervention. The higher-order question is "How do we study ethics?" That is, not "What do we think about?" but "How do we come into a room or to a page to inquire about ethics?" Here we seem linked in a collaborative model of study. Coercion is suspended, even many familiar sorts of it that occur within the university, because we bring our ignorance to the fore, and our willingness to learn about that which we do not expect to endorse. Attention to the historical dynamics within a tradition and to the interplay between traditions in a context where plurality is nurtured challenges a view of ethics or philosophy that is also imperial and coercive. This pedagogic challenge has a substantive parallel in the very complexity we find in jurisprudence in the traditions when the staff of authority is broken and when the divine will is not intervening in the work of jurists and scholars. We have amplified those issues by studying and by writing together.

The ultimate philosophical point, however, is that publishing our writings is designed not only to share insights into the two traditions, but, even more, to open the non-coerced space for law and ethics to interact and for the relation of law's pedagogic and coercive functions to come to light. The plurality of traditions, the plurality of readers, all contribute to a practice that is a kind of philosophical practice to learn new insights in ethics.

List of Contributors

RACHEL ADLER is a professor of modern Jewish thought and Judaism and gender at Hebrew Union College, at the Los Angeles campus. Adler was one of the first theologians to integrate feminist perspectives and concerns into Jewish texts and the renewal of Jewish law and ethics. She is the author of *Engendering Judaism*, one of the first feminist reflections on Jewish law and ethics, as well as a wide range of articles on issues of Jewish law and gender.

RUMEE AHMED is an associate professor of Islamic law at the University of British Columbia. He is the author of *Narratives of Islamic Legal Theory* and other articles on Islamic law. He is engaged in a wide range of professional scholarly activities that reflect his keen interest in thinking across different traditions. He is on the editorial board of the *Journal of Scriptural Reasoning*, as well as co-chair of the Scriptural Reasoning Group at the American Academy of Religion. He is a reviewer for various presses (including Stanford University Press) and leading journals on law and religion.

BETH A. BERKOWITZ is Ingeborg Rennert Professor of Jewish Studies in the Department of Religion at Barnard College. She is the author of *Execution and Invention: Death Penalty Discourse in Early Rabbinic and Christian Cultures* (winner of the Salo Baron Prize for Outstanding First Book in Jewish Studies) and *Defining Jewish*

Difference: From Antiquity to the Present. She is currently at work on a book integrating animal studies with Rabbinics, called *The Clever Ox, The Escaping Elephant, and Other Rabbinic Animalities: Critical Animal Studies in the Babylonian Talmud.* She is also coediting a volume with Elizabeth Shanks Alexander, called *Religious Studies and Rabbinics,* that will explore how the field of religion can contribute to and learn from the study of Rabbinic literature.

AYESHA CHAUDHRY is an associate professor of Islamic studies and gender studies in the Department of Classical, Near Eastern and Religious Studies and the Institute for Gender, Race, Sexuality and Social Justice at the University of British Columbia. She completed her Ph.D. at New York University in the Department of Middle Eastern and Islamic Studies. Her research interests include Islamic law, Qur'anic exegesis, and feminist hermeneutics. She is the author of *Domestic Violence and the Islamic Tradition: Ethics, Law and the Muslim Discourse on Gender.* This book explores the relationship of modern Muslims to the inherited Islamic tradition through a study of legal and exegetical discussions of wife-beating in the pre- and post-colonial periods. Currently, she is collaborating on a book on interfaith feminist hermeneutics, which will explore and challenge the limits of feminist interpretations of patriarchal religious texts in the three Abrahamic faiths, under the title *Difficult Texts or Difficult Women? The Challenge of Scripture to Feminist Readings.*

ARYEH COHEN is Professor of Rabbinic Literature at American Jewish University, where he has held an appointment since 1995. He was chair of Jewish studies in the College of Arts and Science from 1995 to 2000 and chair of Rabbinic studies in the Ziegler School from 2001 to 2005. Cohen has also taught at Hebrew Union College/Jewish Institute of Religion, the Reconstructionist Rabbinical College, and Brandeis University. He is one of the founders of the Shtibl, a Hassidic egalitarian *minyan*, which combines the passion of ecstatic prayer with commitments to egalitarianism and social justice. He is the author of *Rereading Talmud: Gender, Law and the Poetics of Sugyot* and coeditor of *Beginning/Again: Towards a Hermeneutics of Jewish Texts*. He is also a member of the advisory board of *Sh'ma* and an editor of the online journal *Textual Reasoning*. Cohen is a popular lecturer on Talmud, social justice, politics, and the contemporary Jewish scene. His writing on these topics and others has been published in *Conservative Judasim*, *Sh'ma*, *Journal of Jewish Thought and Philosophy*, *Association of Jewish Studies Review*, *Tikkun*, *Reconstructionist*, *Kerem*, *Jewish Spectator*, and *Jewish Journal* and online at Jewschool.com and Jspot.org

ARYE EDREI is Professor of Law at Tel-Aviv University. He teaches a variety of courses on the history and philosophy of Jewish law. His main fields of interest are Talmudic jurisprudence and Jewish law in the twentieth century. He also has written on "law and ideology" and "law and memory." Edrei is the coeditor-in-chief of *Dinei Israel*, a *Journal of Jewish Law*, published jointly by the Tel-Aviv University Law Faculty and the Cardozo Law School of Yeshiva University. Edrei was a senior fellow at the Institute of Advanced Studies, Hebrew University of Jerusalem (2005) and a fellow at Oxford University, Center for Hebrew and Jewish Studies. Edrei is the co-author, with Doron Mendels, of *Zweierlei Diaspora: Zur Splatung der antiken Judischen Welt*. With Hanina Ben-Menachem he published *Windows onto Jewish Legal Culture: Fourteen Exploratory Essays*. His current primary project is a book entitles *Halakhah in the Twentieth Century*, which focuses primarily on contemporary halakhic reactions to Jewish sovereignty.

ANVER M. EMON is Professor of Law and Canada Research Chair in Religion, Pluralism and the Rule of Law at the University of Toronto Faculty of Law. Emon's research focuses on pre-modern and modern

Islamic legal history and theory, pre-modern modes of governance and adjudication, and the role of sharia both inside and outside the Muslim world. The recipient of numerous research grants, he was named as a 2014 Guggenheim fellow in the field of law. In addition to publishing numerous articles, Emon is the author of *Islamic Natural Law Theories* and *Religious Pluralism and Islamic Law: Dhimmis and Others in the Empire of Law* as well as the coeditor of *Islamic Law and International Human Rights Law: Searching for Common Ground?* He is the founding editor of *Middle East Law and Governance: An Interdisciplinary Journal* and General Editor of the Oxford Islamic Legal Studies Series.

ROBERT GIBBS is the inaugural director of the Jackman Humanities Institute and Professor of Philosophy at the University of Toronto. His current work is located on the borderlines of philosophy and religion, with a comparative and historical focus on law and ethics. He has worked on ethics in relation to the modern Jewish philosophical tradition and has numerous publications in this and related fields in continental philosophy, including two books, *Correlations in Rosenzweig and Levinas* and *Why Ethics? Signs of Responsibilities.* He has taught in the philosophy departments at the University of Toronto and at St Louis University, and in the religion departments at Princeton University and (affiliated) at the University of Toronto. He is cross-appointed to the University of Toronto Departments of French, German, Religion and the Centre for Jewish Studies. He is President of the International Rosenzweig Society and serves on various academic advisory boards and journal editorial boards. He is a member of the advisory board of C.H.C.I. (Consortium of Humanities Centers and Institutes) and was a member of the Humanities Initiative Steering Committee of C.I.F.A.R. (Canadian Institute for Advanced Research). He is a member of the Governing Council of the Social Sciences and Humanities Research Council of Canada (SSHRC).

SHARI GOLBERG is a senior policy advisor at the Ontario Ministry of Training, Colleges and Universities in Toronto. She has served as the project director of Beyond Calligraphy, an art exhibit that brings Muslim and Jewish artists together to explore the relationship between art, public policy, and religious identity. Having completed her Ph.D. at the University of Toronto, she is exploring feminist approaches to Jewish and Islamic texts and contemporary text-based collaborations between Jewish and Muslim women. Her other research interests include Jewish and Islamic law, Canadian public policy and religious accommodation, diversity and conflict mediation, and inter-faith activism. Golberg has taught numerous courses on gender and religiosity in both community-based and academic settings, including Huron College and the University of Toronto. In the summer of 2013, Golberg served as an evaluator of the University of Toronto's Connaught Summer Institute in Islamic Studies, a unique program for international doctoral students exploring issues of diversity in the study of Islam and in living Muslim communities. Golberg is also the Director of Shema & Iqra': The Jewish–Muslim Text Project, a grassroots initiative that brings communities of Muslims and Jews together using classical religious texts as a springboard for dialogue to explore issues of mutual concern, including gender and religious leadership, environmental ethics, and creative expression.

MARION H. KATZ is Professor of Middle Eastern and Islamic Studies at New York University. The author of numerous books and articles, she specializes on various aspects of Islamic law, gender, and ritual. Her first book, *Body of Text*, dealt with the reconstruction of early scholarly debates about the law of ritual purity (*tahara*) and the underlying issues of community boundaries, gender, and attitudes toward the body. *Prayer in Islamic Thought* focused on the ways in which prayer featured in Islamic thought and practice, expounding its various details and their implications for the meaning and construction of devotion.

Her most recent book, *Women in the Mosque*, is an extended historical analysis of space and access in sacred places, and the extent to which both are gendered.

ADAM SELIGMAN is Professor of Religion at Boston University and a research associate at the Institute on Culture, Religion and World Affairs there. He has lived and taught at universities in the United States, in Israel, and in Hungary, where he was a Fulbright fellow. He lived close to twenty years in Israel, where he was a member of Kibbutz Kerem Shalom in the early 1970s. His many books include *The Idea of Civil Society, Inner-worldly Individualism, The Problem of Trust, Modernity's Wager: Authority, the Self and Transcendence,* (with Mark Lichbach) *Market and Community, Modest Claims, Dialogues and Essays on Tolerance and Tradition,* (with Weller, Puet and Simon) *Ritual and Its Consequences: An Essay on the Limits of Sincerity,* and, most recently (with Weller), *Rethiking Pluralism: Ritual, Experience and Ambiguity.* His work has been translated into over a dozen languages. He is Director of C.E.D.A.R. (Communities Engaging with Difference and Religion) (www.CEDARnetwork.org), which leads seminars every year on contested aspects of religion and the public square in different parts of the world.

Index

Sunna 14
Sunni Islam 5–6
supernatural, the 231
synagogues 179, 184
Syria 215

al-Tabari 167
tafsir (exegetical authority)
5–6
Taliban, the 126–7
Talmud 9, 23–4, 28, 66–7,
203
and animals 65, 68–9,
71–3, 89–97, 110
and force 164–5
Talmudists 20, 22
tax 169–70, 177–8, 181–2
Teitelbaum, Rabbi Yoel
193–4
terrorism 196–7
theology xiv, 19–20
tolerance 166, 235–6
Torah 24, 65, 185, 202–3
Tosafists 9, 10, 18–19
tradition xxvi, 5, 25–9,
55–8
and authority 233–5
and dialogue 222–30
and reason 221–2
and religion 243–4
transcendence 231–2

'Umdat al-Salik (al-Misri)
207
usury 233
Uymayyad Dynasty 168–71

vigilantism 120, 127
violence 113–16, 119, 120
virginity xxiv, 30–1, 32, 33–5,
38–9
and testers 122–7
vows 41, 42, 46, 48–9, 53

wali (guardian) 30–2, 38, 39
war xxv, 156–7, 168, 188–95,
200–6, 251–2
and Judaism 162–6,
196–200, 213–14
witnesses 121–3, 125, 127,
146–51
and adultery 134, 137,
144–5
and women 140–4, 145–6,
152–3
women 26–7, 28–9, 56–7,
248–50, 253–4
and adultery 128–40,
144–51
and detention 83–4
and ethics 254–5
and Islam 113–14
and marriage 30–9, 40–2,
43–6, 47–55